SWEET SPACES

Learn to Doodle the Coziest Corners

Erin Siney
Creator of eggsdoodz

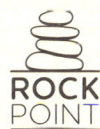

ROCK
POINT

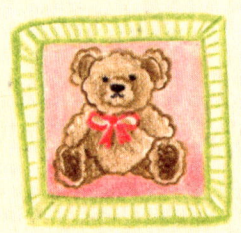

To fellow creatives and crafters who, like me, find comfort and joy in the art of creation. May these pages inspire you as much as they have inspired me.

Contents

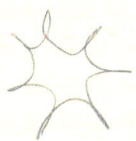

Hiya!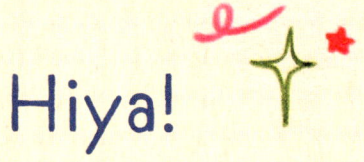

My name is Erin Siney, but I also go by eggsdoodz! I am an illustrator and business owner from the North East of England. I have always loved creating—growing up, I was constantly doodling, painting, sewing, or knitting. I often gravitated toward the arts and crafts-themed classes in school, which eventually led me to pursue my art career by starting my Bachelor of Arts degree in Illustration and Design in 2019.

During the second year of my studies, I developed my own stationery brand "eggsdoodz," and this university project is what started it all! A quick backstory to my alias: I am allergic to eggs and had the sweet nickname "Egg" given to me by my university lecturer Julia Patton, an incredible illustrator and a huge inspiration to me. As the stationery brand I had created consisted of simple colored pencil doodles, I combined the two and formed "eggsdoodz." My deep love for using colored pencils has grown exponentially, and now I use them for all my pieces. Back then, I created extremely realistic lush botanical illustrations in all shapes, sizes, and colors. I rendered delicious, detailed forms inspired by wildlife found around the world, using graphite pencils and sometimes my iPad. Creating eggsdoodz allowed me to express a child-like, carefree approach to creating that really resonates with my inner child. Working on eggsdoodz also formed a new art style for me that is truly such a joy to make!

I have since completed a Master of Arts degree in Fine Art and Ceramics to develop my artistic skill set further and explore new media and techniques. After completing my studies in 2023, I went full-time with eggsdoodz. Although it was a very scary decision to make, I am thankful that my creative career continues to grow. The eggsdoodz brand enables me to share my art no matter what media I use, while further developing my knowledge and experiences within both art and business.

I always try to convey relatable feelings and include words that others may need to hear in my colorful doodles. My words are often a representation of how I am currently feeling or phrases I need to hear to make myself feel a little better. Raising awareness for mental health has been one of my main focuses since eggsdoodz began in 2021. I create with the intention of brightening someone's day and with the hope it makes them feel a bit better. Afterall, my motto is "doodling nice things for lovely people!"

I adore being in cozy, comforting environments, which is why they feature quite often in my art. With this book, I want to share some of my tips and tricks for how to create your own cozy corners! I hope it encourages you to create your own dream rooms and helps you to creatively express your feelings.

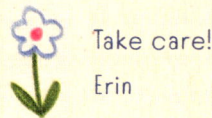 Take care!
Erin

How to Use This Book

After some helpful information here about tools, perspective tips, and quote inspiration, the book contains just over one hundred tutorials divided into eight different rooms: Serene Study Nook, Snug as a Bug Bedroom, Cozy Gathering Room, Berry Sweet Morning, Dinner for Two, Cute Cat Café, Charming Closet, and Colorful Craft Corner. At the end of the book, you'll find a sweet craft and some coloring pages with plenty of doodles to make your own.

Crafting Tools

Feel free to draw your cozy corners with whatever you have available to you, but here are some suggestions.

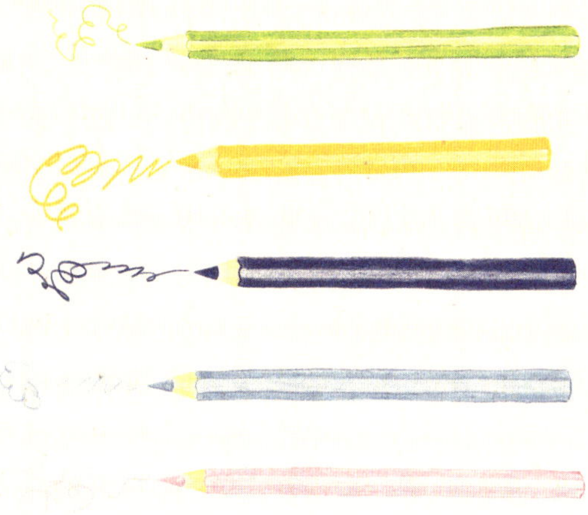

Crayons

Colored Pencils

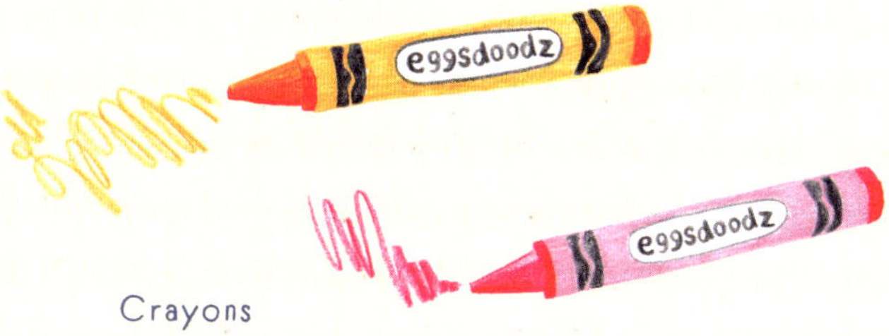

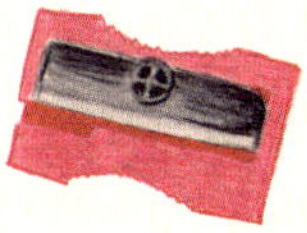

Sharpener

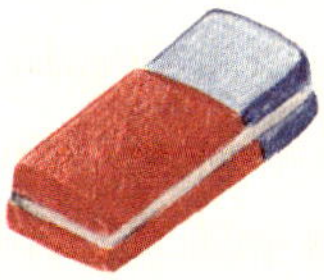

Eraser

Sketchbook

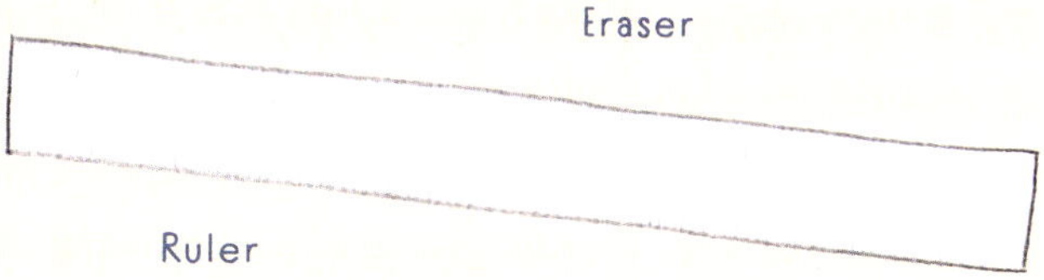

Ruler

Drawing a Room

Use these simple steps to set up a room in perspective, meaning that anything becomes three-dimensional using this technique. Start by using a horizon line (yes, even in a bedroom!) and vanishing points to guide your horizontal lines. Vanishing points will often be located off the sides of your page when drawing, but that's acceptable! Use the points as a guide and make your dream room, closet, or café a reality. This technique, combined with careful shading, pretty patterns, and textures, will give your drawing a sense of realism and bring your imagined sweet space to life!

1. Draw a horizontal line across the paper connecting two crosses at each end. These are called vanishing points.

2. Add a vertical line in the middle. This will be the corner of your room.

TIP

Draw the guidelines very lightly in pencil, as you will need to erase them once you start adding items and furniture to your room.

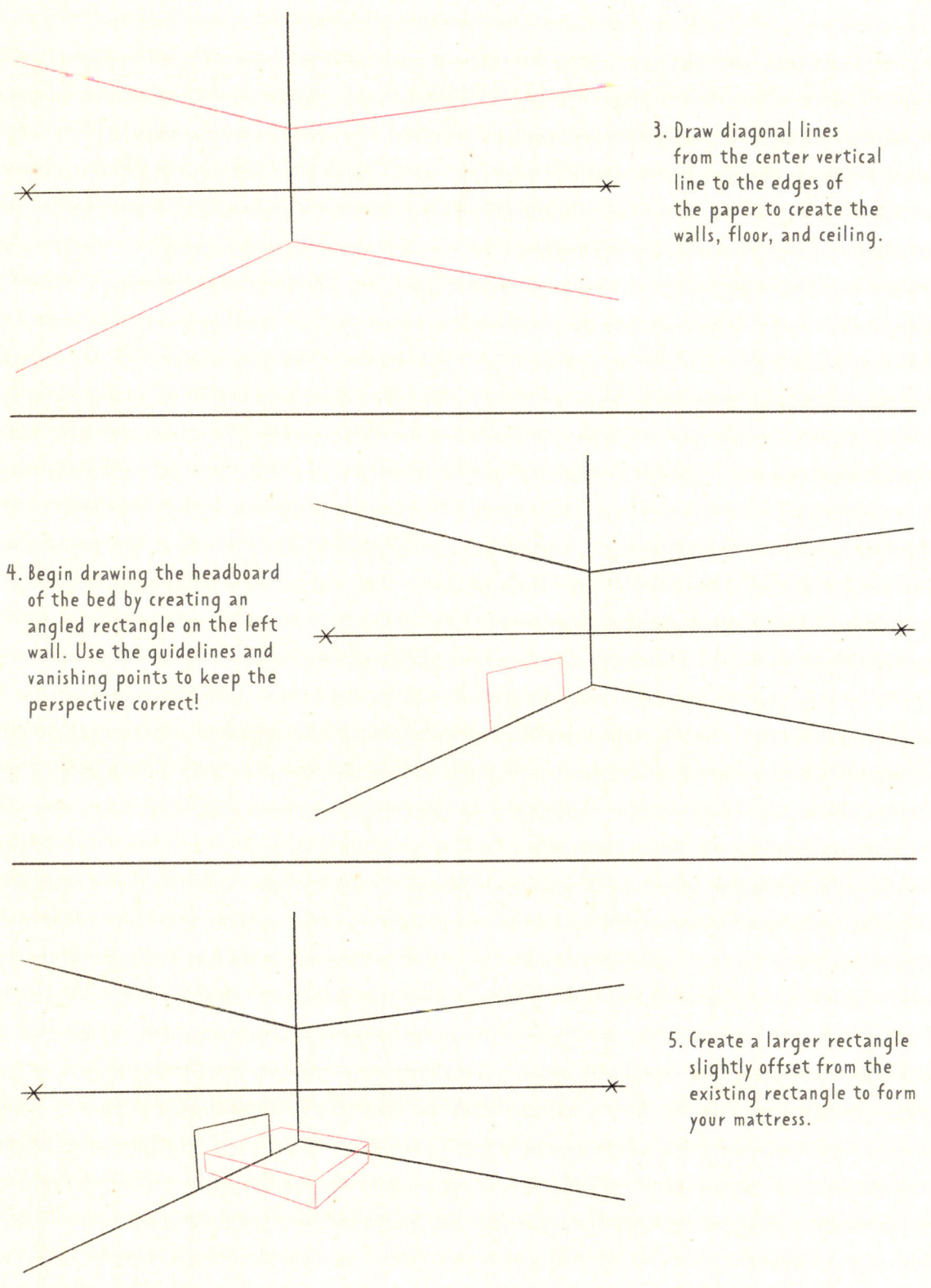

3. Draw diagonal lines from the center vertical line to the edges of the paper to create the walls, floor, and ceiling.

4. Begin drawing the headboard of the bed by creating an angled rectangle on the left wall. Use the guidelines and vanishing points to keep the perspective correct!

5. Create a larger rectangle slightly offset from the existing rectangle to form your mattress.

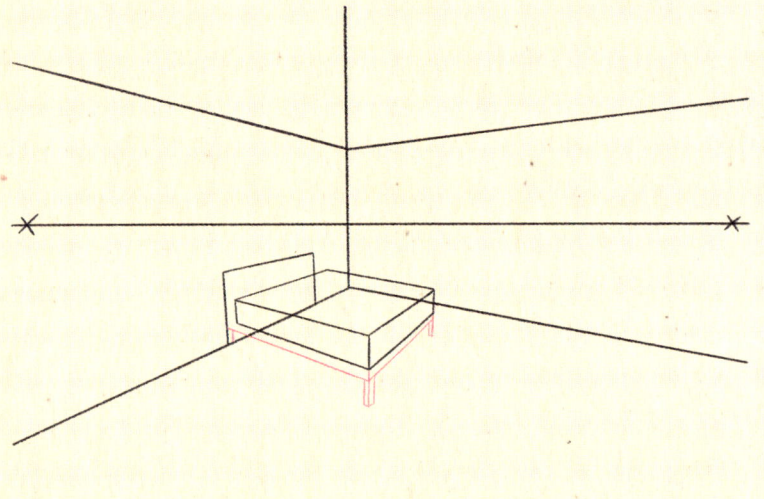

6. Add two more diagonal lines to create the bed frame and short vertical lines to create the legs.

7. Add two comfy pillows by drawing two rectangles with wobbly lines.

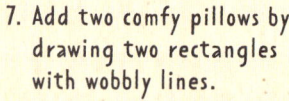

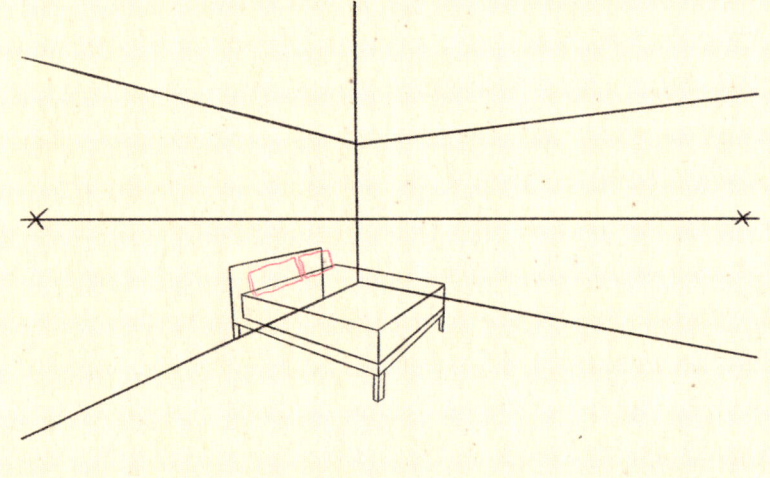

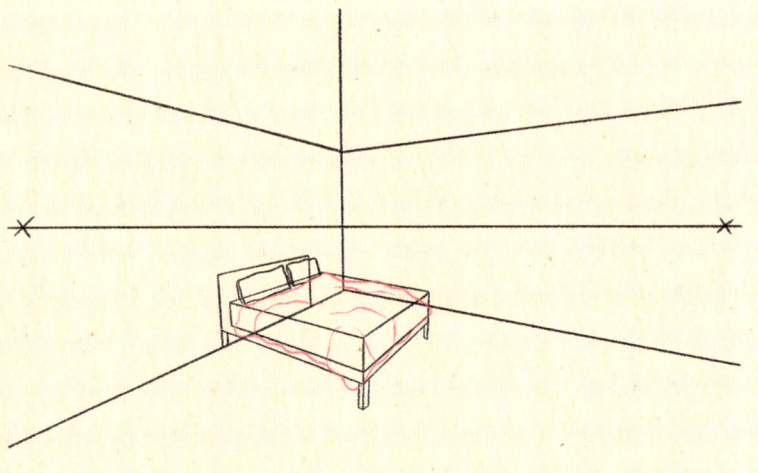

8. Finish the Messy Bed (page 36) by following along the mattress shape using wobbly lines. Erase parts of the guidelines that show through the duvet.

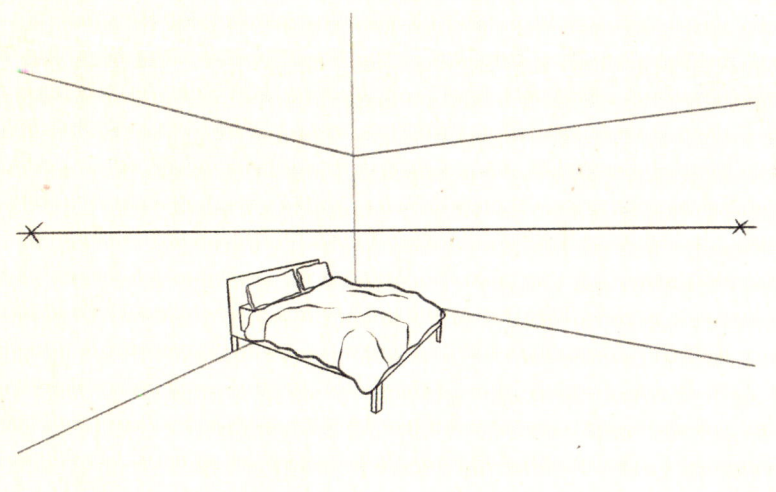

9. This is how your bed
   should look once you have
   erased the guidelines.

10. Use tutorials from the Cozy
    Gathering Room (page 49)
    and Snug as a Bug Bedroom
    (page 35) chapters to add
    more items to your room!
    Draw things such as a side
    table, calendar, plant,
    and window.

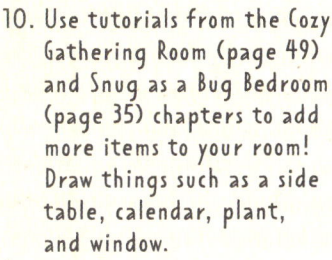

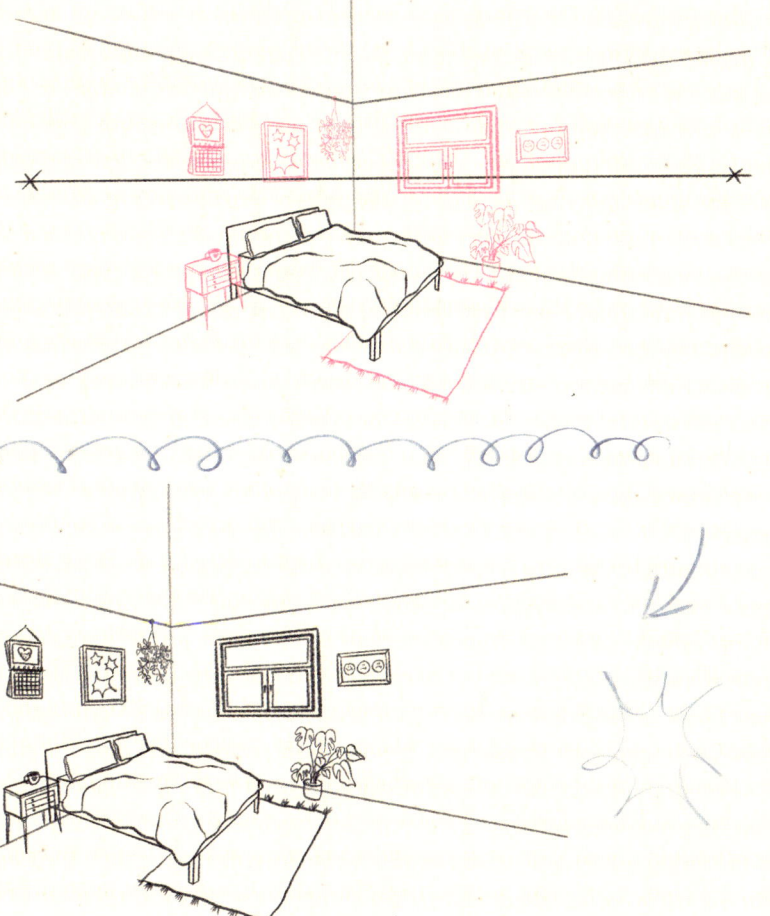

Quote Inspiration

This chapter offers a practical guide to coming up with quotes that enhance your doodles and creations. Discover the joy of pairing your artwork with inspiring, witty, and simple quotes and reminders to help you create unique and authentic pieces.

Let's start simply!

Quite literally, simple reminders such as "Good things are coming" and "It will all be okay" are the best place to start! If you're feeling stuck but want to add something to your design, make a list of simple, encouraging reminders such as:

"I hope you know it's going to be okay."
"I'm glad you're here."
"You are enough!"

These short, positive affirmations will brighten your day!

Often, the best quotes come to you randomly. Make sure to note these down in your phone or a nearby journal. Don't pressure yourself to think of an extravagant, lengthy quote. Keep it short and sweet. For example, let's say you ate an apple, and it was really delicious. A quote that would spring to mind would be something along the lines of "Enjoy the little things." Find small joys in each day to help inspire your quotes.

At times, you may be having a bad day or stuck in an art block, unable to create anything you love. First, this is totally normal, and I experience it myself. Take some time to rest and come back to your sketchbook later. When you experience these down days, speak to yourself like you would a friend.

Sayings like "I'm so proud of you," "Things are going to get better and better," and "You did your best, and that's all that matters" can be extremely encouraging during these times, and these quotes often help me create some wonderful pieces.

And finally, I try to add some humor and honesty to my pieces now and then! For example, I wrote on one piece "I don't need luck!! I need 2 days of sleep and a new teddy bear." On that day, I was awaiting my university results and everyone kept telling me "Good luck!" But I was truly exhausted from working so hard that I just wanted to nap and reward myself with a new teddy bear—things that bring me immense joy!

Quotes like this really resonate due to their realness and personal touch. Use your experiences and feelings to influence your quotes. Write reminders and words of affirmation that you may need to hear yourself!

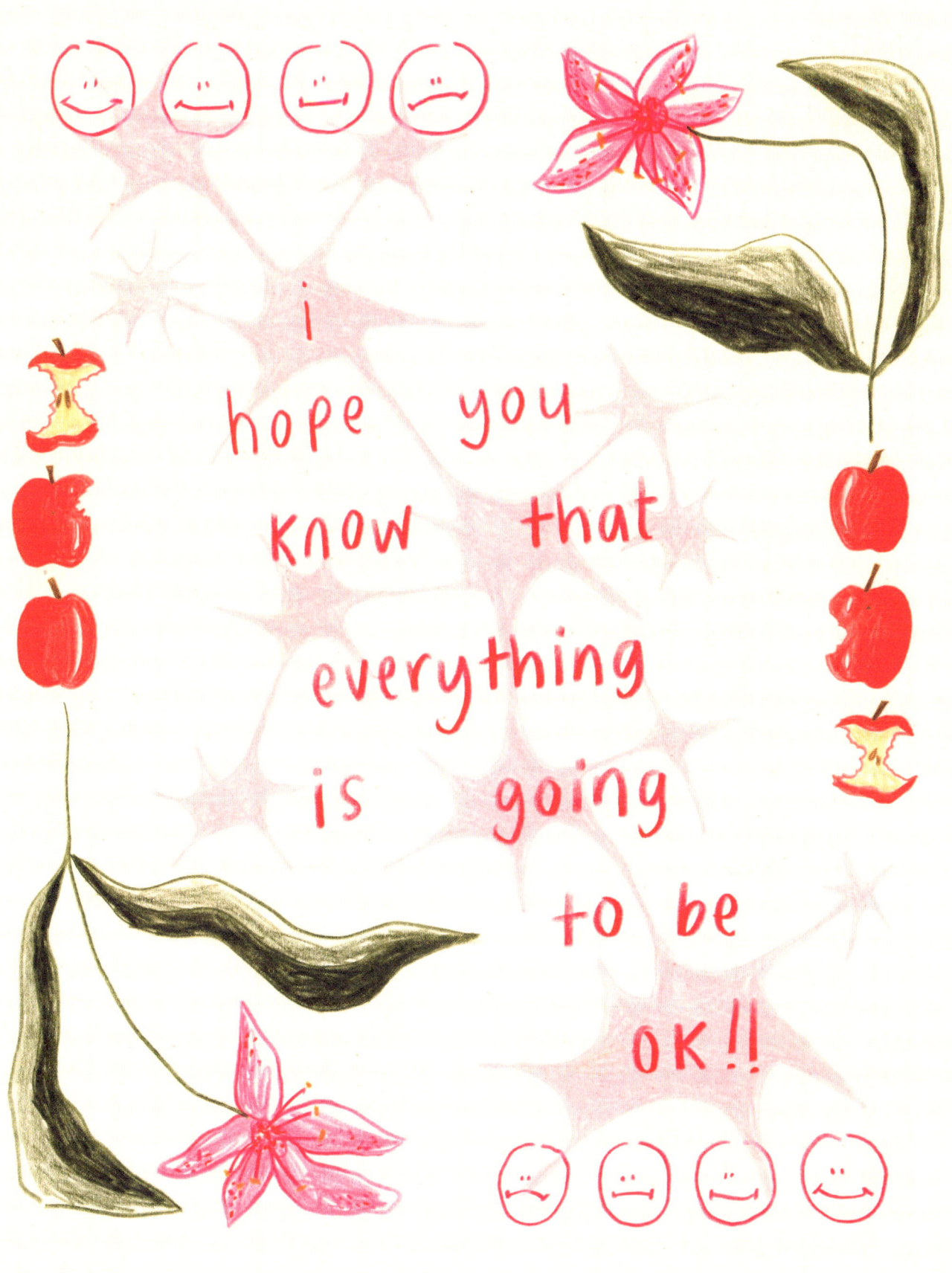

Common Things in Your Room

I like to use a lot of repeated elements, designs, and figures in my work. Here, I show you some of my most popular things that you'll find in almost every room in this book. You'll even find some steps to draw Ed the Ted—he always fits right in!

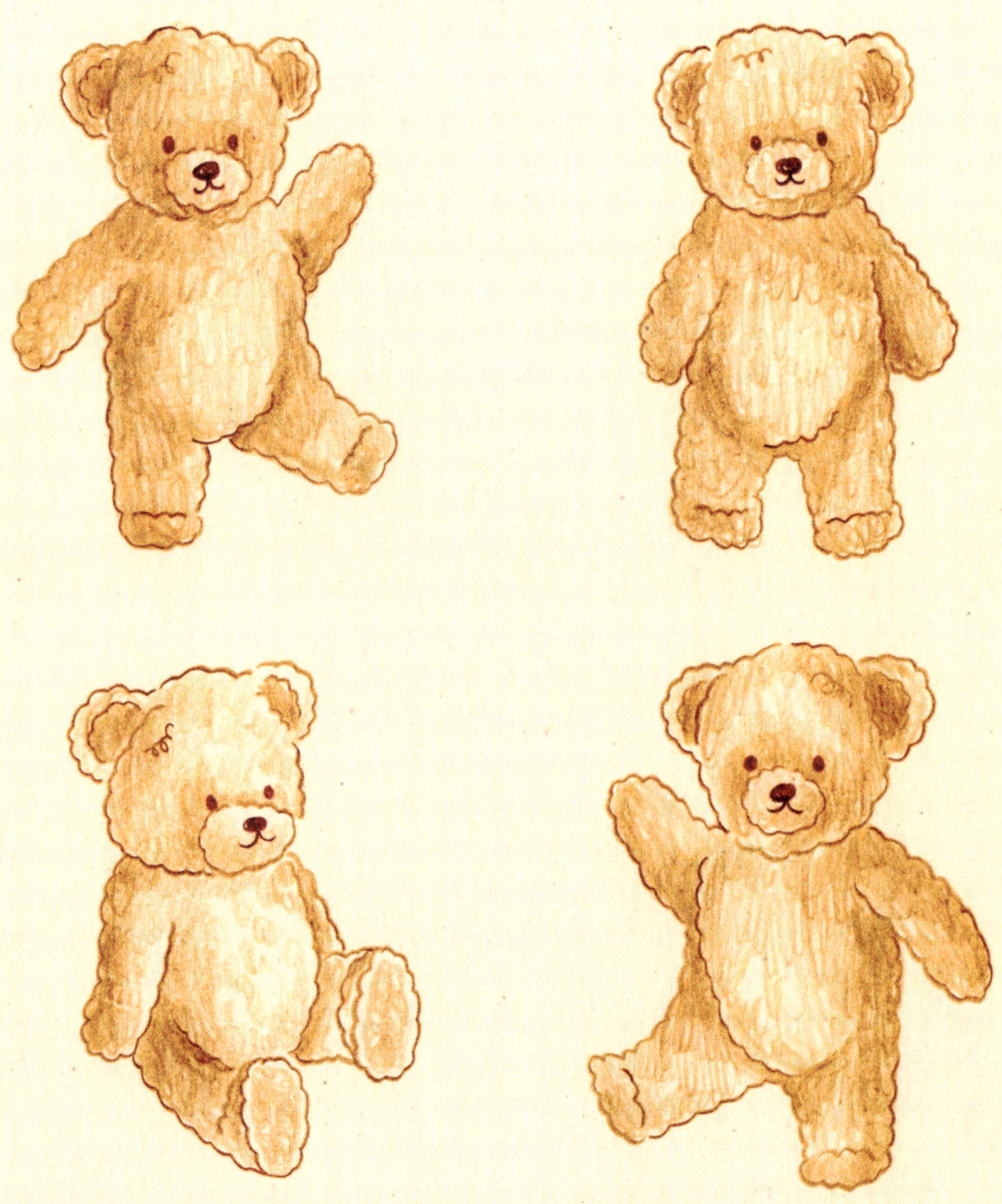

Flowers

DAISY

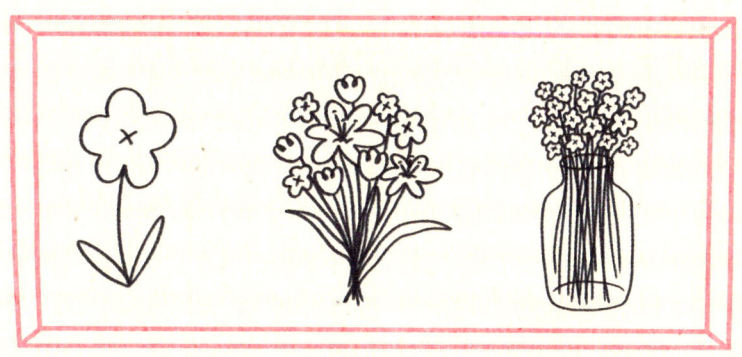

TULIP

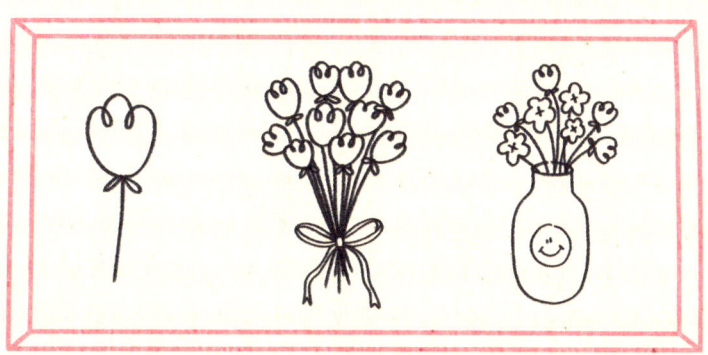

POPPY

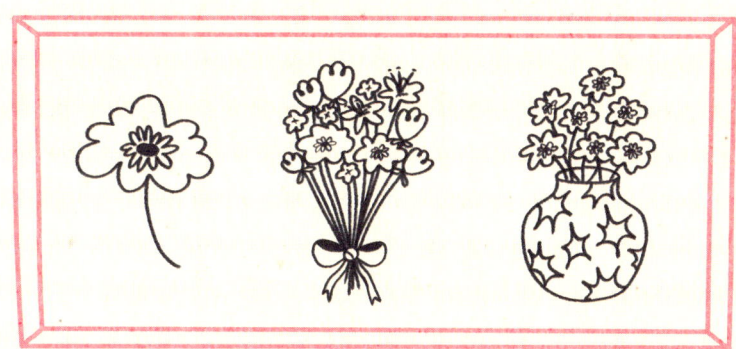

LILY

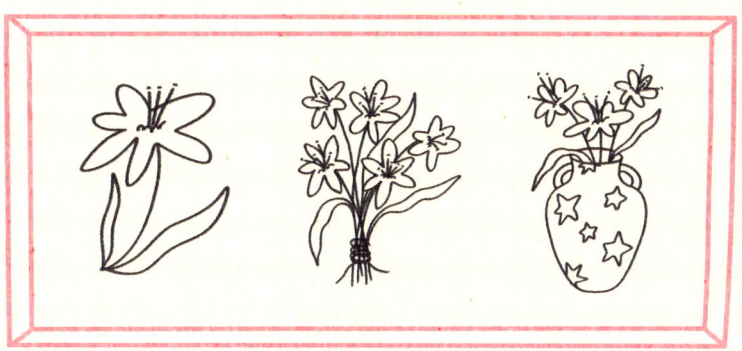

Simple Designs

STARS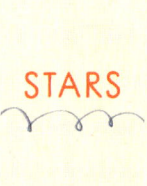

RAINBOW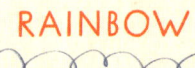

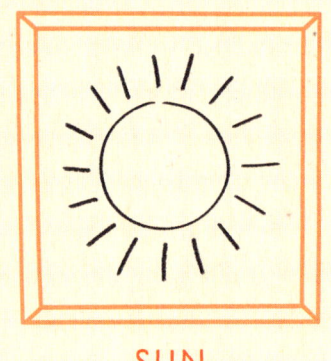

SUN

CLOUD

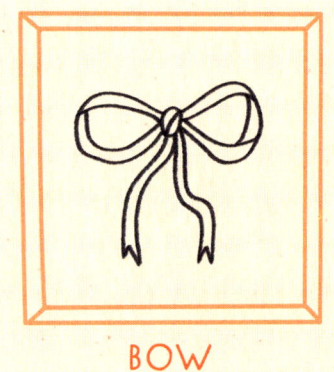

BOW

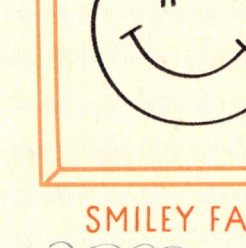

SMILEY FACE

CLOVER

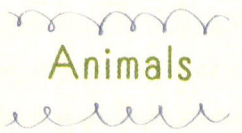 Animals

ED THE TED

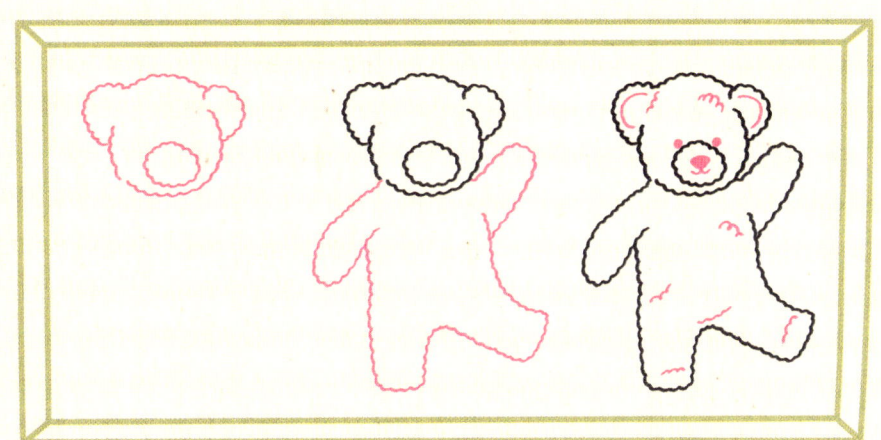

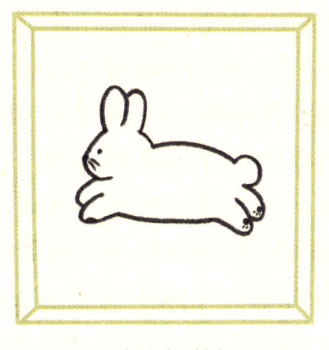

BUNNY

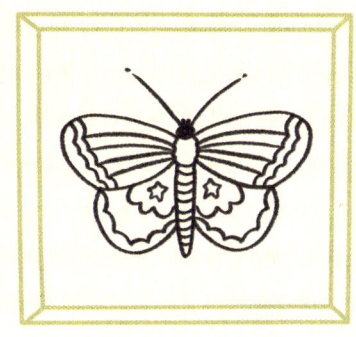

BUTTERFLY

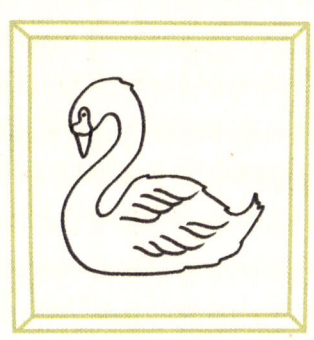

SWAN

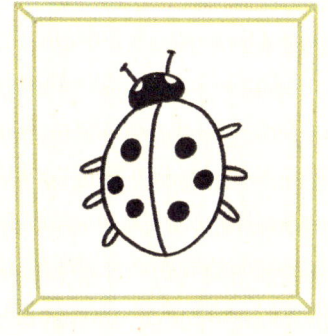

LADYBUG

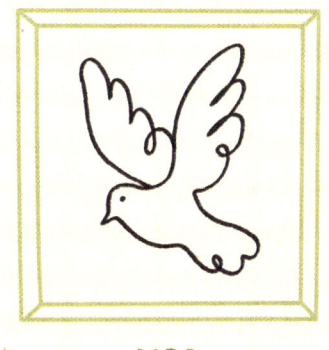

BIRD

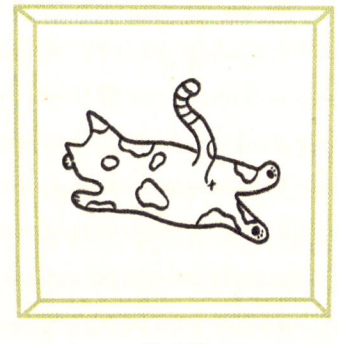

CAT

Food

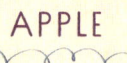

APPLE
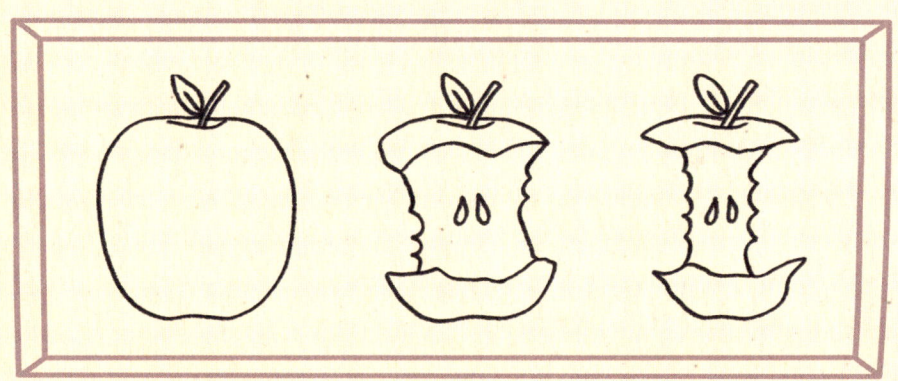

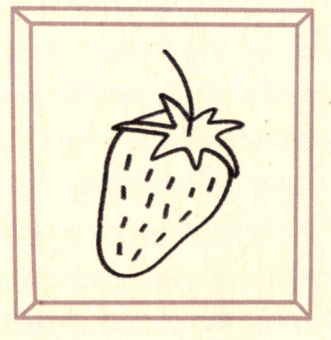

STRAWBERRY

CHERRY

TOMATOES

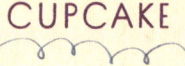

CUPCAKE

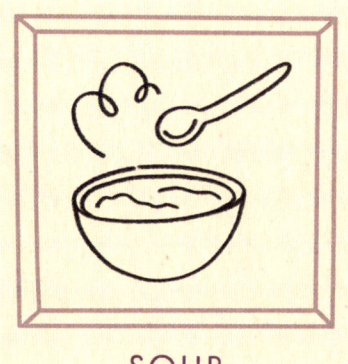

SOUP

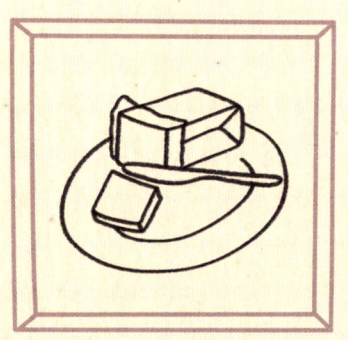

BUTTER

Now put everything together! Add your common things to each room or draw a doodle using some animals and fruit surrounding an encouraging or funny quote from Quote Inspiration (page 12). With these tools and by following the step-by-step directions in the following chapters, you can draw anything! Make your cozy corner your own.

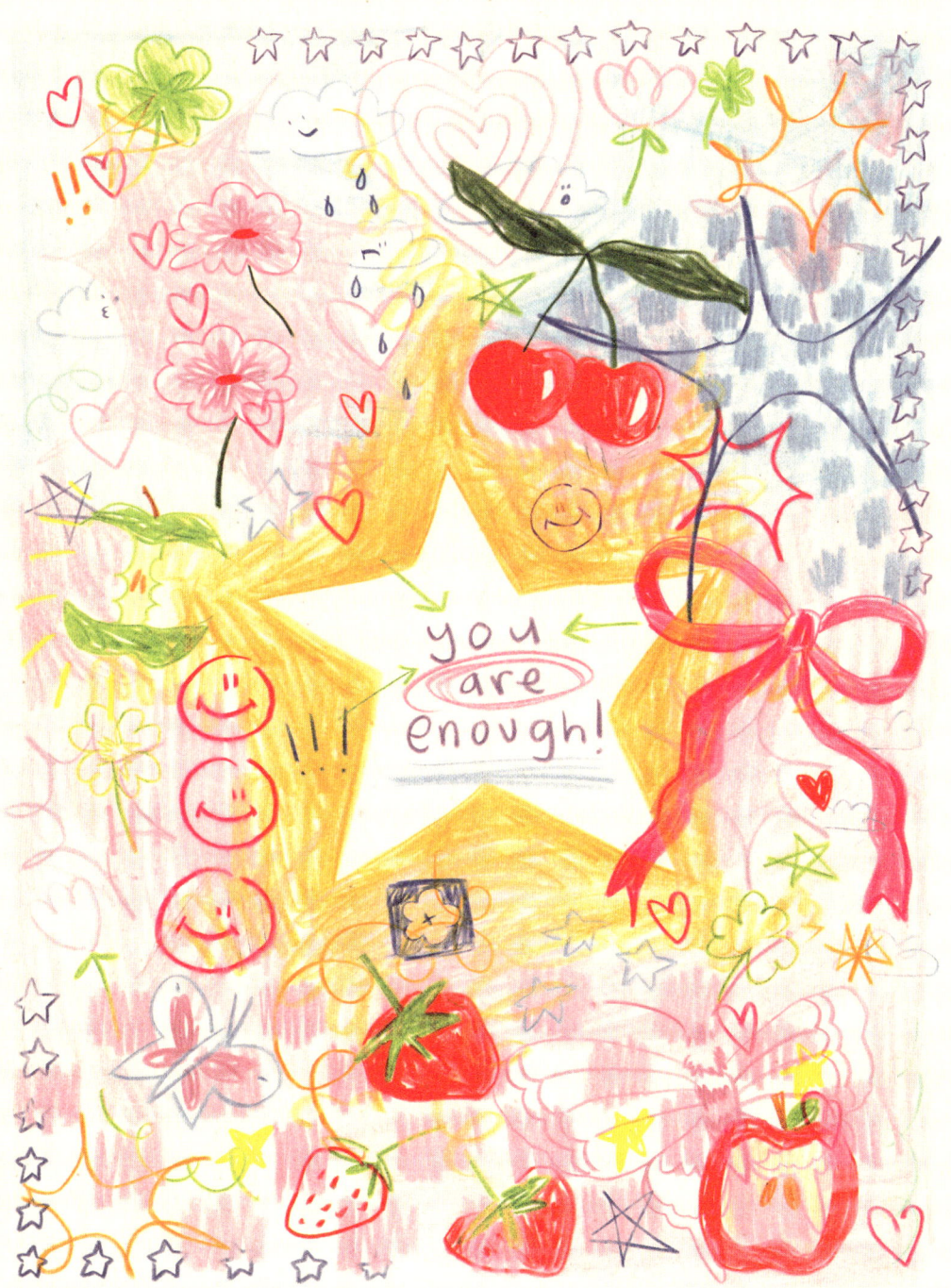

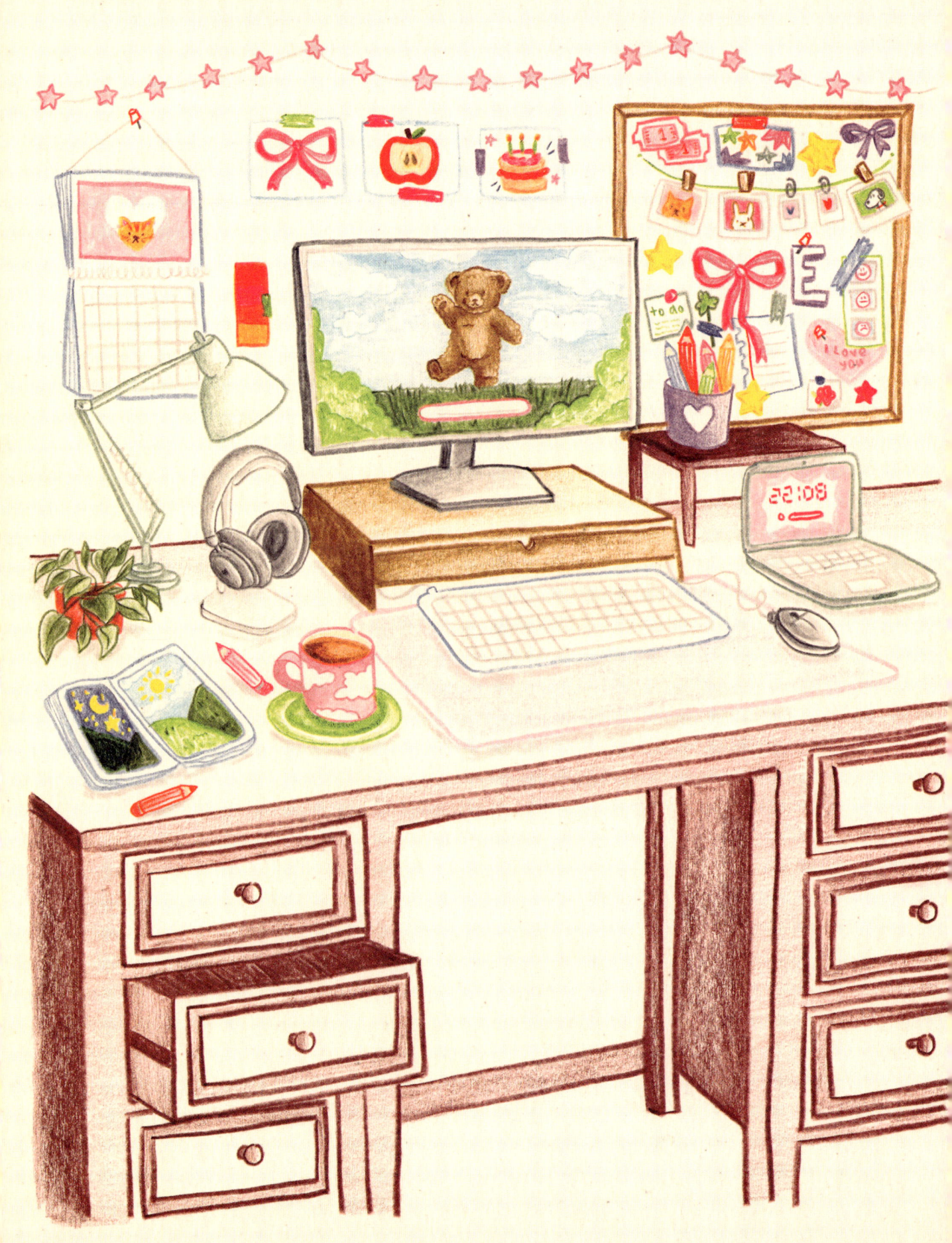

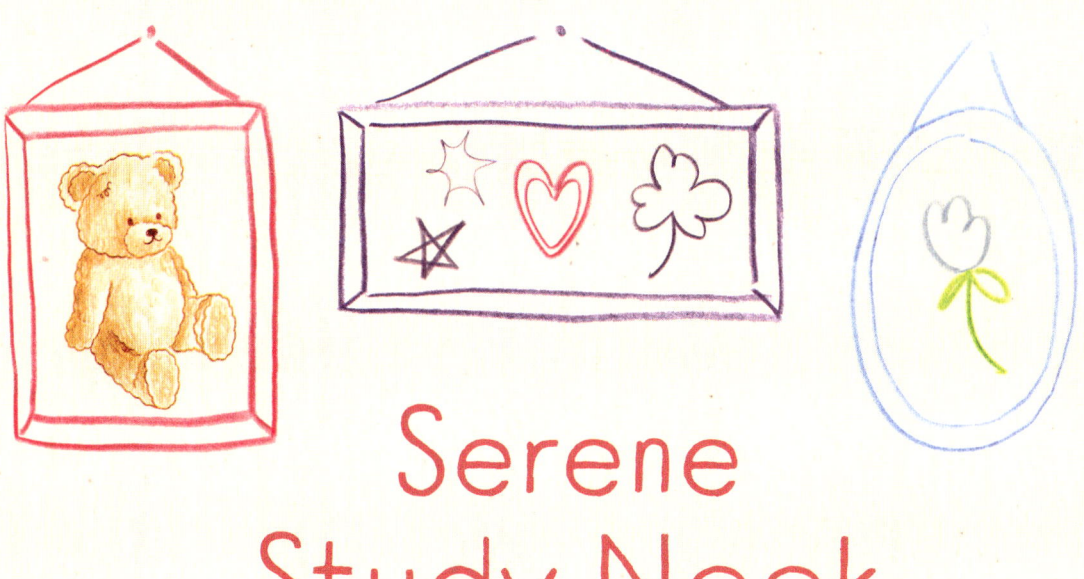

Serene
Study Nook

Hunker down and get to work . . . on something cute! Make your study space your own by adding elements from Common Things in Your Room (page 14), Colorful Craft Corner (page 119), and Cozy Gathering Space (page 49). Decorate the bulletin board, personalize photographs with illustrations of your friends, and clutter your desktop!

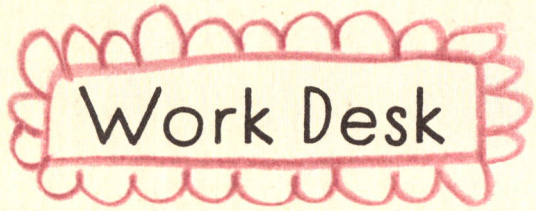

Work Desk

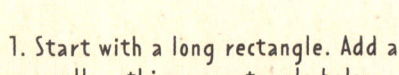

1. Start with a long rectangle. Add a smaller, thinner rectangle below.

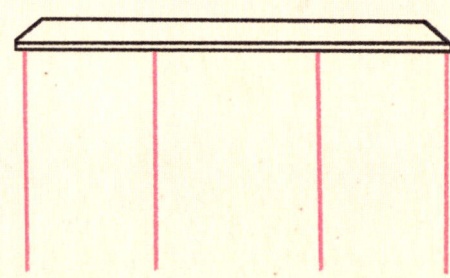

2. Draw four lines perpendicular from the corners and spaced evenly.

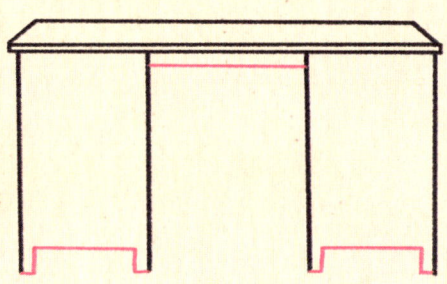

3. Add lines to make the legs, and add a horizontal line for the middle support.

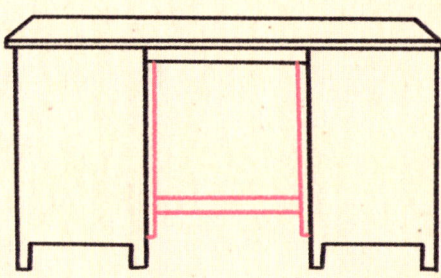

4. Create lines inside the panels for the back legs. Connect them with a horizontal beam.

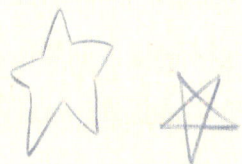

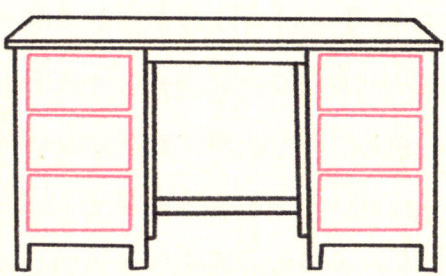

5. Draw six evenly spaced and sized rectangles. These will be the drawers!

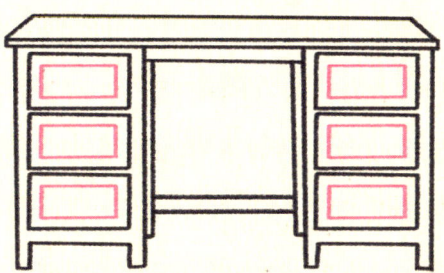

6. Add six smaller rectangles inside the bigger ones.

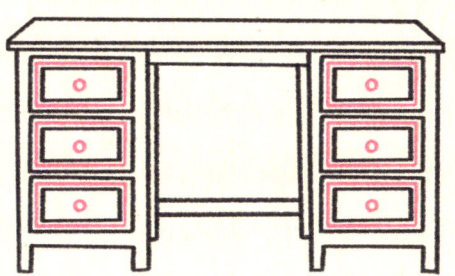

7. Finish by drawing six more rectangles in the drawers and adding circles to the center of each for the handles.

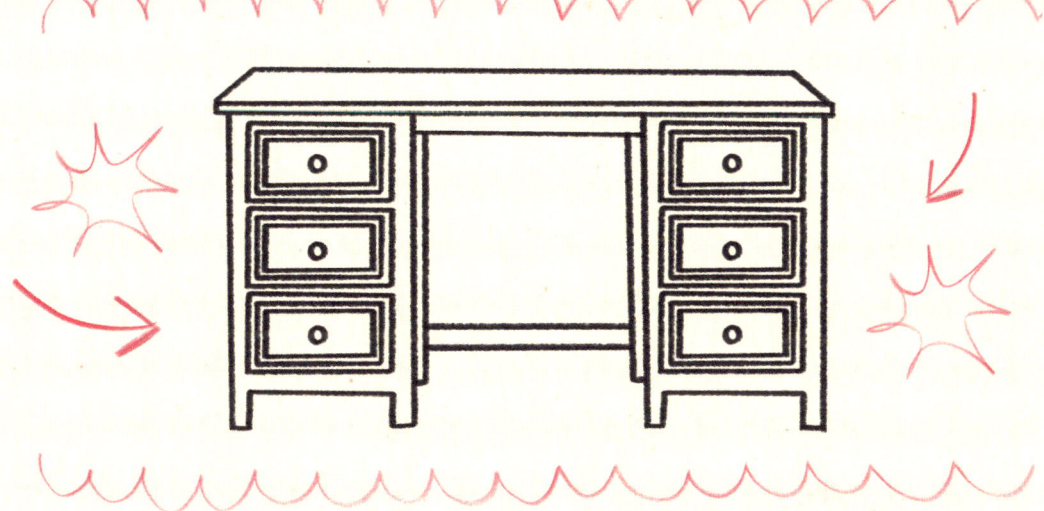

Computer Monitor

1. Draw a rectangle for the screen.

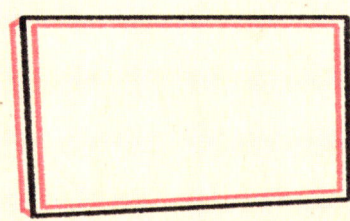

2. Create a smaller rectangle inside the bigger shape and a thin line on the left side of the bigger rectangle.

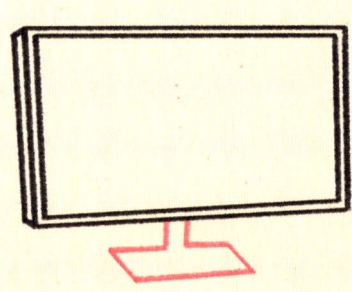

3. Draw a smaller rectangle at the bottom with an opening for two parallel lines. This is the stand of the monitor.

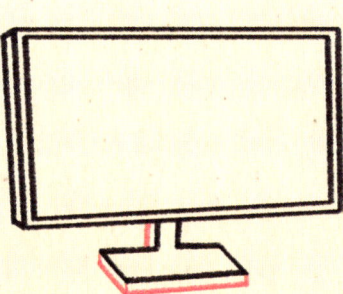

4. Add a thin edge to the computer stand.

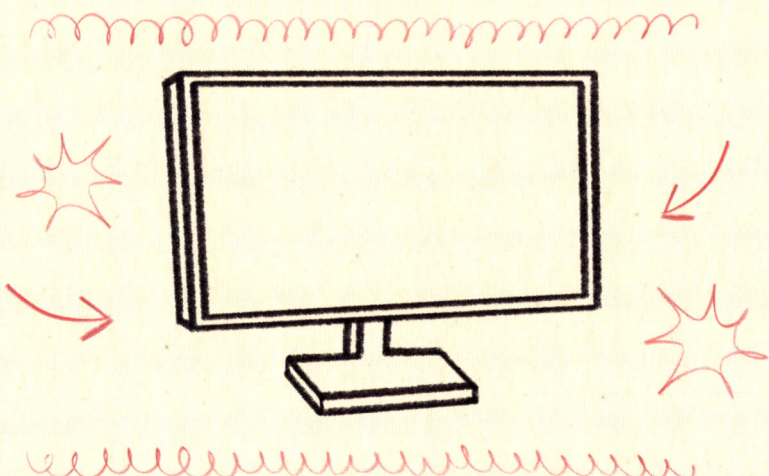

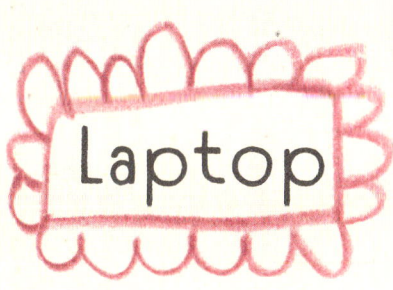

Laptop

1. Draw a rectangle for the screen with rounded edges.

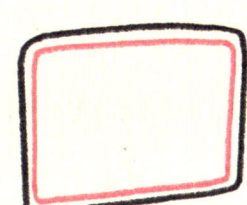

2. Add a smaller, rounded rectangle inside the bigger one.

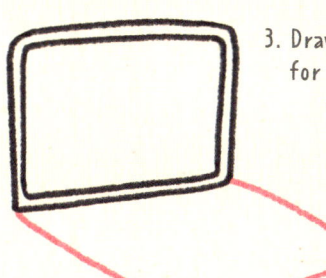

3. Draw an angled square for the laptop base.

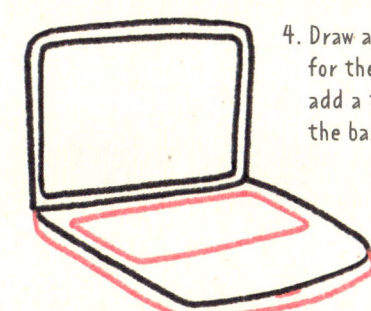

4. Draw a small rectangle for the keyboard and add a thin edge to the base.

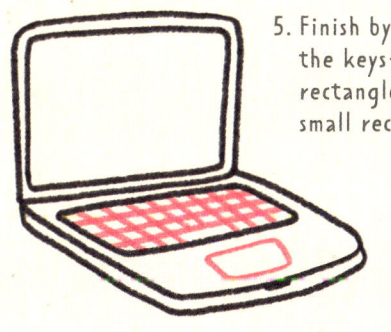

5. Finish by drawing checkered lines for the keys—make sure there's a longer rectangle for the spacebar—and a small rectangle for the touchpad.

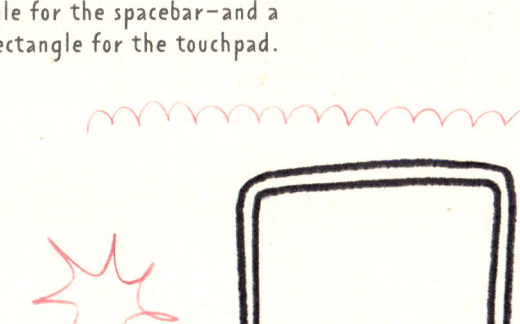

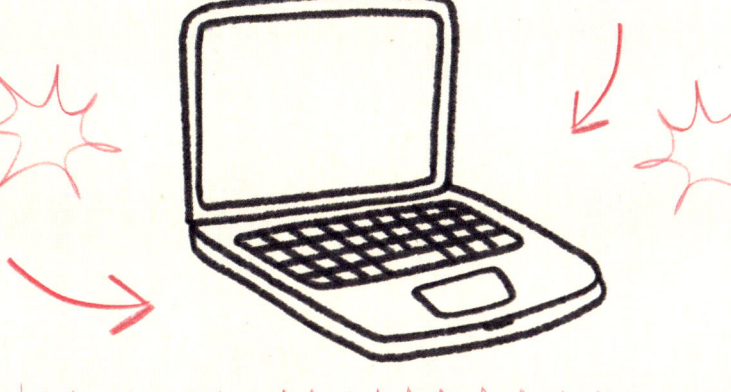

Clicky Keyboard

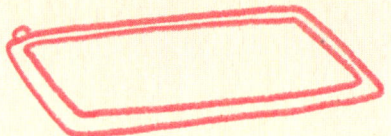

1. Draw two rounded rectangles. Draw a small, rounded shape on the top left for the cable.

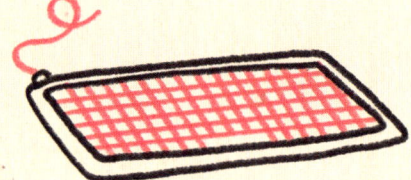

2. Add a grid for the keys and a curly line for the cable. Make sure there's a longer rectangle for the spacebar.

Mouse

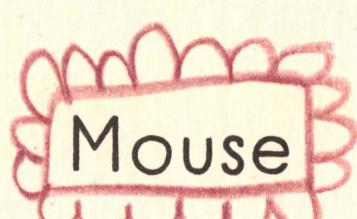

1. Draw an oval and add a curved line for the base. Draw a small circle for the cable.

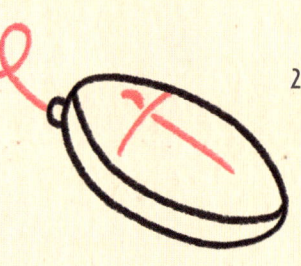

2. Add a T-shaped line for the buttons and a curly line for the cable.

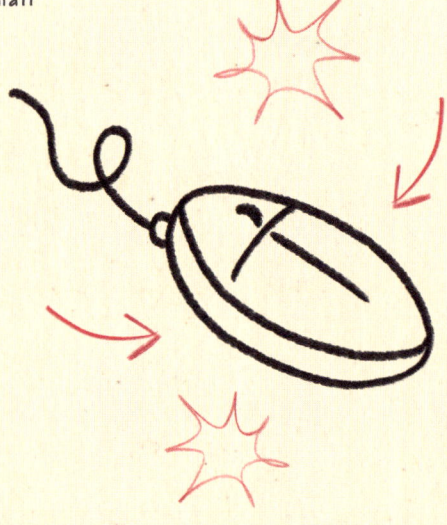

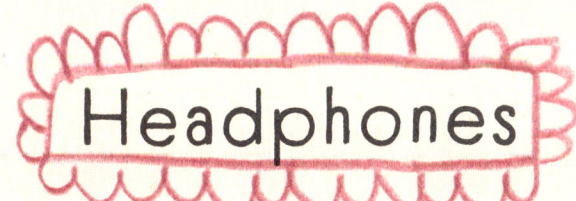

Headphones

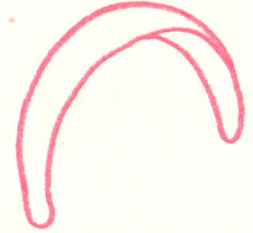

1. Draw a curved shape with rounded ends like a sideways C. Add a curved line below the right side of the curved shape for dimension.

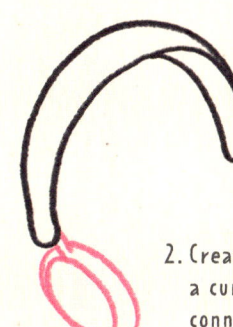

2. Create an oval for the ear. Add a curve inside and add lines to connect it to the headband.

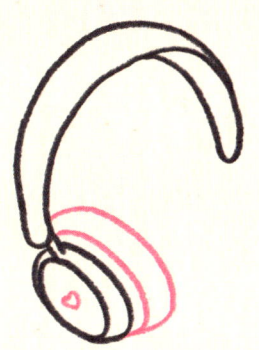

3. Draw a bigger curved line for the padding. Add a small heart detail!

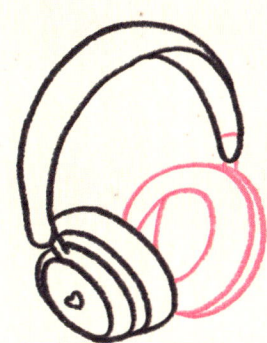

4. Create a bigger circular shape on the other end of the headband. Draw a smaller oval inside this and color in.

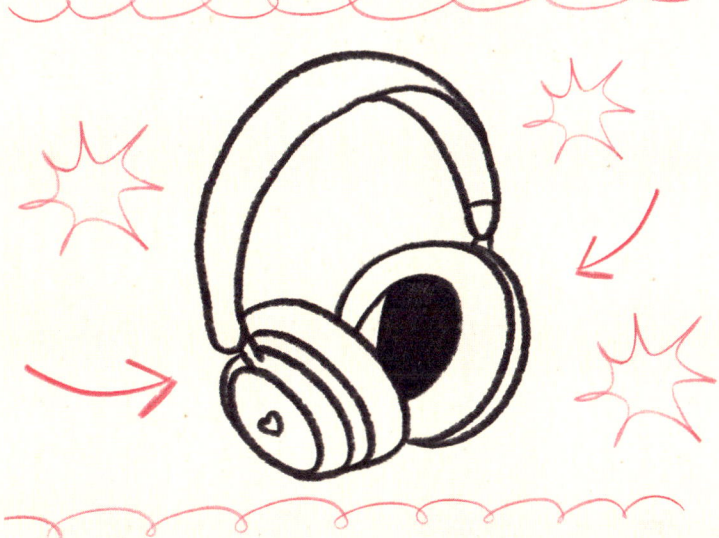

Pencil

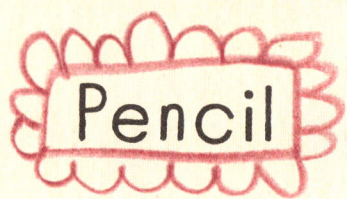 

1. Create the tip of a triangle, then add long, curved lines on either side for the pencil body. Draw two horizontal, curved lines for the eraser.

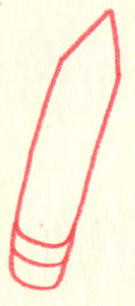

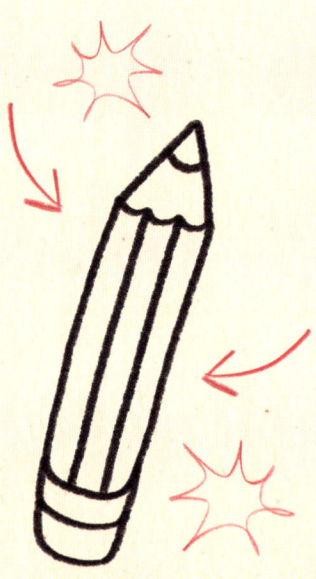

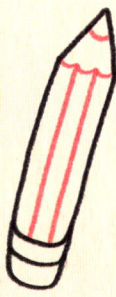

2. Draw a curved line at the tip and a scalloped edge at the bottom of the triangular shape. Draw straight lines down the body for detail.

Pencil Pot

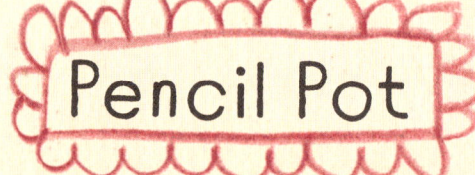

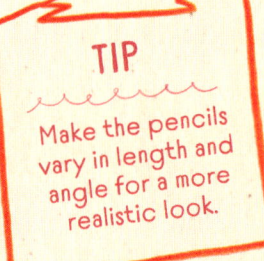

TIP

Make the pencils vary in length and angle for a more realistic look.

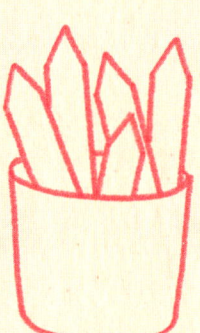

1. Draw a rectangle for the pot with curved lines for the top and bottom. Add pencils coming out of the pot.

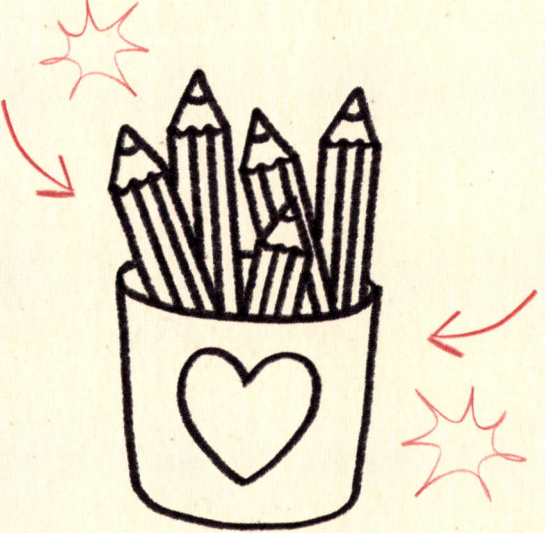

2. Add the pencil details to each shape. Draw a heart on the front of the pot.

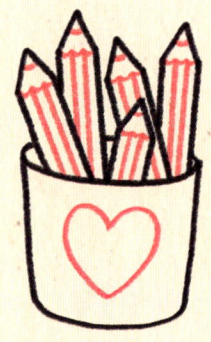

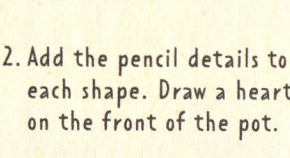

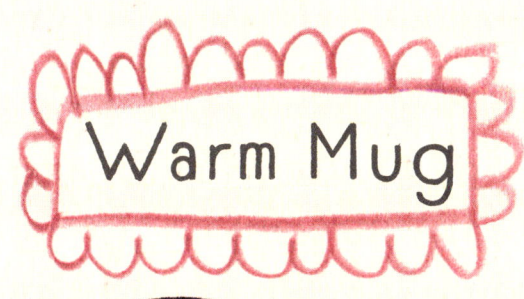

Warm Mug

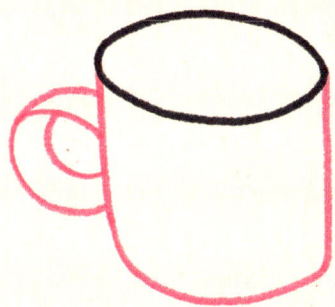

1. Start with an oval for the opening of the mug.

2. Add the base of the mug with two straight lines and a curved line at the base. Draw a C-shaped handle on the left side with a line through the shape for dimension.

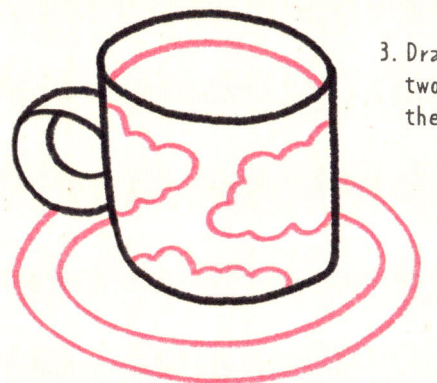

3. Draw a liquid line inside the opening and two circles around the mug's base to create the saucer. Finish with a cloud pattern!

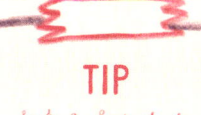

TIP

Add your own pattern to the mug! Check out Common Things in Your Room (page 14) for inspiration.

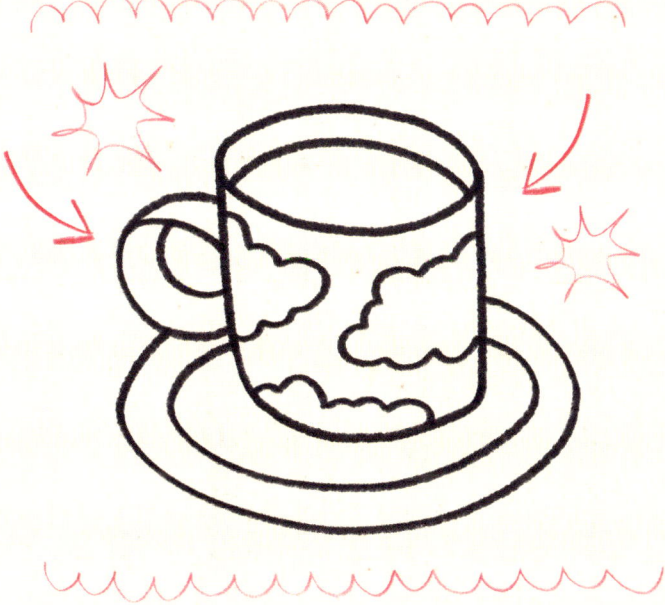

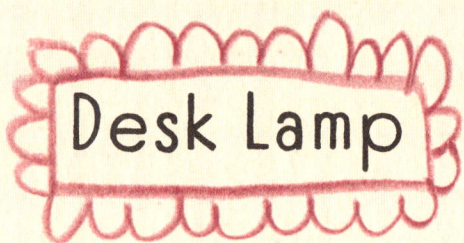

Desk Lamp

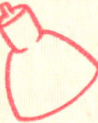

1. Draw the head of the lamp. Create a curved triangle shape with a rectangle shape on top with a point for the cord.

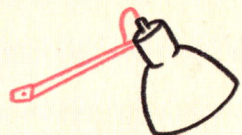

2. Draw two parallel lines to the left of the head with a cord extending from the top. At the end of the lines, draw a small rectangle with a dot in the center.

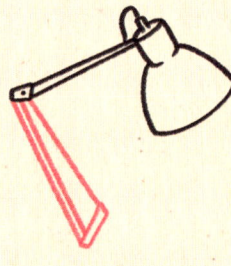

3. Draw another three lines so that the lamp arm bends at a ninety-degree angle. Add a rectangle at the end of the lines.

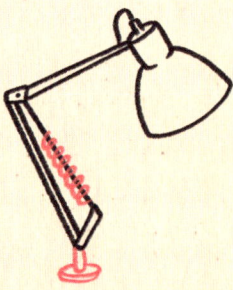

4. Draw a curlicue on the bottom right line of the arm. Add a stand with a short rectangle connected to the circular base.

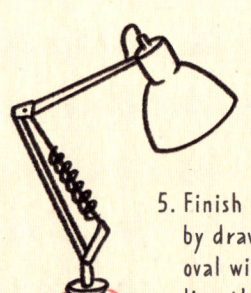

5. Finish the base by drawing an oval with a curved line through the middle.

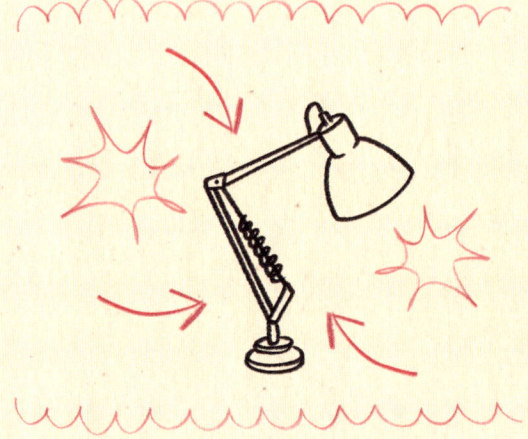

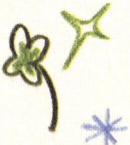

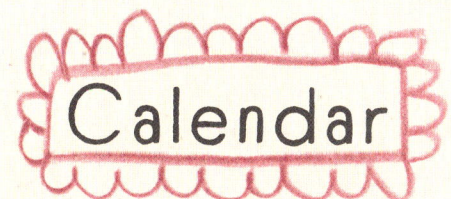

1. Start by drawing a vertical rectangle.

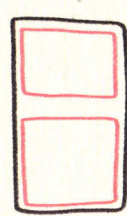

2. Draw a square below a wide rectangle inside the vertical rectangle.

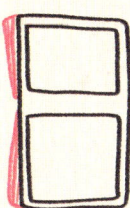

3. Add dimension to the pages of the calendar by drawing lines close together on the top and bottom half of the calendar.

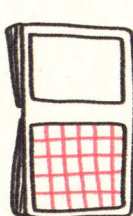

4. Draw a grid in the square of the calendar (the bottom shape).

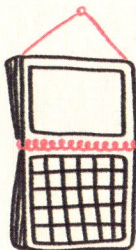

5. Add a curlicue line through the middle of the calendar and two lines meeting above the calendar toward a circle.

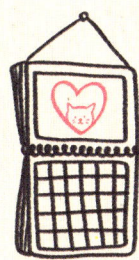

6. Decorate your calendar! Draw a heart with a friendly feline inside.

TIP

Add whatever designs you want to your calendar, like a few of your favorite things from Common Things in Your Room (page 14).

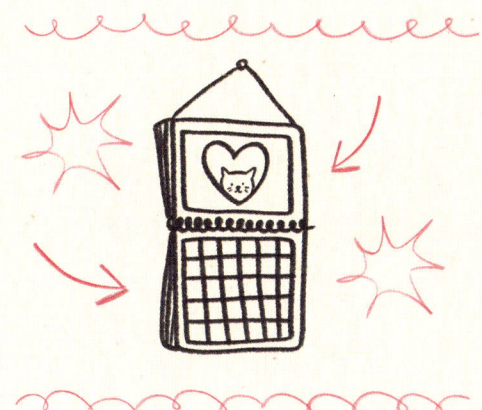

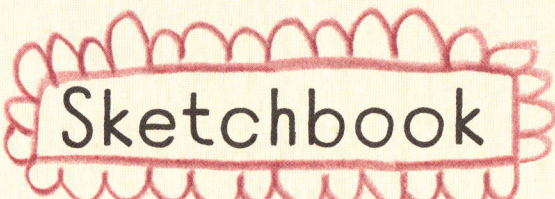

Sketchbook

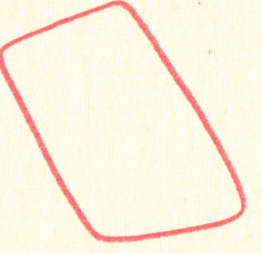

1. Start by drawing an angled rectangle with rounded corners.

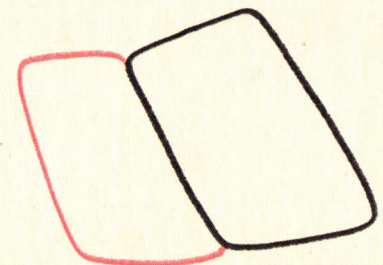

2. Duplicate the rectangle on the left side.

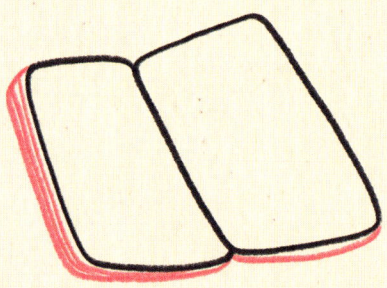

3. Add pages to your open sketchbook by drawing lines on the left side and below the book.

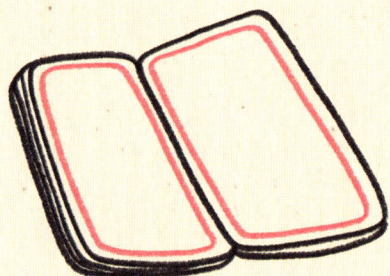

4. Draw two rectangles inside the pages of the sketchbook.

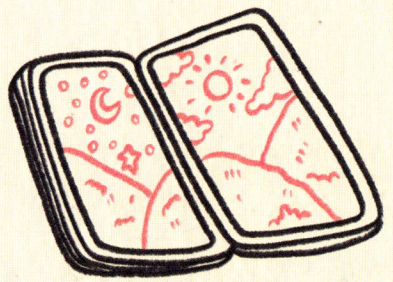

5. Decorate your sketchbook pages! Draw a natural scene or a room from this book.

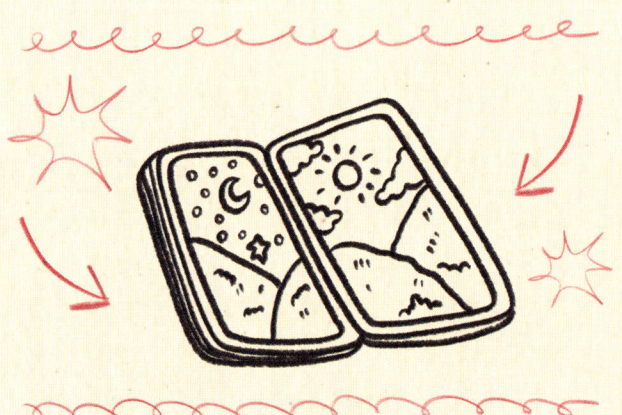

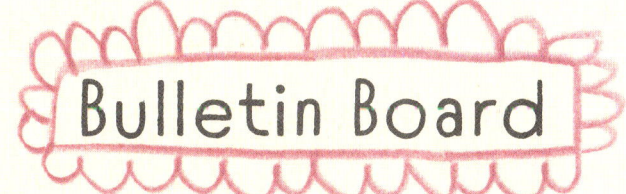

Bulletin Board

1. Draw a square with another slightly smaller square inside. Connect the corners with lines to create the frame.

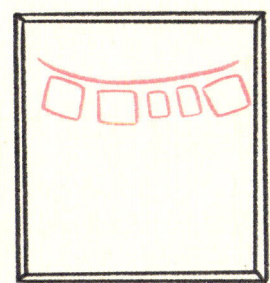

2. Add a curved line on the top half of the bulletin board, with five rectangles of various sizes below.

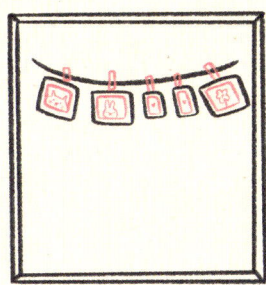

3. Draw another rectangle inside each shape and a design inside each photo. Add long, thin rectangles to connect the photos to the string.

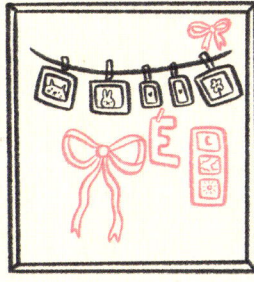

4. Draw two bows in different sizes. Add a letter of your choice taped to the bulletin board and a photobooth strip.

5. Finish with details from Common Things in Your Room (page 14) like a star or clover, a to-do list, and a landscape photo.

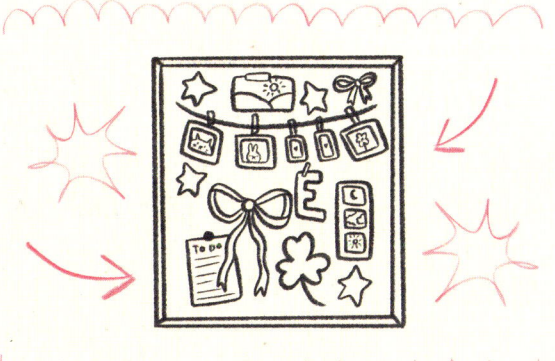

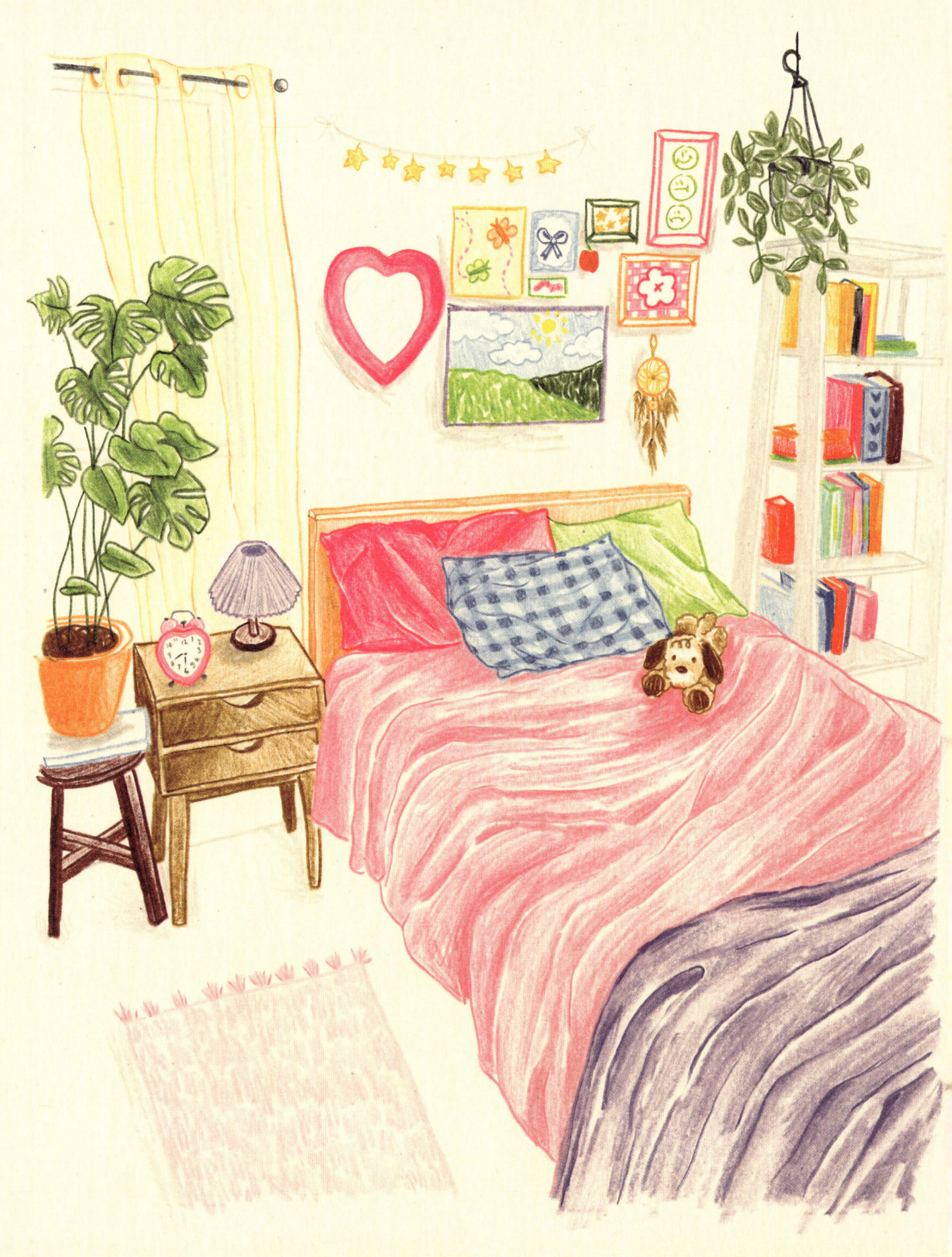

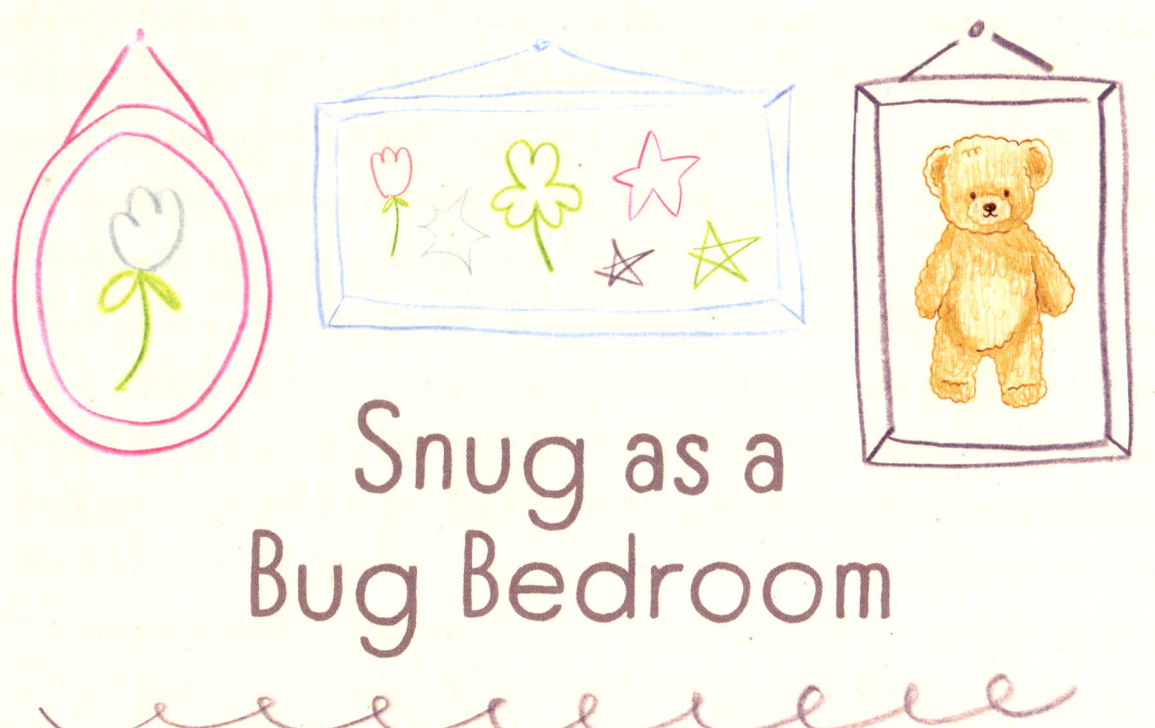

Snug as a
Bug Bedroom

Grab your favorite book and get cozy in bed! Surround yourself with luscious plants and curate your own gallery wall by adding designs from Common Things in Your Room (page 14) to your art prints and posters and a dreamy star garland from Cozy Gathering Space (page 49).

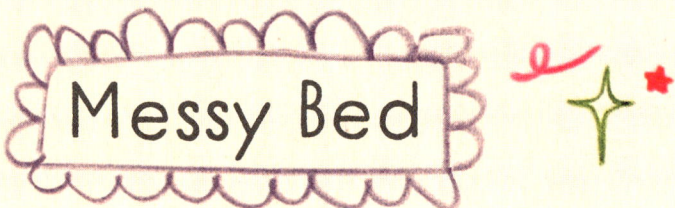

Messy Bed

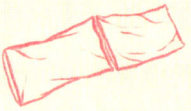

1. Start with the Pillows (page 43). Draw two rectangles side by side at an angle, with an open end on the left pillow. Add lines for pillowcase creases.

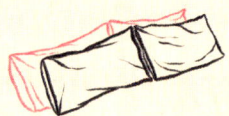

2. Add two more pillows behind the front pillows. Only the tops and the left opening will be visible. Add creases to the back pillows.

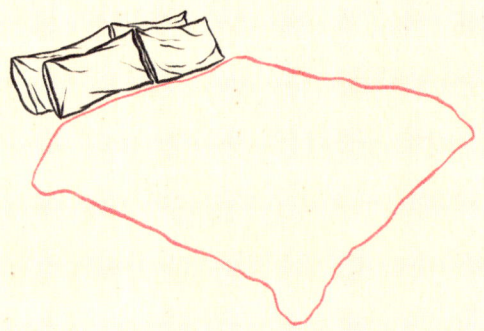

3. Draw the rectangular bedspread with the bottom three corners hanging lower.

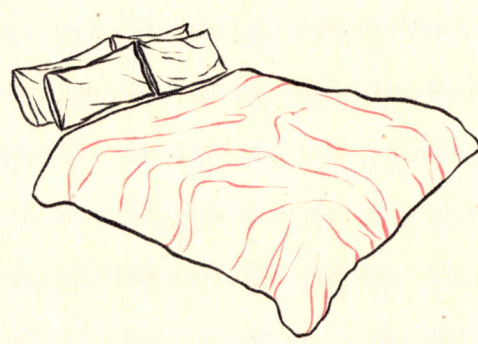

4. Add creases to the bedspread in wavy lines and short, curved lines.

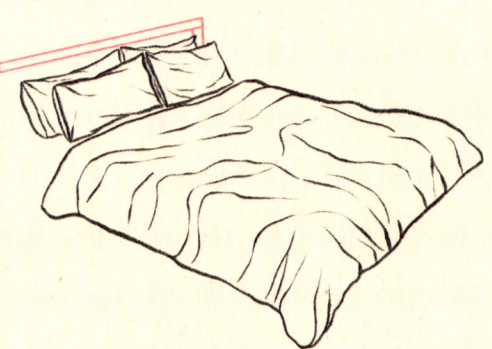

5. Start the headboard by adding one short rectangle beside the back right pillow and a long, wide rectangle above and parallel to the pillows and bedspread.

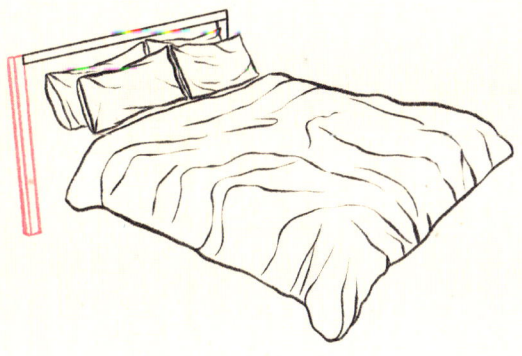

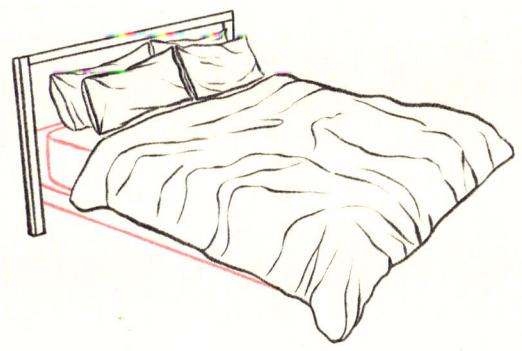

6. Draw a tall rectangle with a vertical line through the middle for dimension. Connect the rectangle to the long, wide rectangle of the headboard.

7. Finish the headboard with a short line connecting the vertical rectangle to the back left pillow. Draw the bottom of the bed with two parallel lines and add the mattress with the corner of a cube below the left pillows.

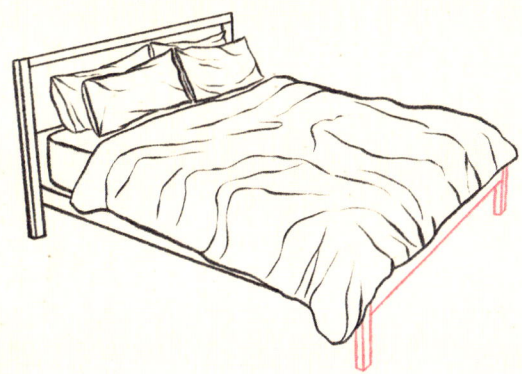

8. Draw the end of the bed with a straight line parallel to the edge of the bedspread and two legs at each corner. Draw a vertical line through each leg for perspective.

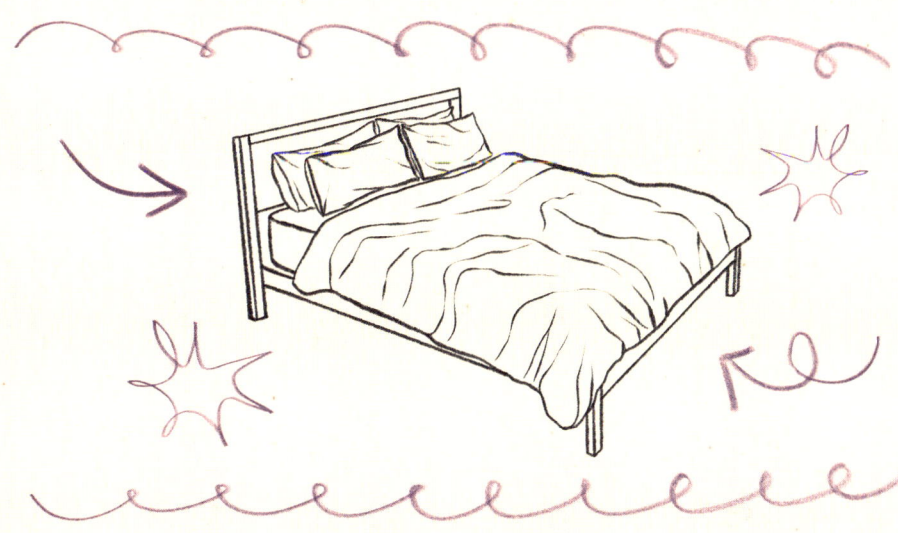

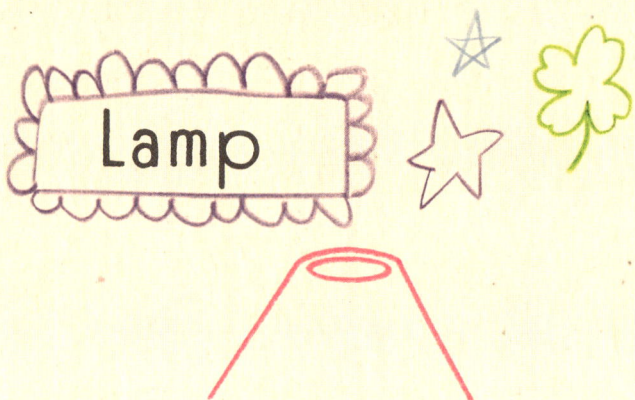

Lamp

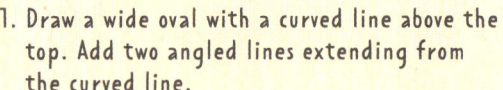

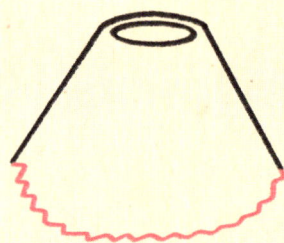

1. Draw a wide oval with a curved line above the top. Add two angled lines extending from the curved line.

2. Draw a zigzagged half circle connecting the two extended lines.

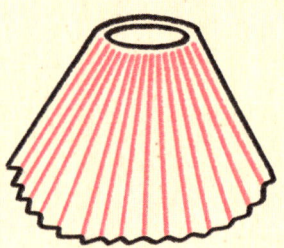

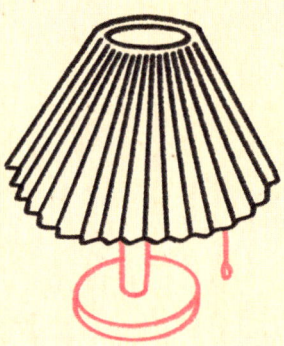

3. Draw a series of lines connecting the top of the lamp shade to the zigzags; there should be more space between the lines at the bottom.

4. Finish with the base of the lamp using a short rectangle connected to a wide oval with a curved line below for dimension. Add a vertical line with a small circle below the lampshade for the light switch.

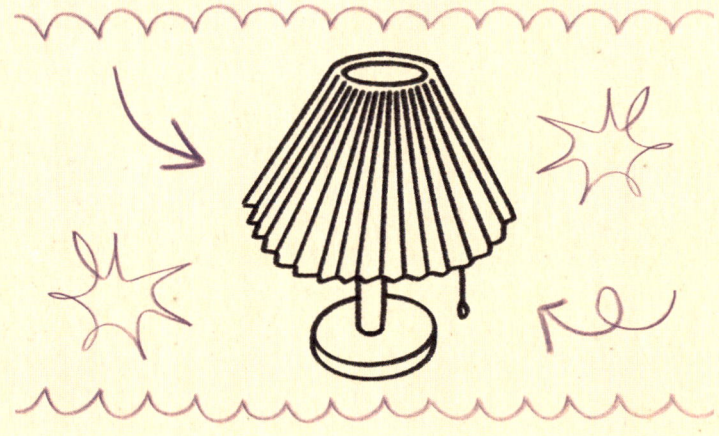

1. Draw an open-topped cylinder. Add two curved lines inside the pot for the dirt.

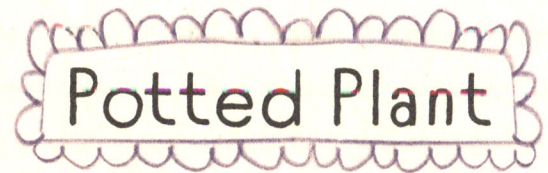

Potted Plant

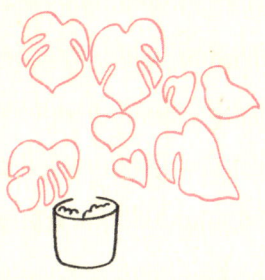

2. Draw a group of leaves above the pot. Start with an approximate heart shape with finger shapes cut out of the sides of the larger leaves.

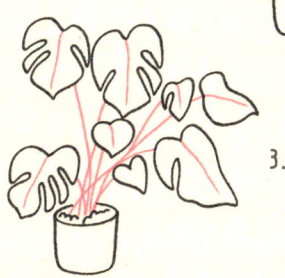

3. Draw a stem from the dirt towards the direction of the center of the leaf. Draw a line through the center of the leaves, like broken hearts.

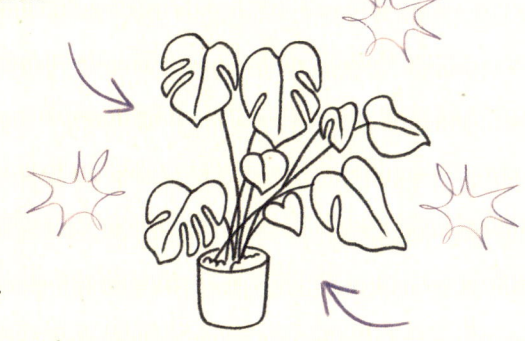

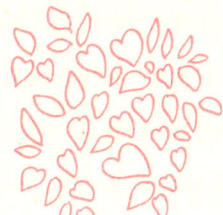

1. Draw a cluster of heart shapes and leaf shapes.

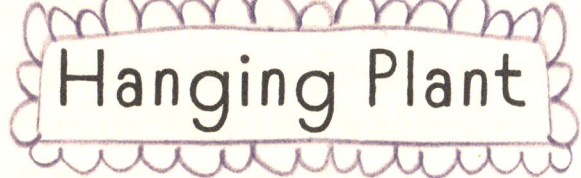

Hanging Plant

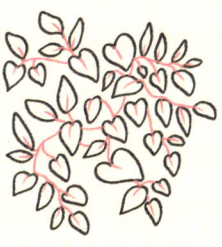

2. Draw stems connecting all the shapes, with a longer line through the entire cluster and shorter lines from the main stem to the leaves.

TIP

Remove the grooves in the leaves to make a different plant species! Turn your monstera deliciosa into a spider plant or a flowering plant.

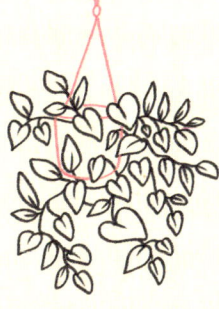

3. Finish with a rounded pot in the center of the cluster behind the leaves, below a triangle shape topped with a C-shaped hook.

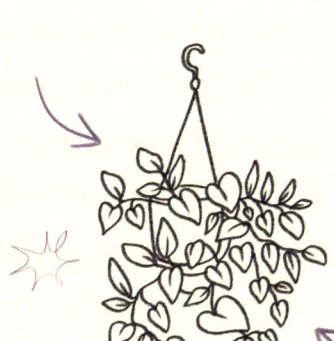

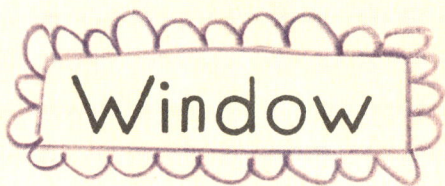

Window

1. Draw two rectangles, one inside the other.

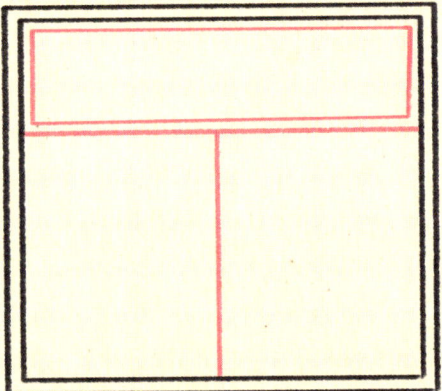

2. Draw a horizontal line across the top third of the interior rectangle. Draw a rectangle inside the top third and split the space between the remaining two-thirds with a vertical line.

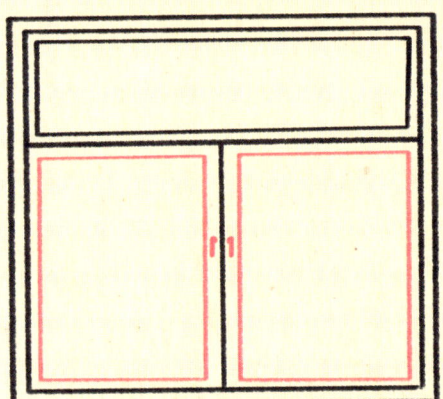

3. Draw two rectangles inside the bottom windows. Add two knobs.

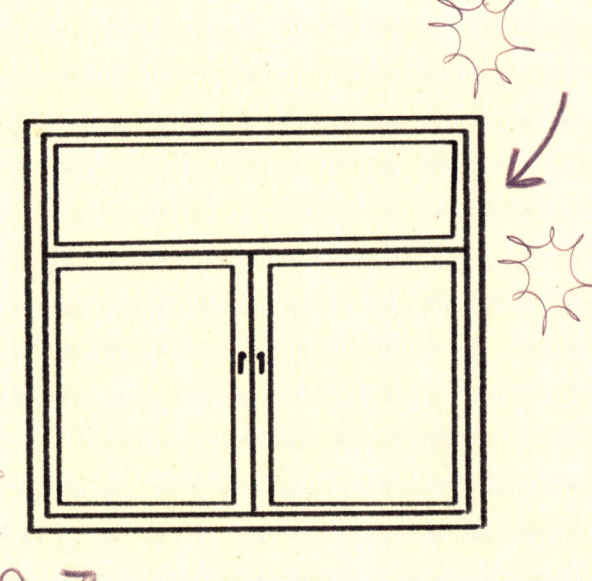

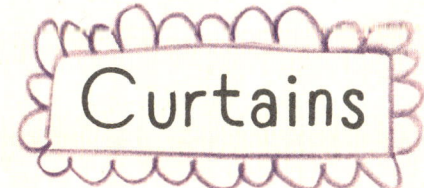

Curtains

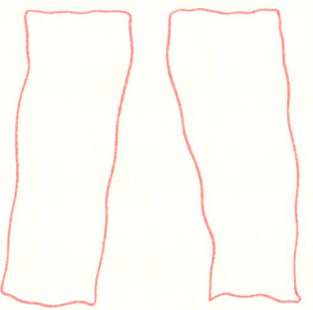

1. Draw two tall rectangles side by side, but make sure the shapes are imperfect and that the lines are shaky.

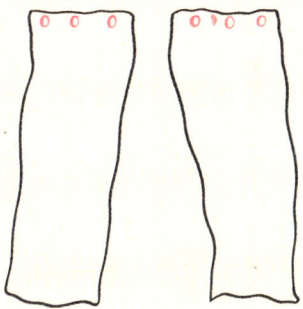

2. Add circles along the top of the shapes.

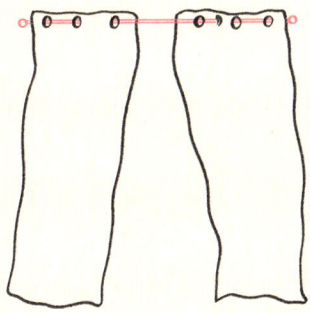

3. Draw the rod between the circles, skipping every other circle. Add circles at each end of the rod.

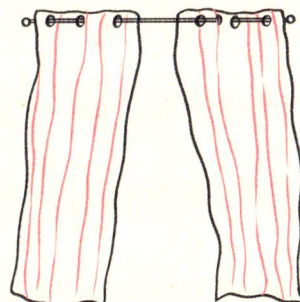

4. Finish with vertical, wavy lines on the curtains.

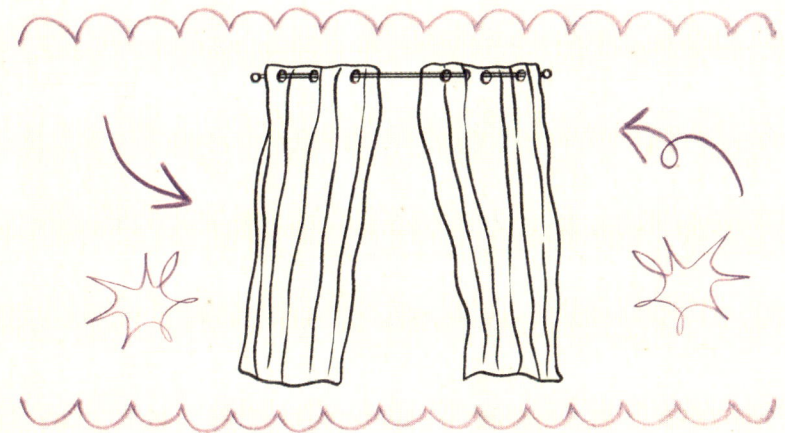

Dream Catcher

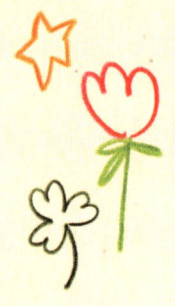

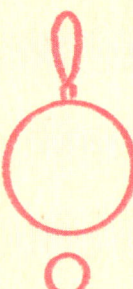

1. Start by drawing two circles. The top circle should be approximately triple the size of the bottom circle. Above the top circle, add a loop to hang the dream catcher.

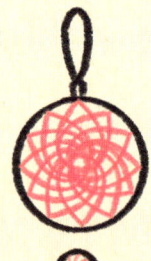

2. Add the woven patterns in each circle. In the bottom circle, draw a pinwheel pattern. In the top circle, add a lotus-like pattern using a repeated leaf shape.

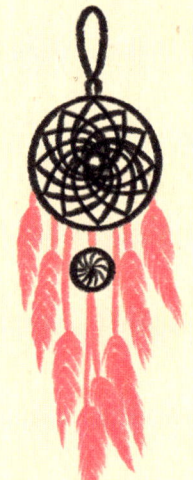

3. Finish by drawing lines for the feathers' quills hanging from the circles—one in the center and three on each side—with a feather at each end.

TIP

You can get the feather effect by drawing short, soft lines on either side of the quill line. Make the lines shorter as you get to the end and angle them in the shape of a point.

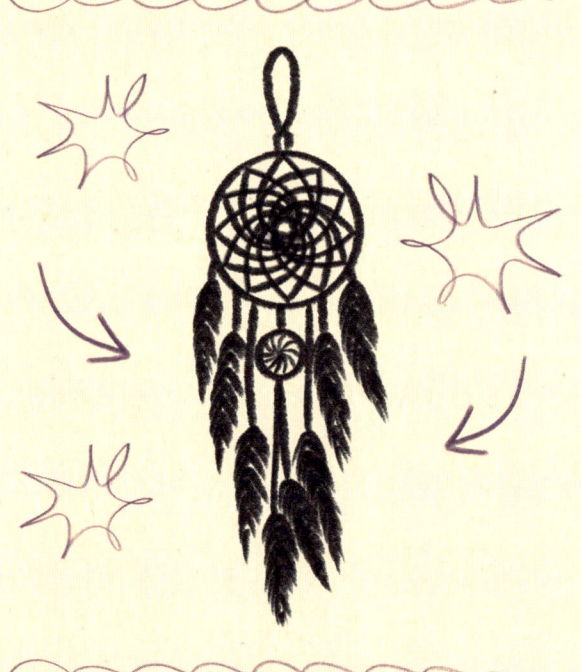

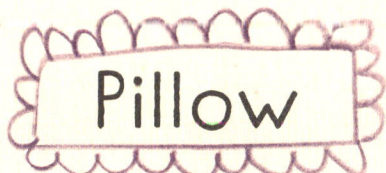

Pillow

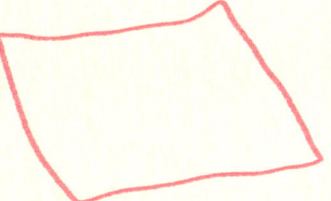

1. Draw a rectangle with rounded edges and pinched corners.

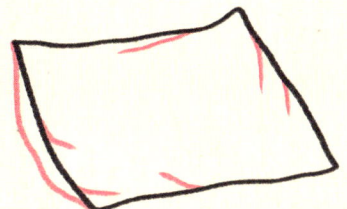

2. Draw a curved line on the left side. Add creases with short, straight lines along the rectangle's edges.

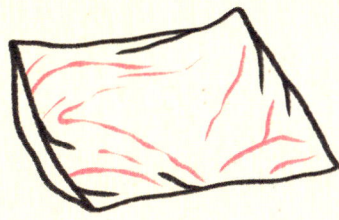

3. Add more creases! Draw curved lines, V shapes, and short Y shapes inside the rectangle.

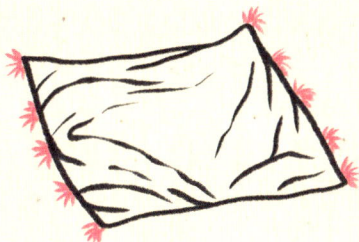

4. Add tassels by drawing five half-asterisks along the sides of the pillow.

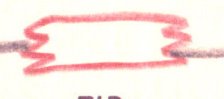

TIP

Draw small hearts or flowers, add tassels to the corners, or even draw a square instead, like the Throw Pillows (page 59) from the Cozy Gathering Space.

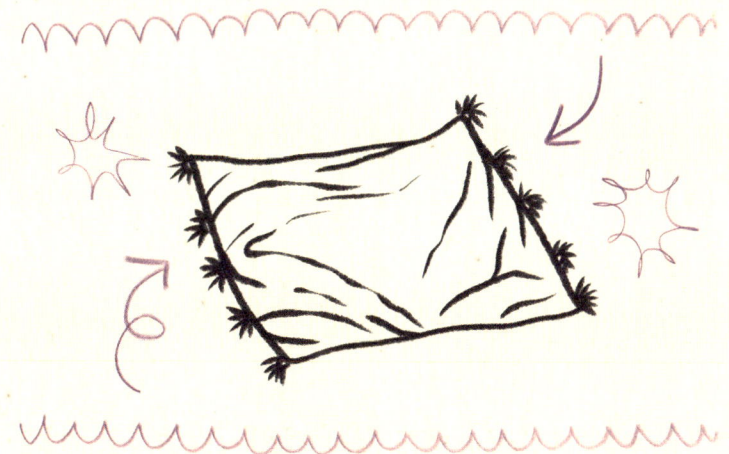

Bookcase

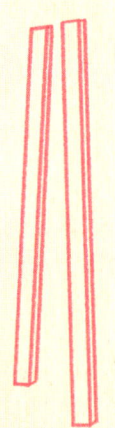

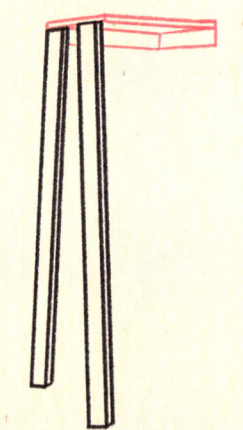

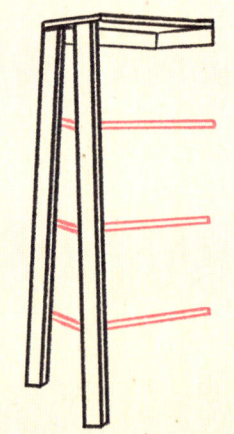

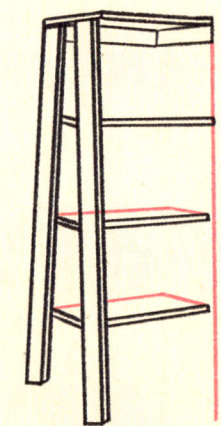

1. Draw two tall rectangles leaning toward each other in perspective. Draw a thinner rectangle of the same length off the right side of each rectangle.

2. Draw the top of the bookcase with a series of rectangles making up a square. The front two rectangles are thinner than the back two.

3. Draw the shelves by adding double lines connecting the legs of the bookcase. Add three angled, wide rectangles connected to the right leg.

4. Add perspective to the shelves by adding a bent line to the top of two shelves. Add a straight line connecting the shelves and the top of the bookcase.

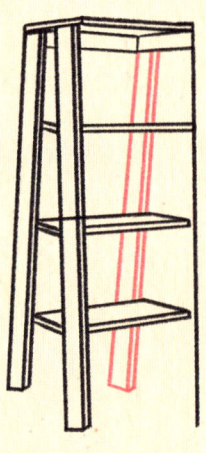

5. Draw the back, right leg of the bookcase.

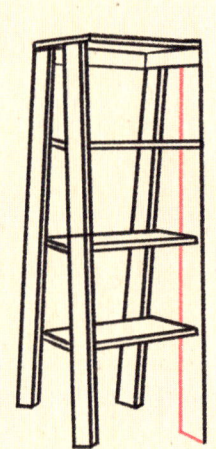

6. Finish with a line to the front, right leg along the length of the existing line and connected at the bottom with a short line.

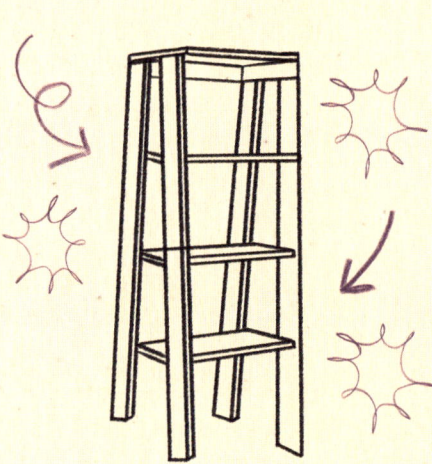

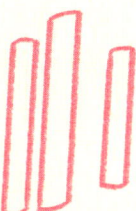

1. Draw three rectangles beside each other at different heights and at varying distances.

2. Add lines at an angle from the top and bottom of the rectangles. Connect the angled lines with vertical lines to complete the book shape.

3. Finish with lines on top of the books for the pages and decorations on the covers and spines. Take, for example, a star for *Peter Pan* or a ruby slipper for *The Wizard of Oz*!

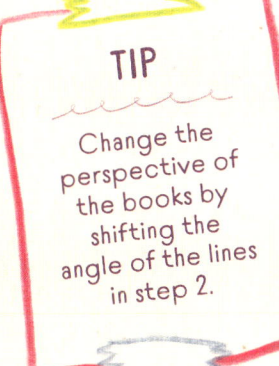

TIP

Change the perspective of the books by shifting the angle of the lines in step 2.

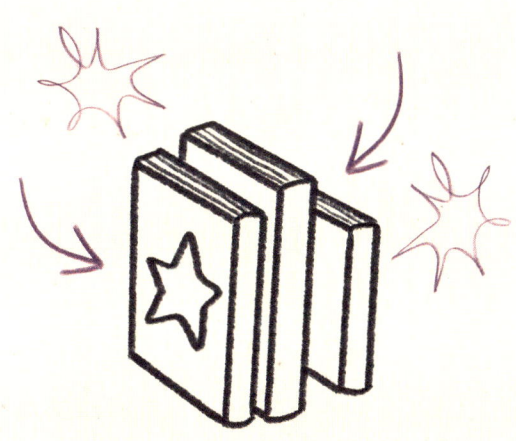

Alarm Clock

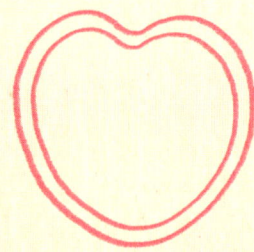

1. Draw two heart shapes with no sharp edges, one inside the other.

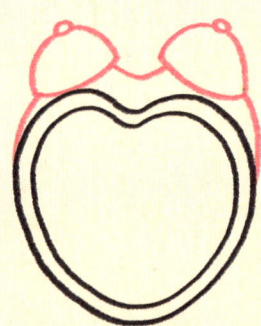

2. Add two bells above each curve using angled half circles, a curved edge to close the shape, and a small circle on the top of the bell. Draw a curved line parallel to the top and through the bells.

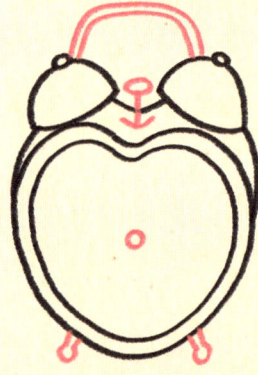

3. Add the details: a small circle in the middle of the clock face, the button between the bells, two short legs on the bottom of the clock, and a double-lined and curved handle.

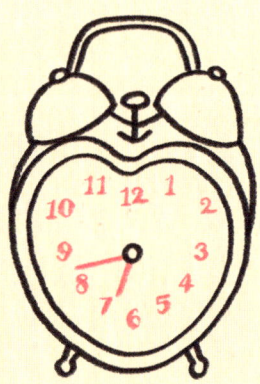

4. Finish with the numbers of the clock and the hour and minute hands. Twelve goes at the top!

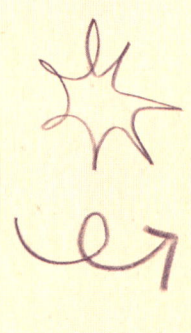

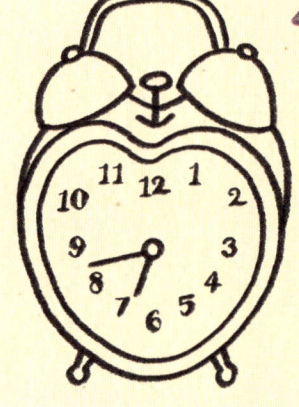

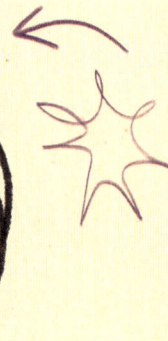

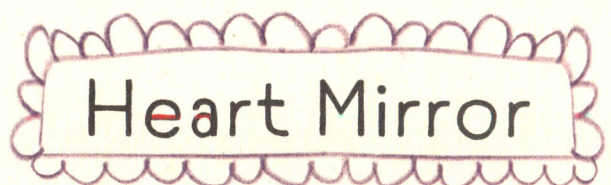

Heart Mirror

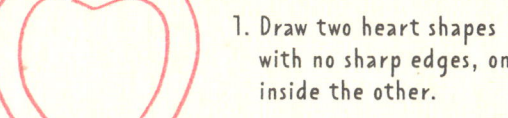

1. Draw two heart shapes with no sharp edges, one inside the other.

2. Add scalloped decoration around the edge of the mirror. Finish with delicate lines in the center of the mirror for a reflective effect.

ADD EVEN MORE DETAIL!

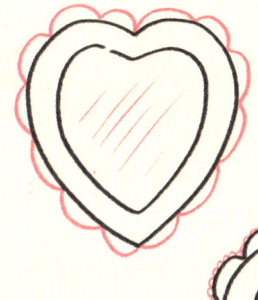

1. Add larger scalloped decoration around the edge of the mirror.

2. Add smaller scalloped decoration around the edge of the larger scalloped decoration.

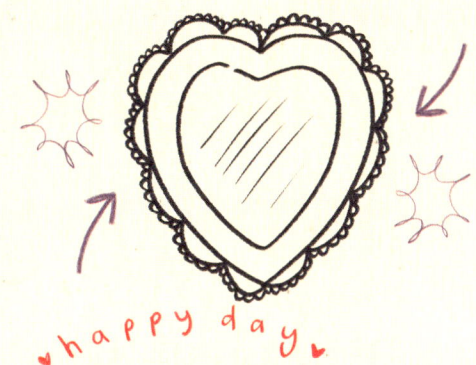

happy day

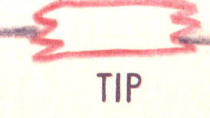

TIP

When coloring, get the reflective effect by adding delicate lines. Add some colors from the room, too, for an added effect!

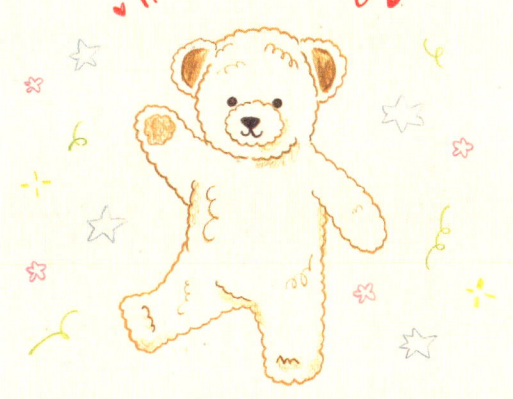

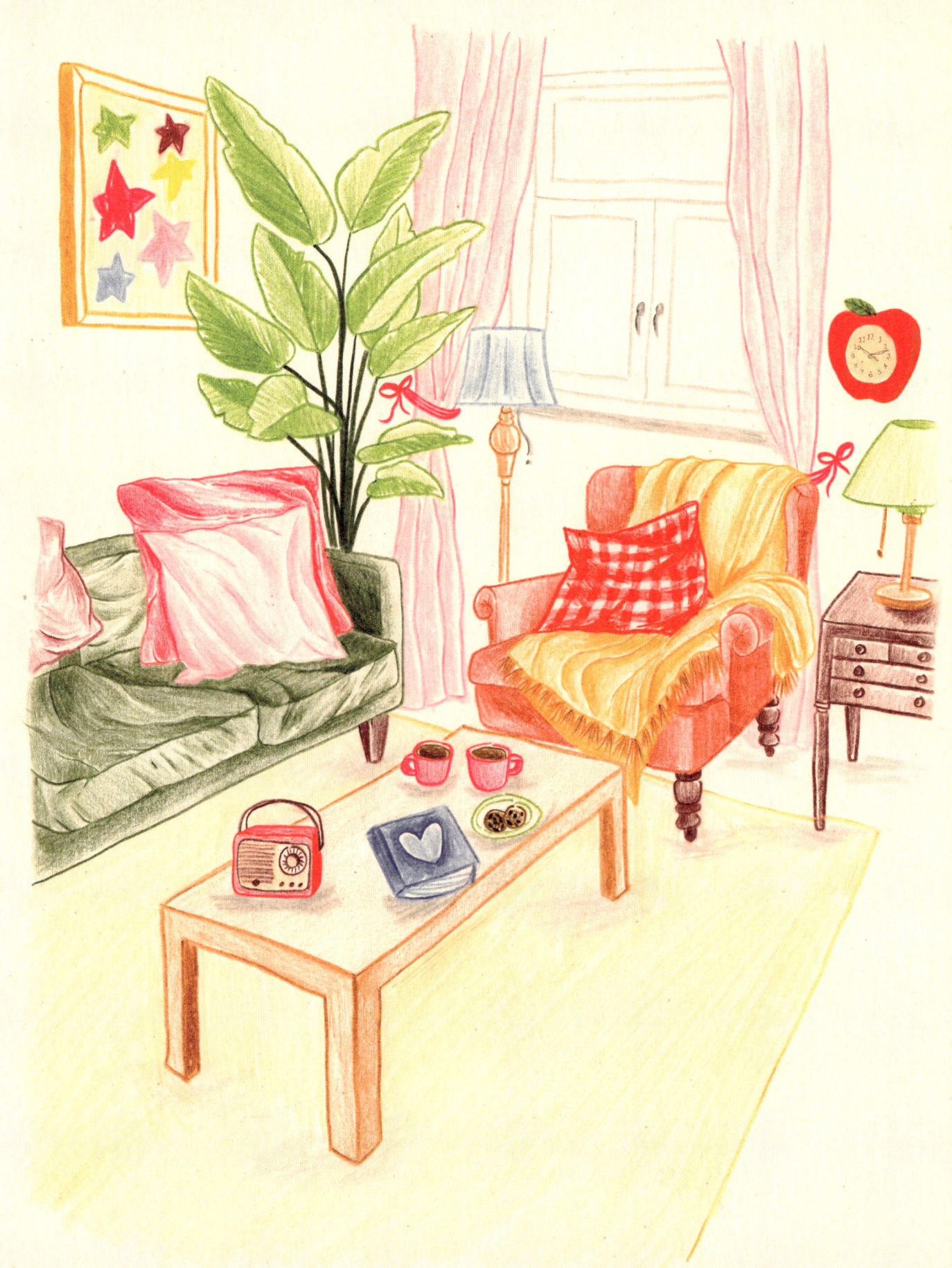

Cozy Gathering Space

Make your room a haven of warmth and comfort! Use your favorite colors to decorate the throw pillows in an array of patterns. Add a plate of your favorite sweet treats on a nearby side table by taking elements from Cute Cat Café (page 93).

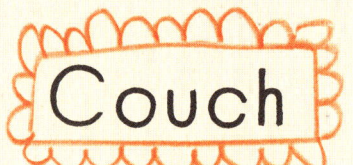

Couch

1. Start by drawing a straight, horizontal line. Then, add two legs at each end using angled rectangles with an extra line inside for perspective and the front arms of the couch with two vertical lines that turn toward the center.

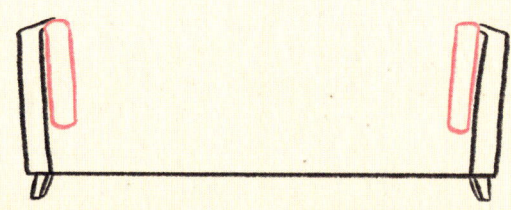

2. Draw two tall rectangles with rounded edges at each end of the couch.

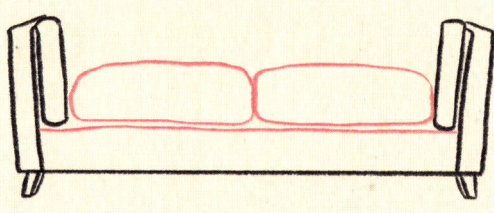

3. Draw a horizontal line below the round-edged cushions of the couch. Add two more larger cushions for the seats with round-edged, wide rectangles.

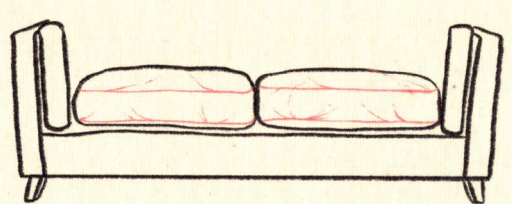

4. Add creases and dimension to the seat cushions with two horizontal lines along the top and bottom, along with short, straight lines.

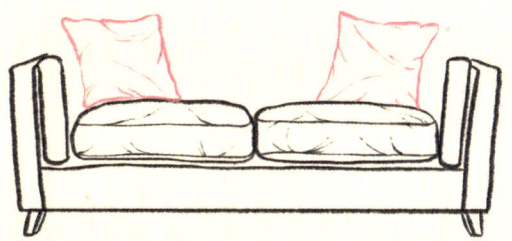

5. Add two Throw Pillows (page 59) to the couch.

6. Finish by drawing the back of the couch. Add two wide, symmetrical, and creased cushions behind the throw pillows. Draw two lines from each armrest toward the back of the couch.

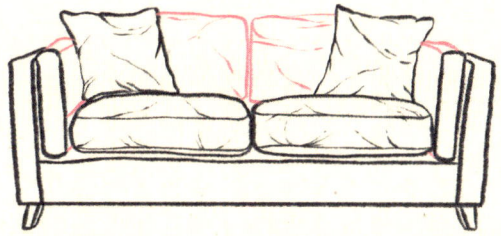

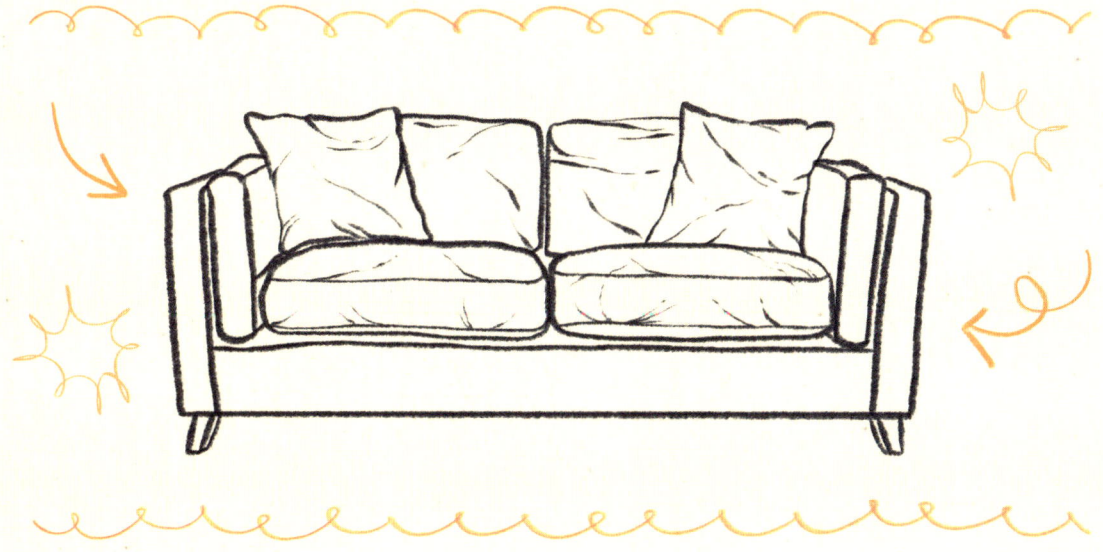

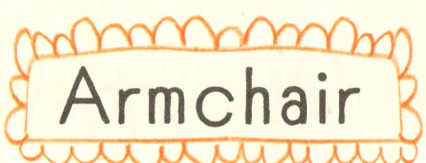 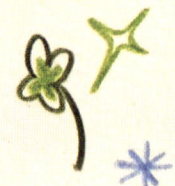

Armchair

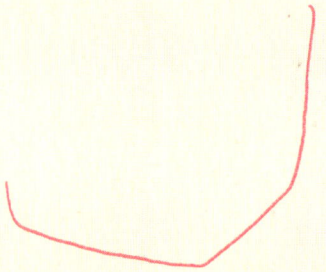

1. Start by drawing the base and right side of the chair. Draw a line with four curves.

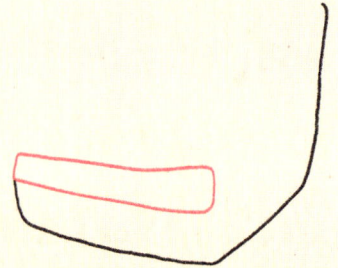

2. Draw a rectangle parallel to the bottom of the armchair.

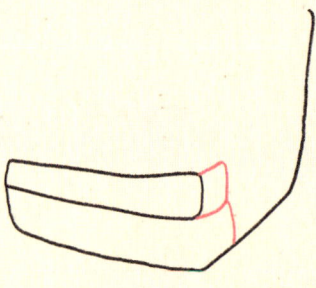

3. Draw a square to the right of the rectangle. Add a short, vertical line below the square.

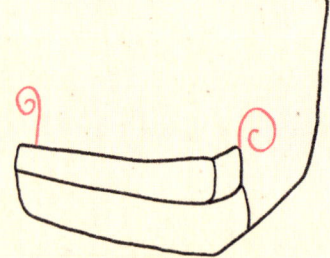

4. Draw mirrored P-shaped curlicues on either side of the rectangle/square.

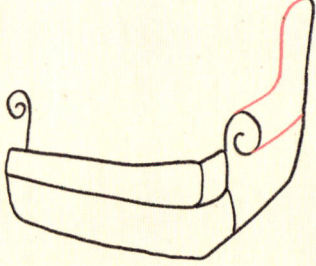

5. Add a bent line connecting the right P shape to the top of the armchair. Add a line connecting the P shape to the back of the armchair.

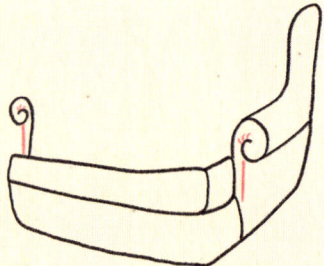

6. Draw a vertical line beneath the curlicue P shape.

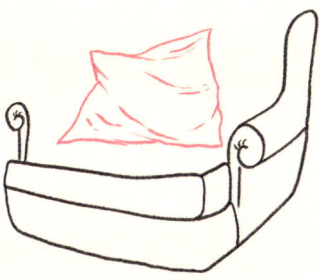

7. Draw a Throw Pillow (page 59) between the arms of the armchair.

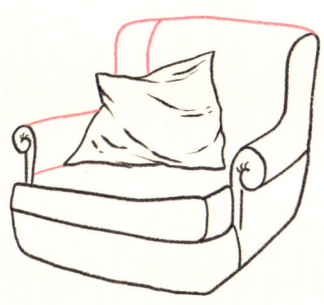

8. Draw the back of the chair with a curved line from the top right of the chair to the left P-shaped arm. Draw a line parallel to the left armrest and a vertical line above the pillow.

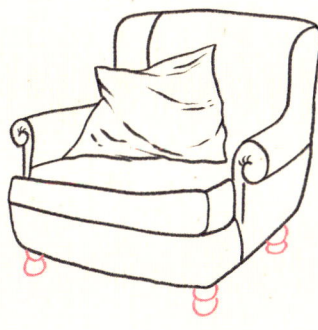

9. Draw the front legs of the chair and the back right leg by drawing two ovals stacked for each leg.

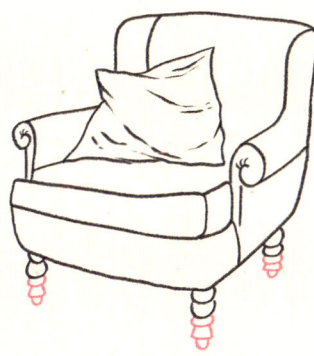

10. Finish the rest of the chair legs by adding more oval shapes to add height.

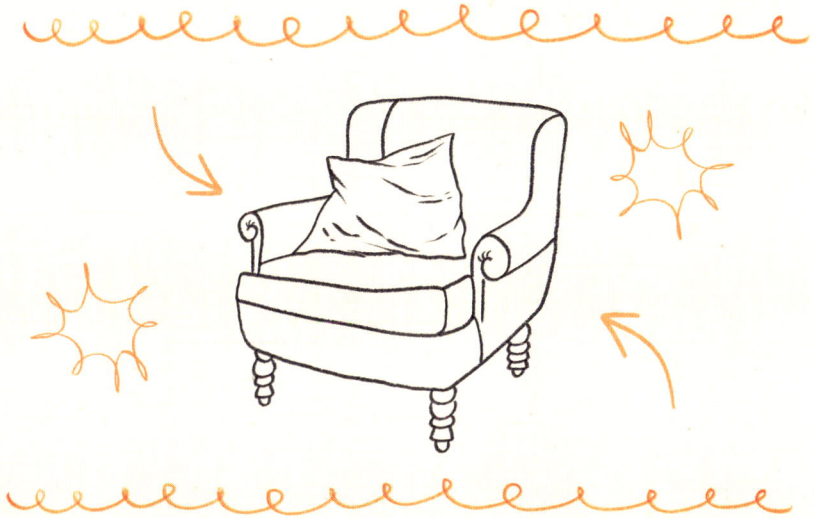

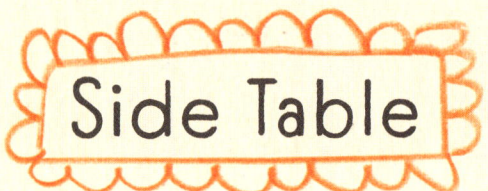

Side Table

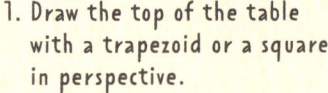

1. Draw the top of the table with a trapezoid or a square in perspective.

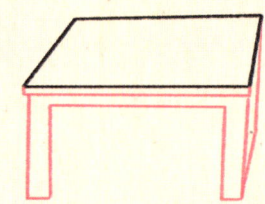

2. Add a staple-like shape below the tabletop. Connect the top right corner to the bottom right of the staple shape with a bent line.

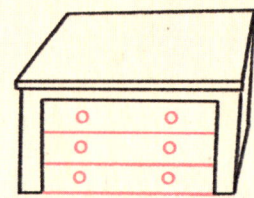

3. Within the staple shape, add three horizontal lines for the drawers. Add two circles on each drawer for the handles.

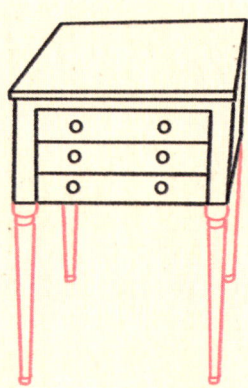

4. Finish with the four legs extending from each corner of the tabletop. The front legs start with circles below the table, then a rectangle and two long lines meeting together to a square. The back legs are half the length of the front legs.

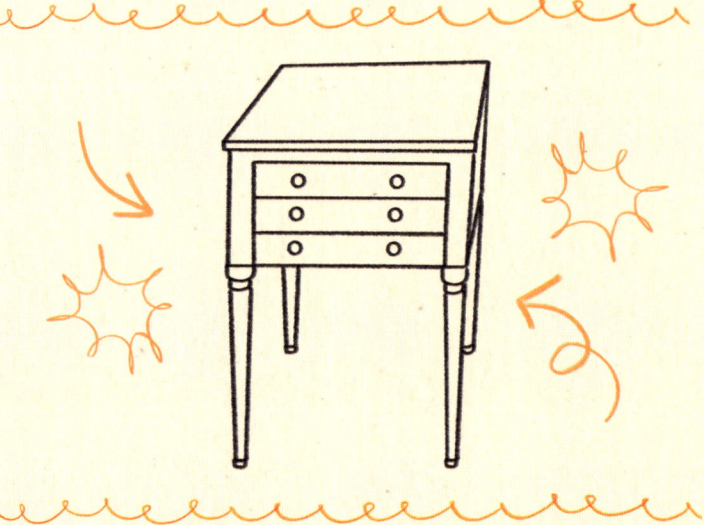

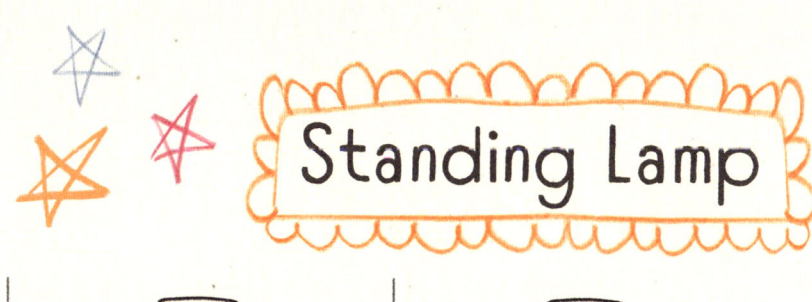

Standing Lamp

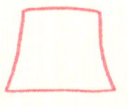
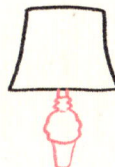

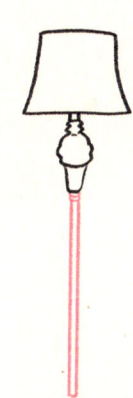

1. Draw a trapezoid with curved sides.

2. Draw a rectangle, a circle with ridged edges, and then a rectangle below.

3. Draw a tall, thin rectangle for the stand of the lamp.

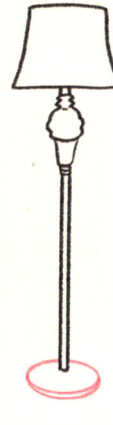

4. Add the base at the bottom using a wide oval and a curved line below it.

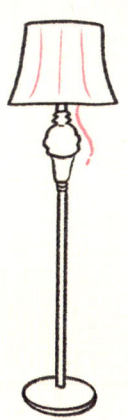

5. Finish with details, like three curved lines on the shade and a curvy line below one side of the shade for the light switch.

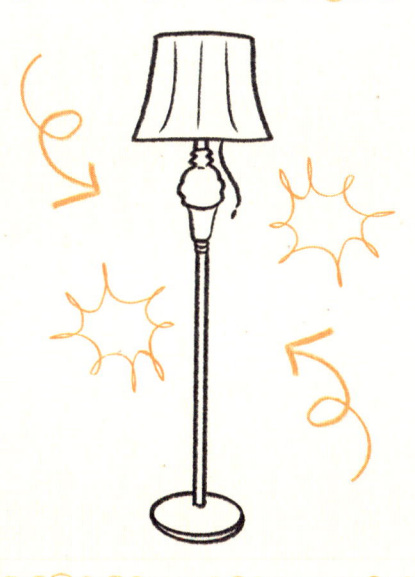

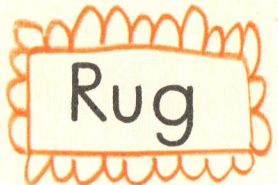

Rug

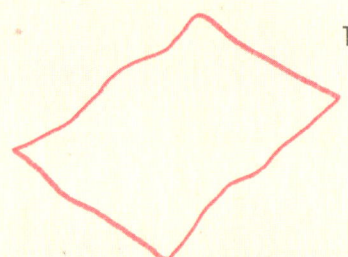

1. Draw a rectangle at an angle with wavy edges.

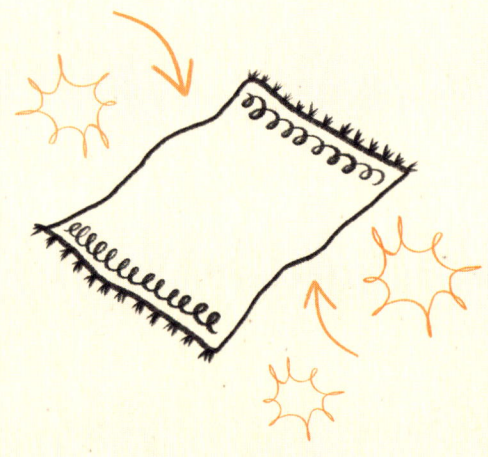

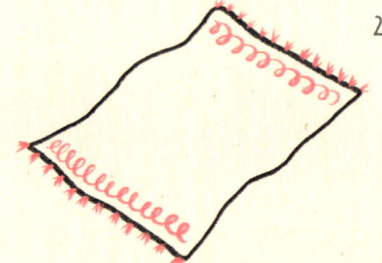

2. Add detail to the rug with curlicues along the ends and tassels—using three short, connected lines—along the edges.

PERSONALIZE YOUR RUG!

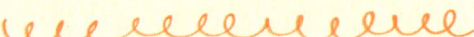

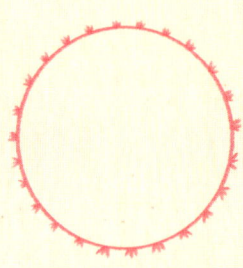

1. Draw a circle with tassels—using three short, connected lines—along the edges.

Decorate your rug with stripes or polka dots. Make it a circle or a star! Or even . . . add a bunny.

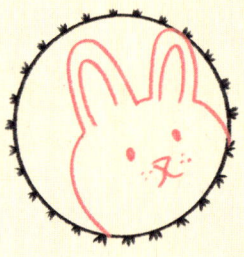

2. Add a bunny to your rug! Draw the head with two tall ears, a triangle nose and upside-down V mouth, three dots on each cheek, and dot eyes.

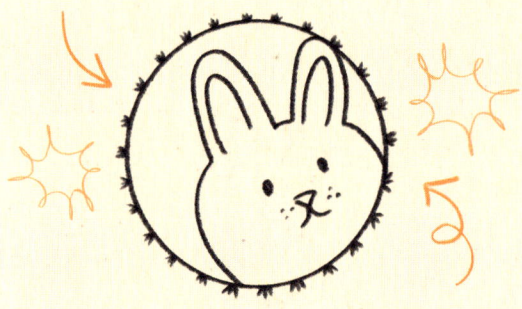

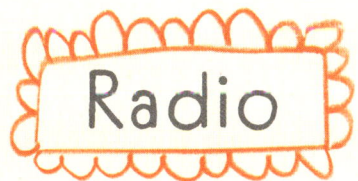

Radio

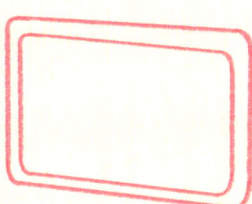

1. Draw two rectangles, one inside the other.

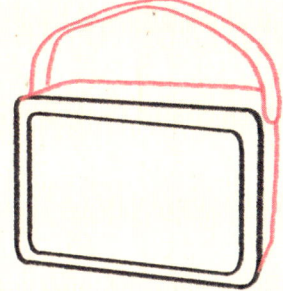

2. Draw the body of the radio with a line connecting the top left to the bottom right of the larger rectangle. Add a handle with two lines close together at varying widths.

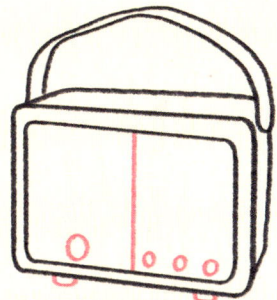

3. Add the buttons of the radio in the smaller rectangle. Draw a line splitting the rectangle in half, a circle on the bottom of the left side, and three smaller circles on the right side.

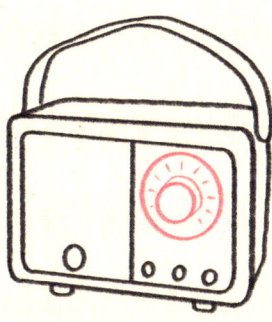

4. Add the larger knob on the right side of the radio. Draw a doughnut shape with short lines within the shape.

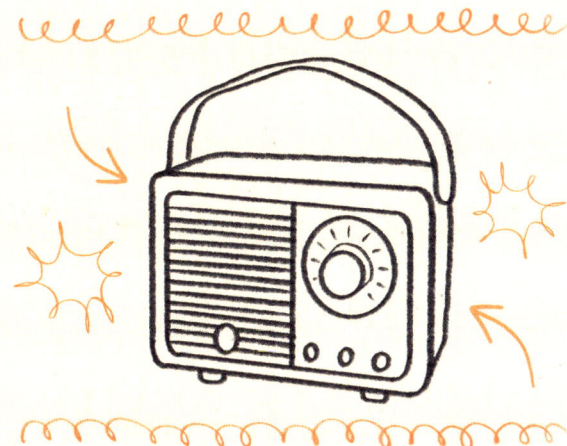

5. Finish with horizontal lines on the left side of the radio.

Picture Frame

1. Draw two tall rectangles, one inside the other.

2. Connect the corners of the rectangles. Add dimension by drawing parallel lines along the left side and the bottom and then connect each of these corners to the rectangle.

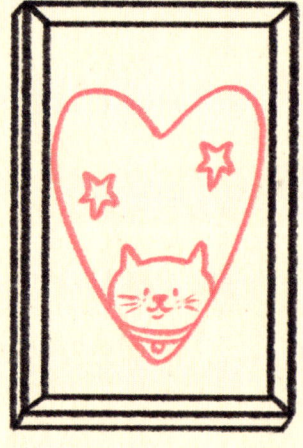

3. Add a portrait to your frame. Inside a heart, draw a cat's smiling face with stars above, as found in Common Things in Your Room (page 14).

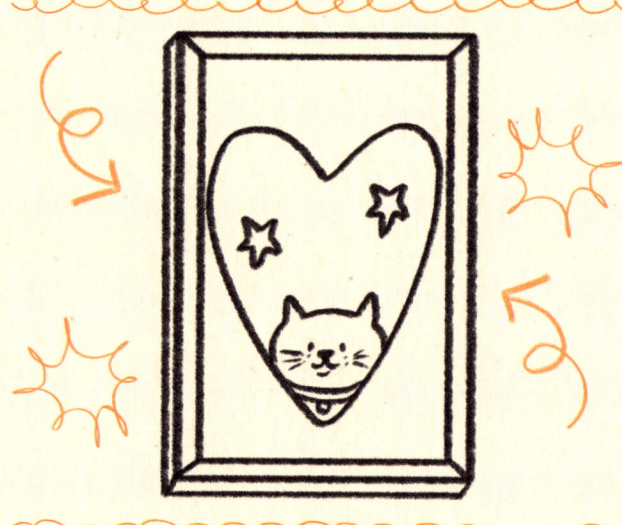

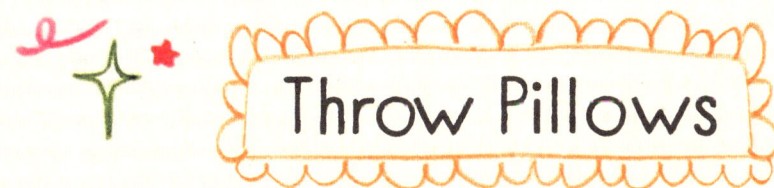

Throw Pillows

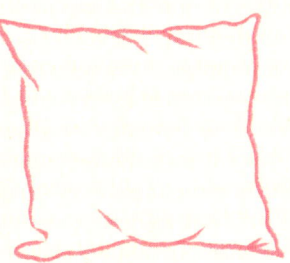

1. Draw a square with jagged edges and pointed corners. Add some creases and folds along the edges with short, straight lines.

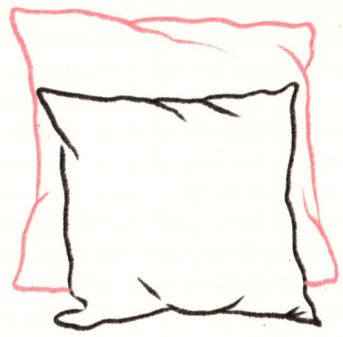

2. Draw another, larger square with jagged edges and pointed corners with creases and folds.

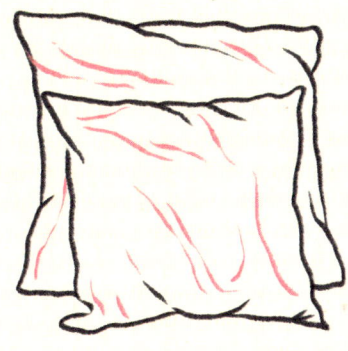

3. Finish with more texture details using straight and curved lines.

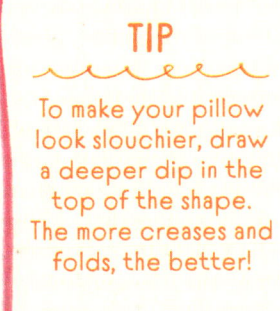

TIP

To make your pillow look slouchier, draw a deeper dip in the top of the shape. The more creases and folds, the better!

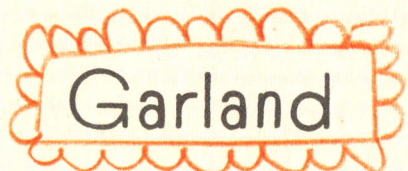

Garland

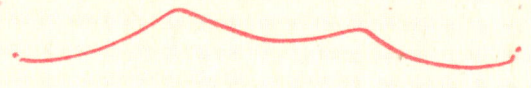

1. Start by drawing a curved line with two peaks. Draw dots at each end.

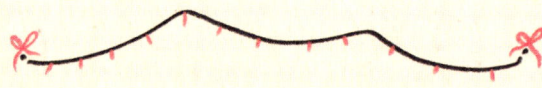

2. Draw a series of short lines along the bottom of the curved line. Add one bow at each end of the line.

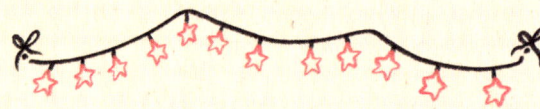

3. Finish with star shapes at the end of each short line.

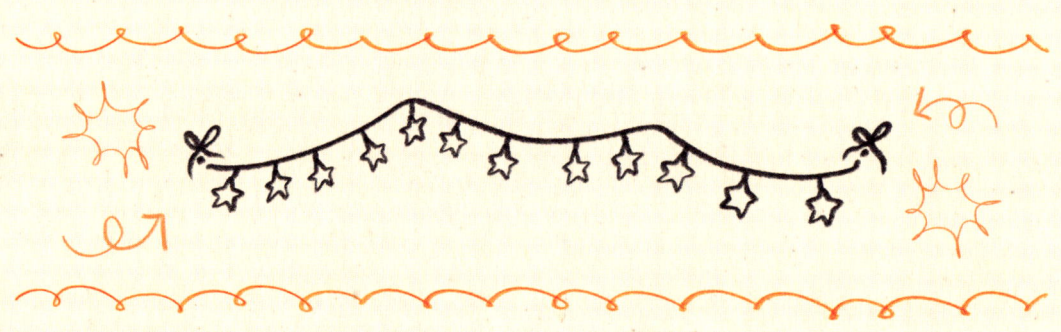

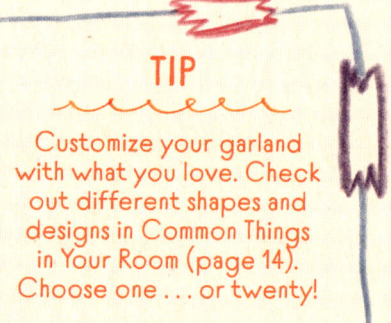

TIP

Customize your garland with what you love. Check out different shapes and designs in Common Things in Your Room (page 14). Choose one . . . or twenty!

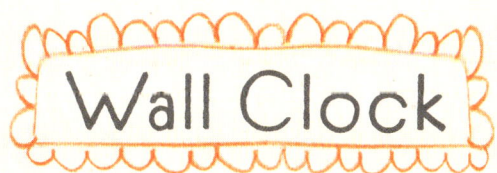
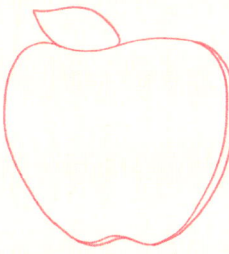

1. Draw an apple with a leaf on the top. Add a line on the right side connecting the top and bottom of the shape and a line on the left bump on the bottom to add dimension.

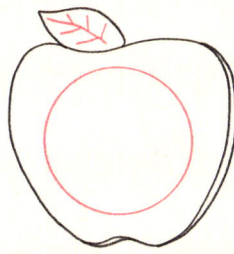

2. Draw a circle in the center of the apple. Add lines on the leaf.

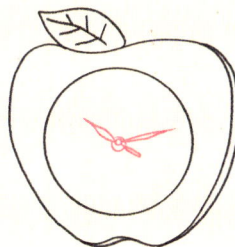

3. Draw a small circle in the center of the clock face. Add the hour and minute hands with pointed shapes.

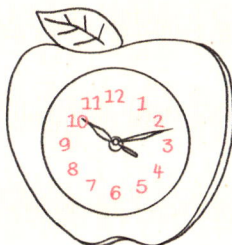

4. Finish the clock by adding the numbers. Twelve goes at the top!

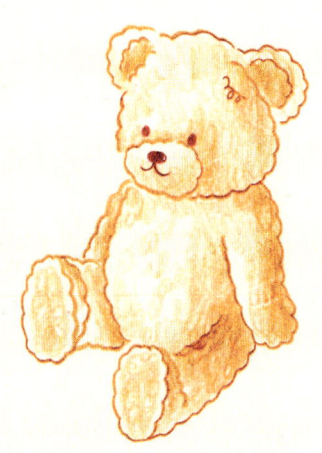

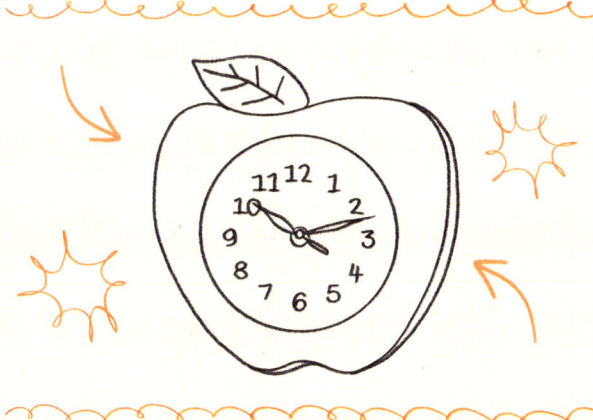

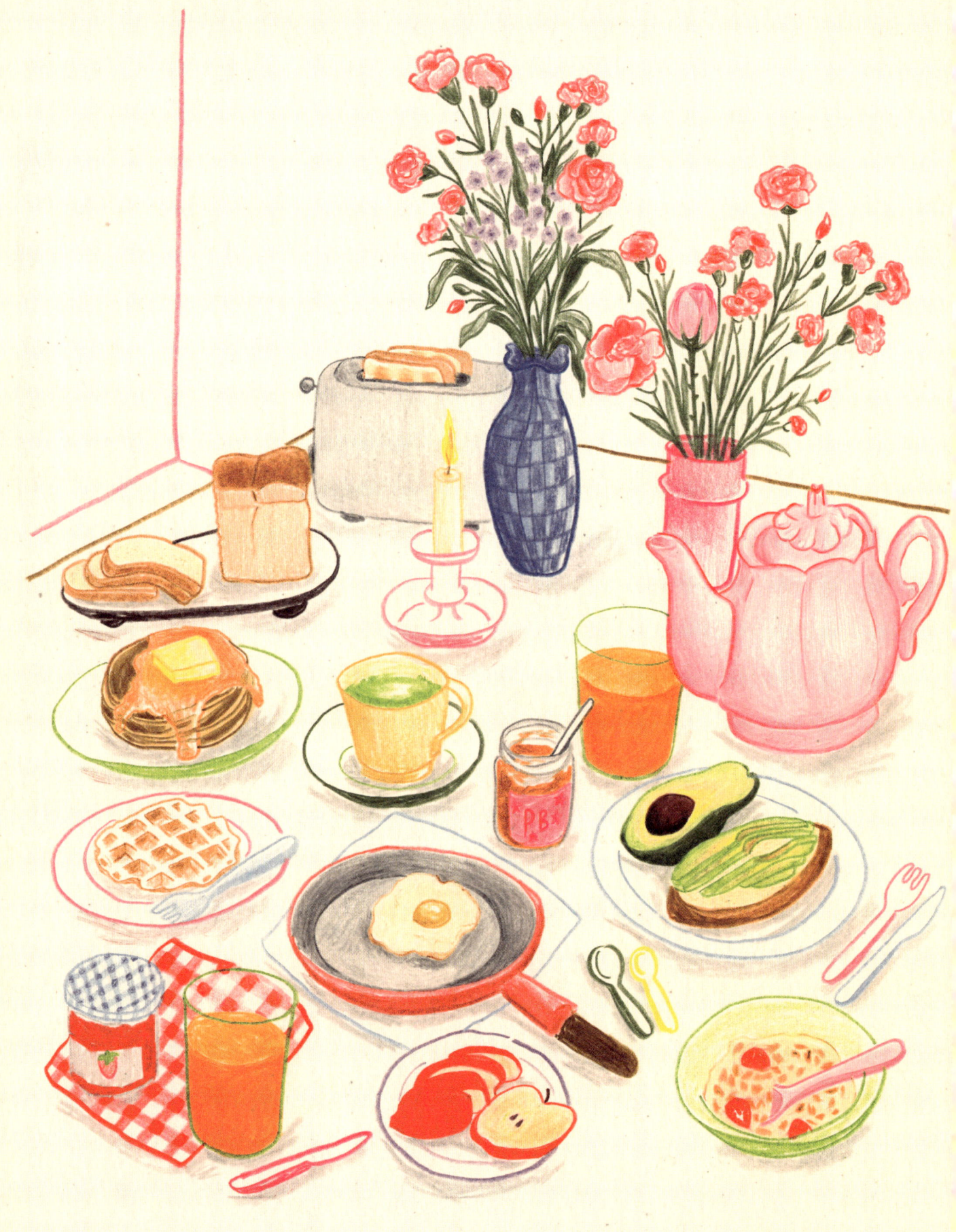

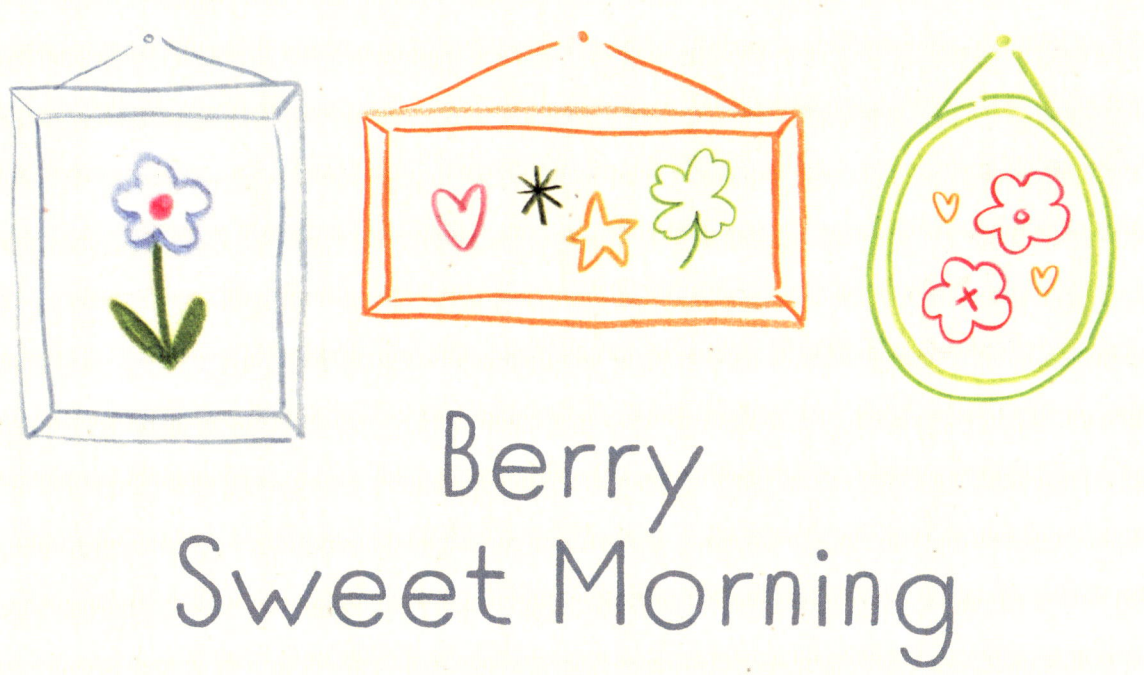

Berry
Sweet Morning

Good morning . . . let's eat! Some days, happiness is a stack of warm pancakes with sugary syrup. Why not also add a yummy bowl of cereal or a warm mug of matcha! Add a beautiful bouquet centerpiece for the table by taking inspiration from Common Things in Your Room (page 14) and Dinner for Two (page 79).

Little Teapot

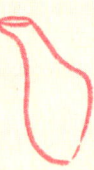

1. Start by drawing the spout with two curved lines meeting toward an oval opening. Connect both ends of the curved lines.

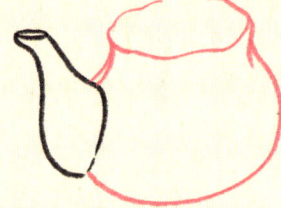

2. Draw the circular body of the teapot with a wide oval opening on top. The oval's lines are wavy.

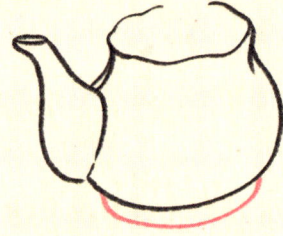

3. Add a line below the pot for the base.

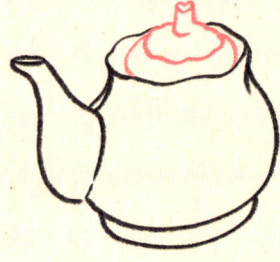

4. Draw the lid of the pot with an oval and a stem, like the top of an acorn.

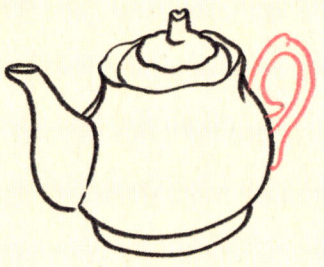

5. Draw the handle in the shape of a question mark.

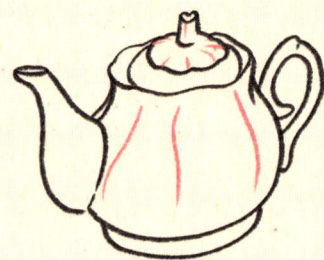

6. Draw curved lines on the pot and the lid.

Teacup

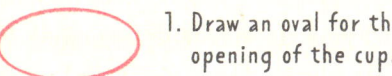

1. Draw an oval for the opening of the cup.

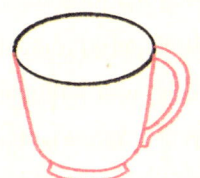

2. Draw the rest of the cup—a curved line for the cup, an open-topped rectangle for the base, and a backward C-shaped handle.

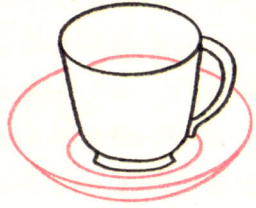

3. Finish with the saucer. Draw a circle around the cup, a smaller circle around the base, and a curved line connecting each end of the saucer. Add another curved line inside the cup for the tea.

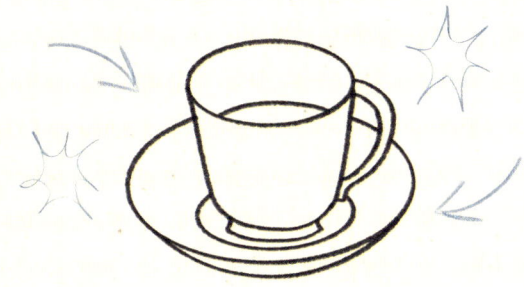

Silverware

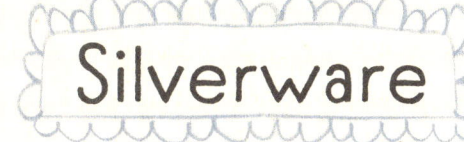

1. Draw a butter knife and a fork with three prongs.

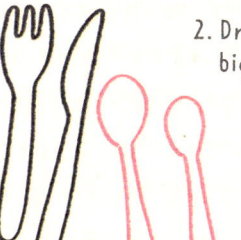

2. Draw two spoons, one big and one small.

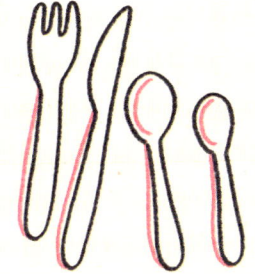

3. Finish with dimension details. Draw a curved line along each handle and a curved line inside each spoon.

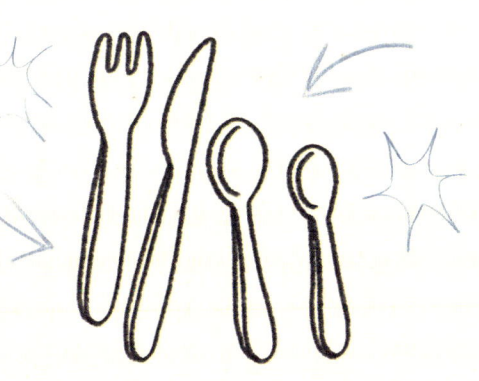

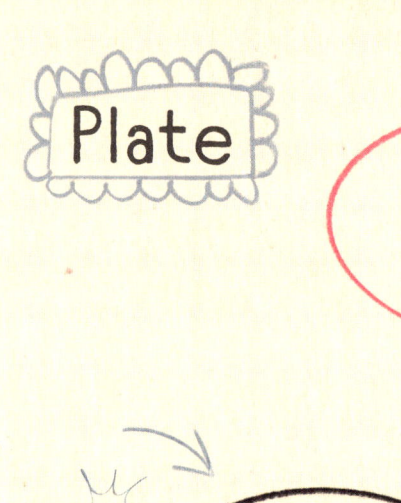

Plate

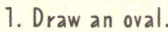

1. Draw an oval.

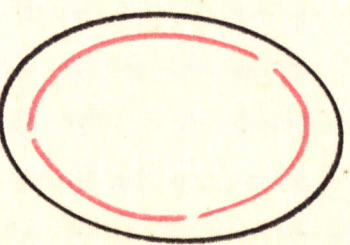

2. Draw another oval inside, but with a few openings.

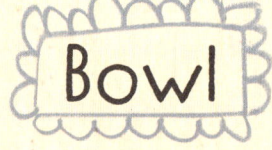

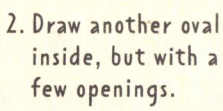

Bowl

1. Draw an oval.

2. Add curved lines below the oval—connected to each side of the oval—and inside the oval for the bottom of the bowl.

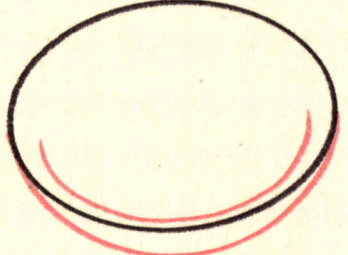

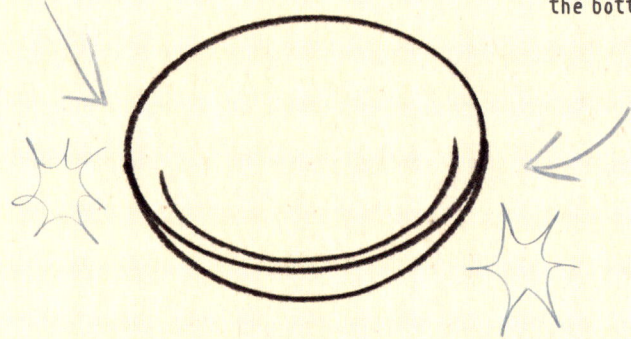

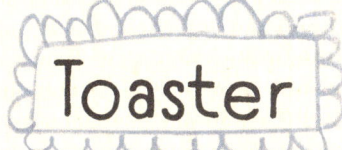

1. Draw a wide oval.

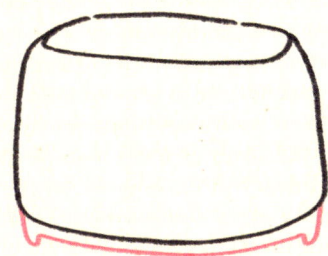

2. Draw a rectangle connected to the oval with curved edges and corners.

3. Draw the base with two small curves on each side and a line following the bottom curve of the toaster.

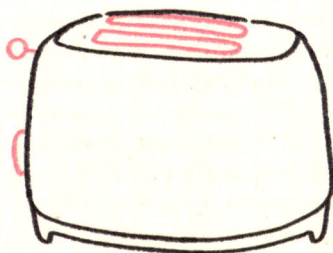

4. Finish with the details of the toaster. Draw two wide rectangles on the top, a line with a dot at the end on the left side for the lever, and a C-shaped curved line on the left side for a button.

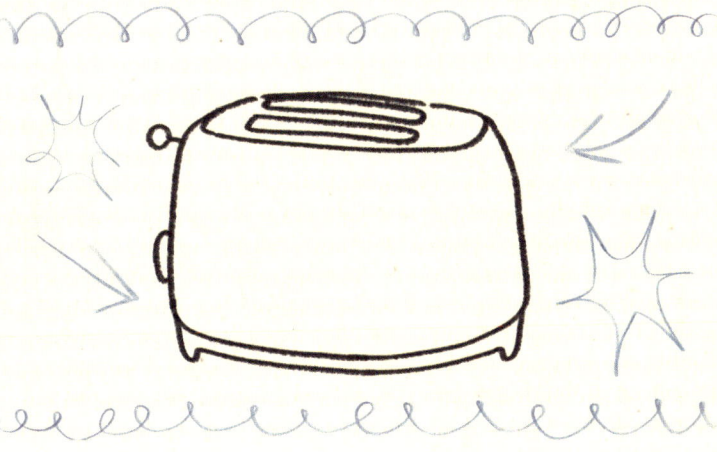

Bread

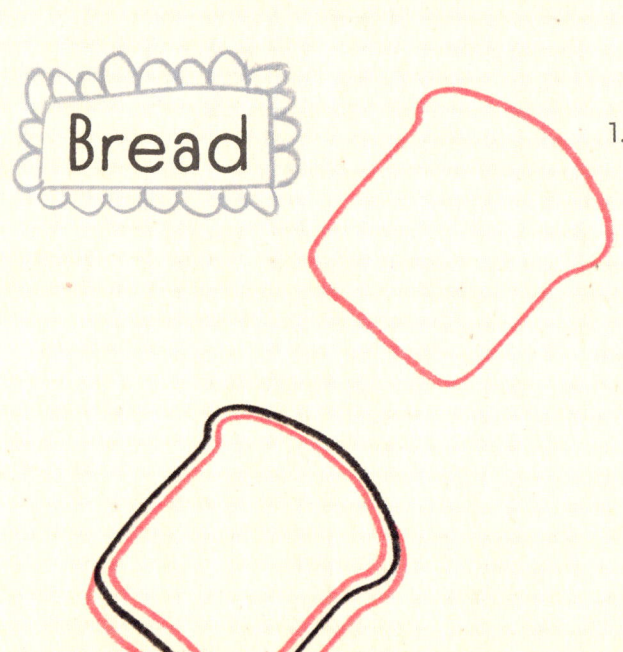

1. Draw a bread shape, or a rectangle with a curved top and two bumps on the top corners.

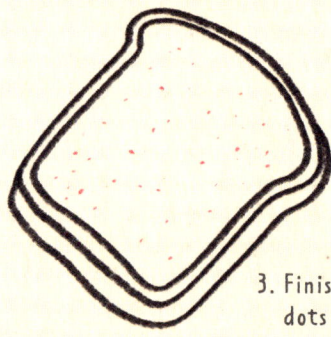

3. Finish with delicate dots on the bread.

2. Draw another bread shape inside and a line along the bottom and right side of the bread for dimension.

BUTTERED TOAST

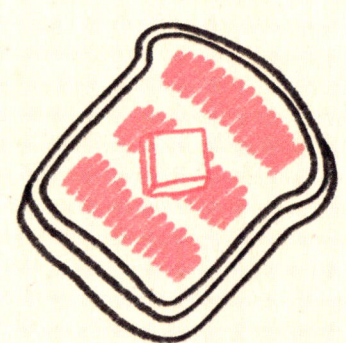

Toast the bread! Draw three jagged lines along the bread so that it looks almost colored in, then add a cube of butter on top.

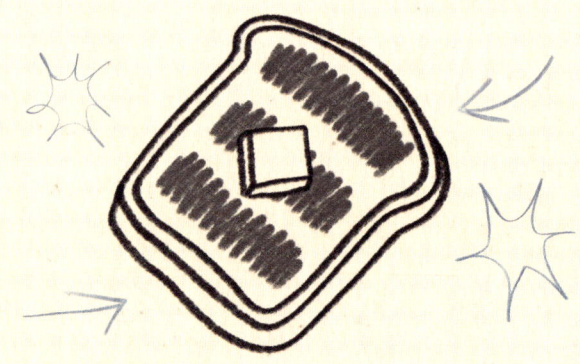

EGG & AVOCADO TOAST

Add an Egg (page 71) on top of Bread (opposite). Add an irregular shape inside the edge of the crust for the mashed avocado.

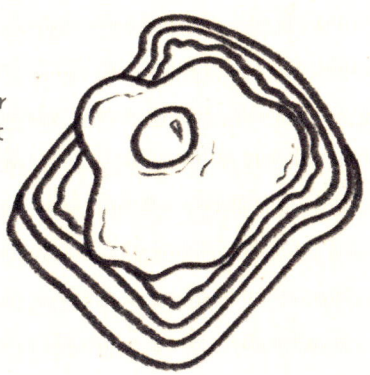

BANANA & PEANUT BUTTER TOAST

Add an irregular shape inside the edge of the crust and circles for the banana. Draw curved lines along the banana slice edges and dots in the center.

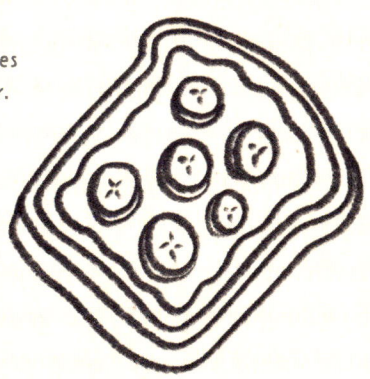

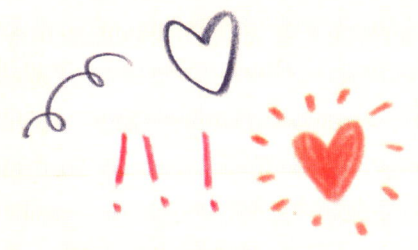

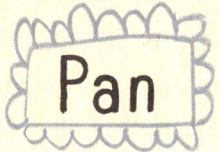

Pan

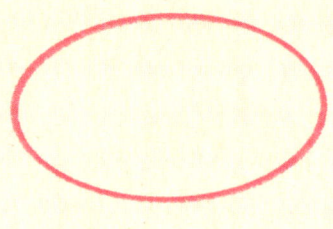

1. Draw an oval.

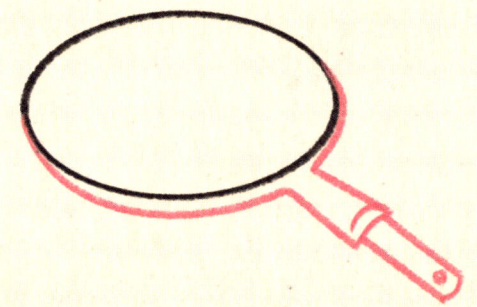

2. Draw a curved line along the bottom of the oval with a rectangle extending from the bottom right. Add another rectangle on the end of the handle with a dot at the end.

3. Finish with curved lines inside the pan.

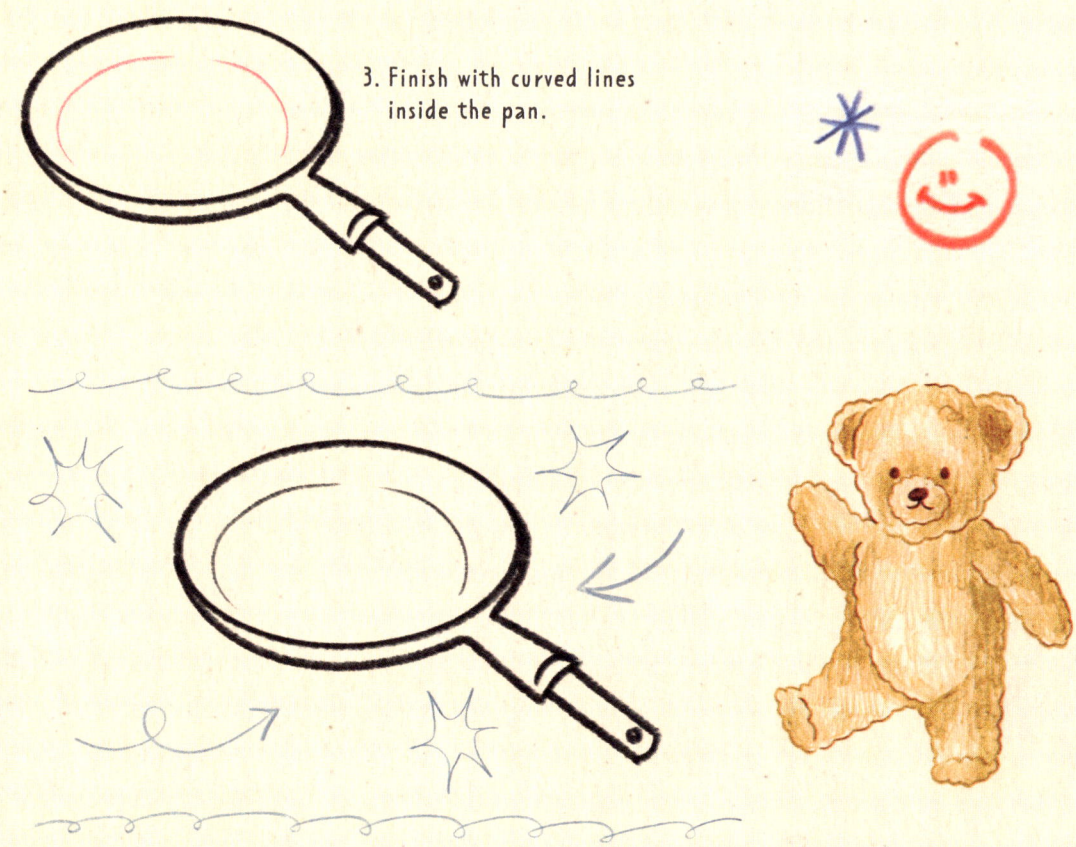

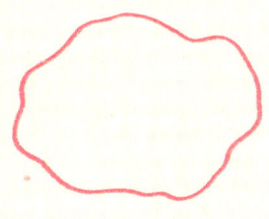

1. Draw an oval with wavy lines.

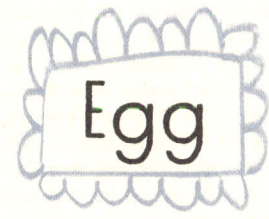

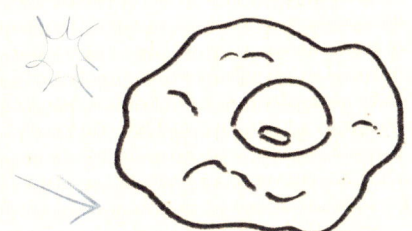

2. Draw the yolk with two curved lines almost connecting to make an oval. Add a small oval inside the yolk for a reflection.

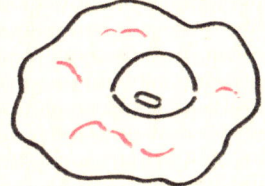

3. Finish with small, curved lines on the egg white.

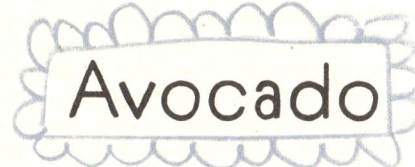

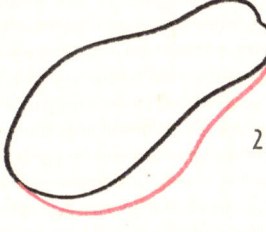

1. Start by drawing a peanut shape.

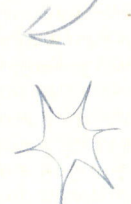
Avocado

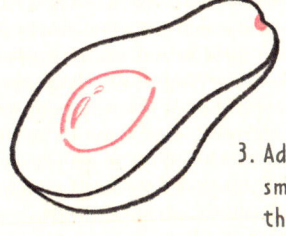

2. Draw a curved line on the bottom connecting each end of the avocado.

3. Add a dot at the tip of the smaller end of the avocado and the pit with two curved lines almost connecting to make an oval. Add a circle and water drop shape on the pit for reflection.

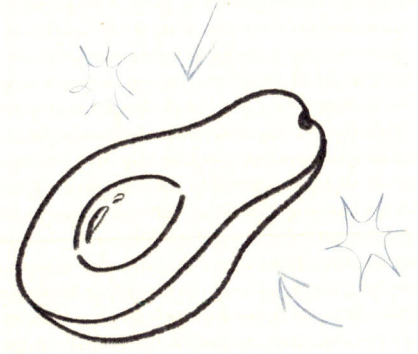

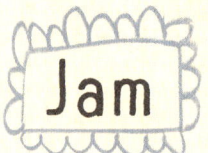

Jam

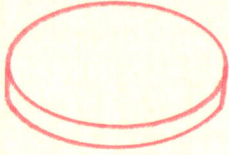

1. Draw an oval with a curved line beneath, connected at each end. This is the lid.

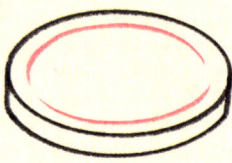

2. Draw curved lines inside the lid on the top and bottom.

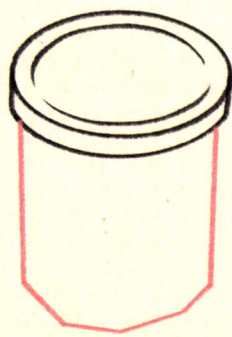

3. Draw two vertical lines on each side of the lid. Connect the lines at the bottom with a line with three bends as if drawing a decagon.

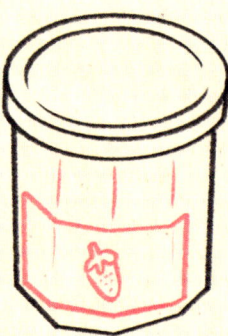

4. Add a wide rectangle on the jar, with the same three decagon-like bends. Finish with light vertical lines along the bends and a strawberry on the label.

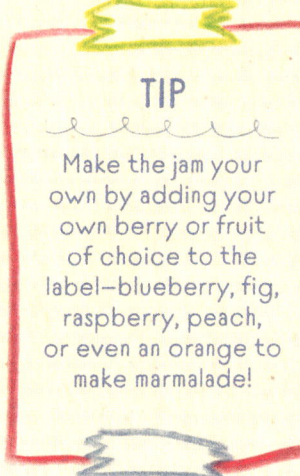

TIP

Make the jam your own by adding your own berry or fruit of choice to the label—blueberry, fig, raspberry, peach, or even an orange to make marmalade!

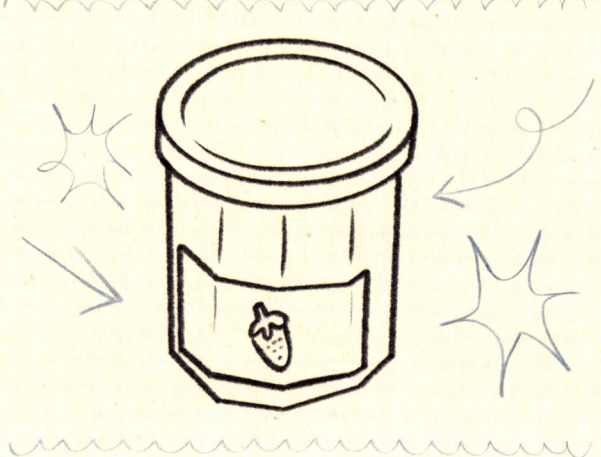

Peanut Butter

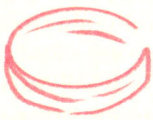

1. Draw an oval with curved lines along the edges for the jar opening.

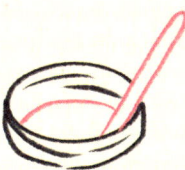

2. Add a curved line through the center of the opening with a long, rounded shape leaning on the edge. This is the handle of a spoon or knife.

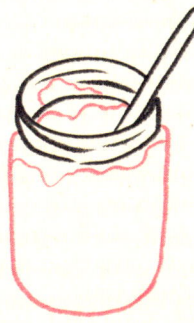

3. Draw straight lines down the sides with a curved line connecting the two at the bottom. Add a wavy line along the top of the jar and around the opening for the peanut butter.

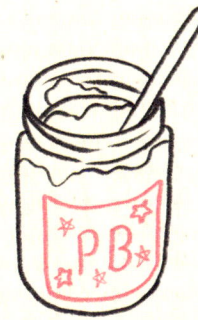

4. Finish with a label! Draw a rectangle on the jar with curved edges, write "PB" for peanut butter, and decorate with stars.

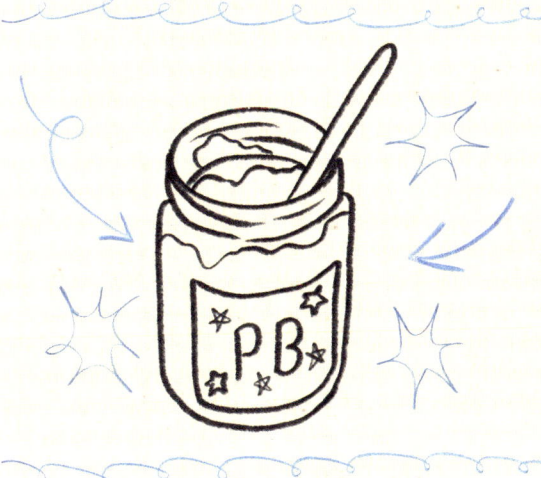

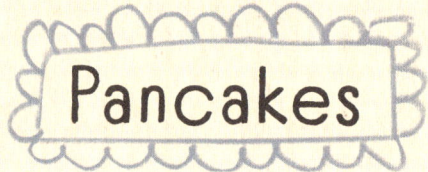

Pancakes

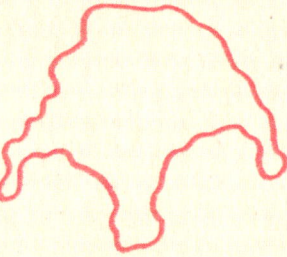

1. Create an irregular shape with a rounded top, three dripping shapes, and wavy lines.

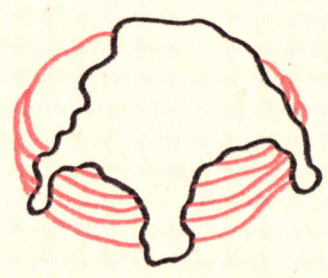

2. Draw an oval under the shape with curved lines below to create a stack of five or so pancakes.

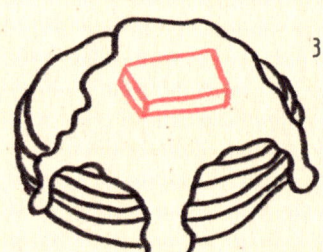

3. Finish with a cube of butter on the pancakes.

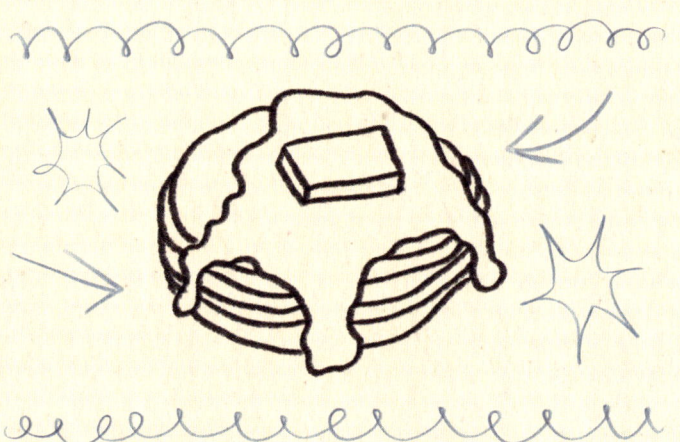

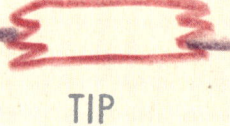

TIP

When coloring, leave a small gap along the edges of each pancake blank, or color the gaps with a lighter beige shade! This creates more dimension and highlights your pancakes to look oh-so delicious. See page 62 for an example!

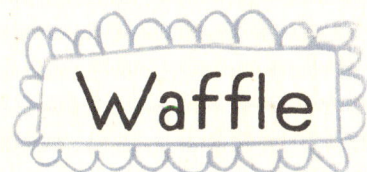

Waffle

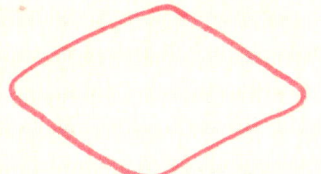

1. Start by drawing a square at an angle

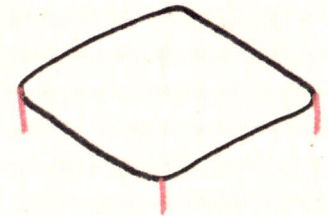

2. Add short, vertical lines below the three bottom edges.

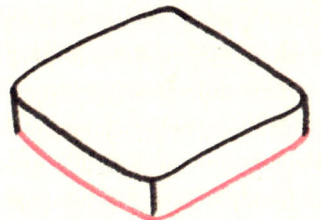

3. Connect the vertical lines with two straight lines.

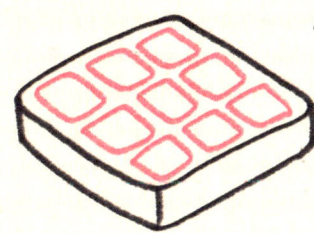

4. Draw a three-by-three grid of angled squares inside the bigger square.

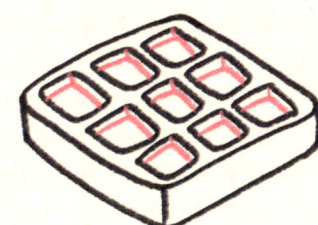

5. Finish with upside-down Y shapes inside each small angled square.

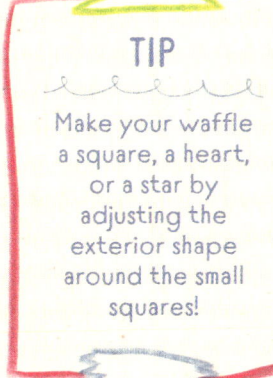

TIP

Make your waffle a square, a heart, or a star by adjusting the exterior shape around the small squares!

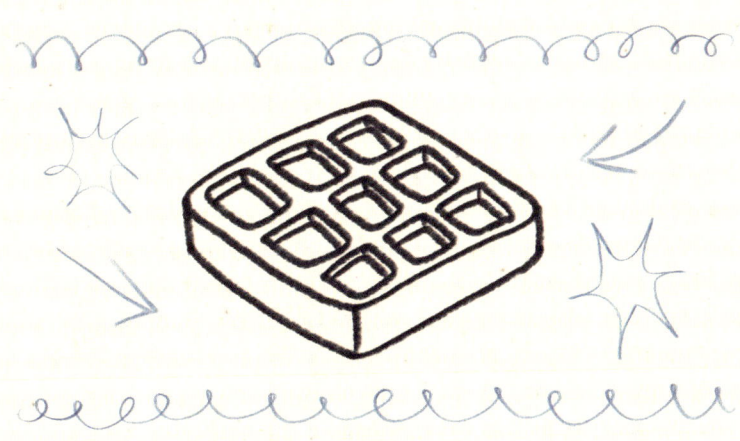

Sliced Apple

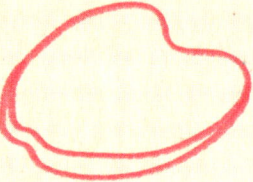

1. Draw an angled heart shape with curved lines and a ridge at the bottom.

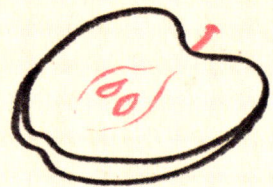

2. Add two ovals for the seeds in the center of the shape and curved lines beside the seeds. Add the stem with a short line and dot at the top.

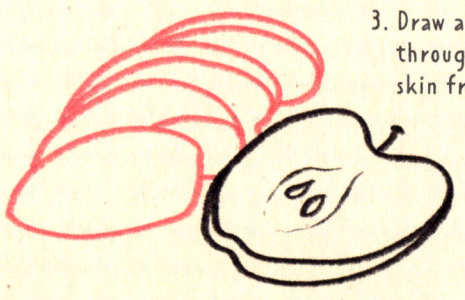

3. Draw a series of ovals with horizontal lines through their tops. This differentiates the skin from the apple.

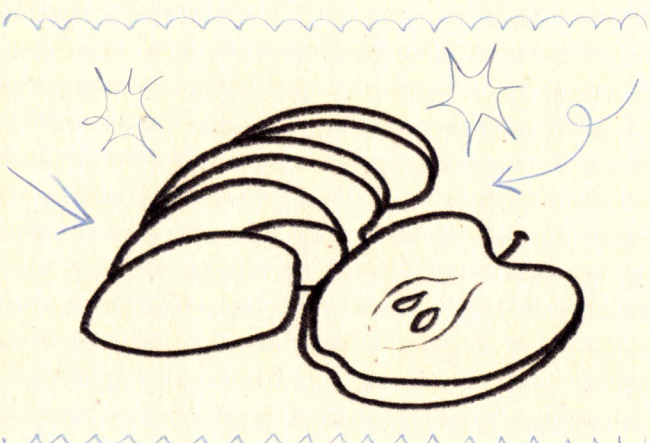

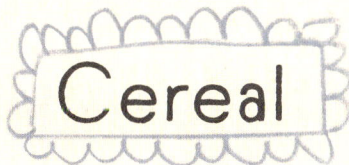

Cereal

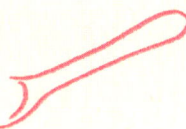

1. Draw the handle of a spoon. Before the bowled part, draw a curved line.

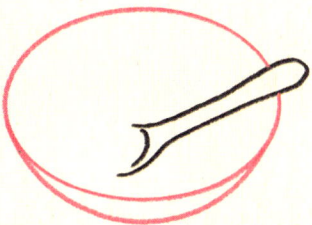

2. Draw an oval around the spoon. Add a curved edge connected to each end of the oval.

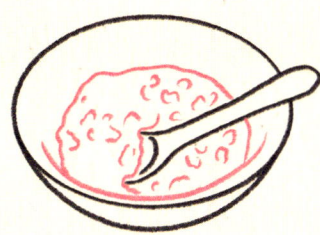

3. Inside the bowl and around the spoon, add the cereal by drawing a wavy-lined circle with a curved line beneath. Add half circles inside, or even add small doughnut shapes for loops.

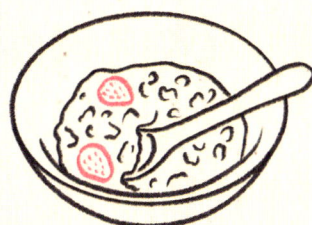

4. Finish with two stemless strawberries in the cereal mix.

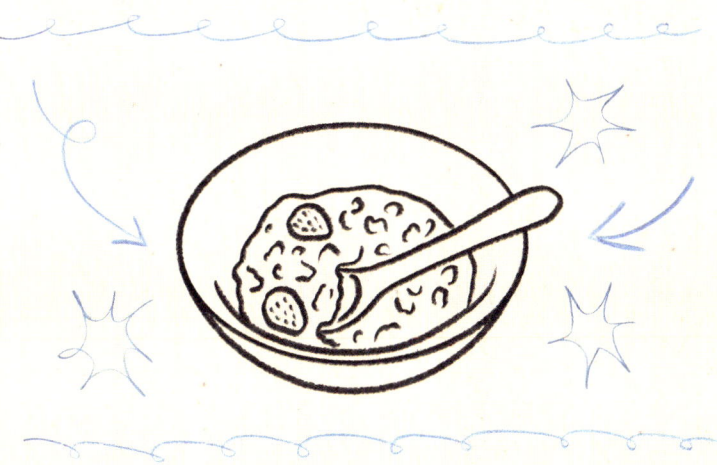

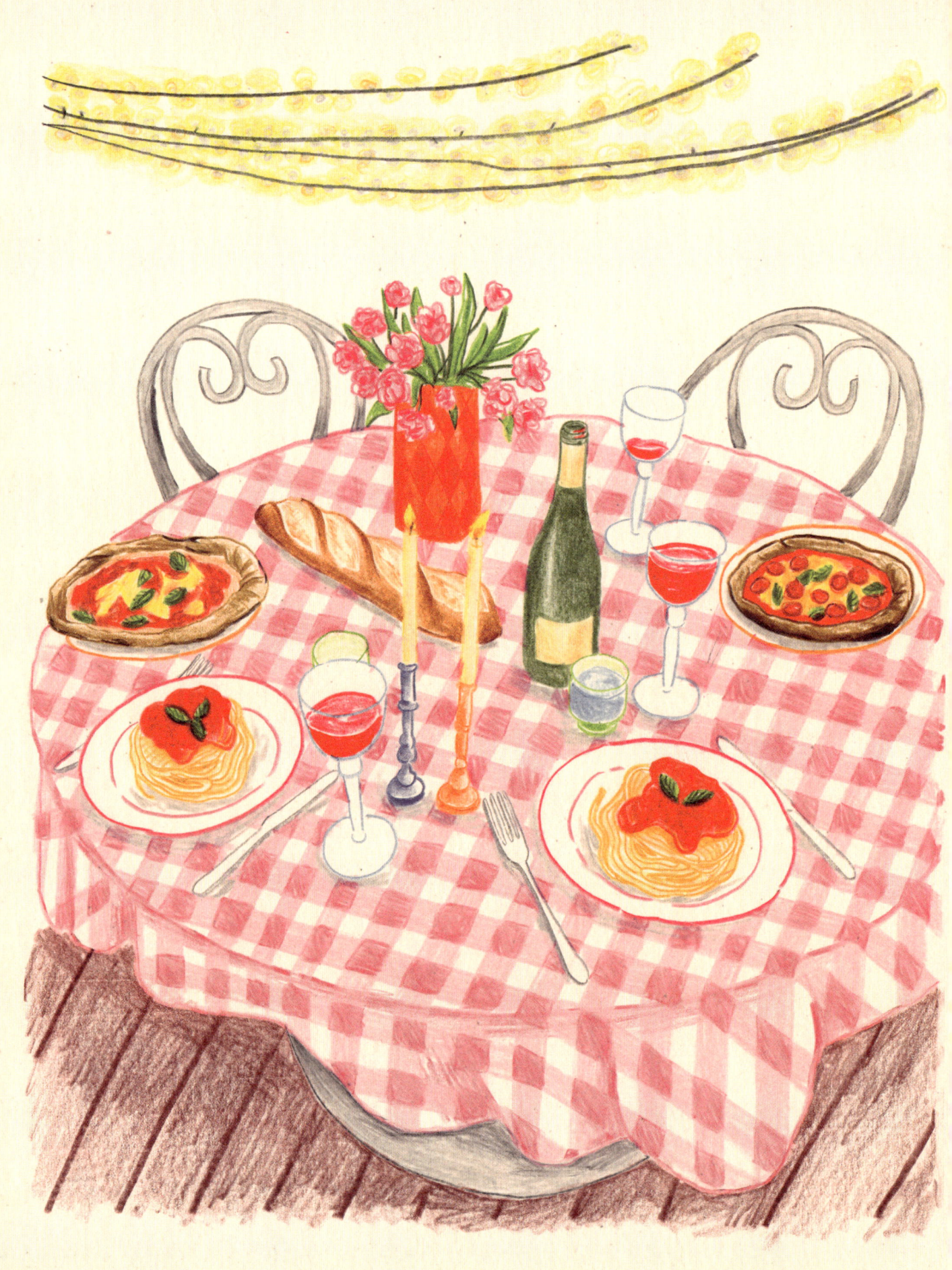

Dinner for Two

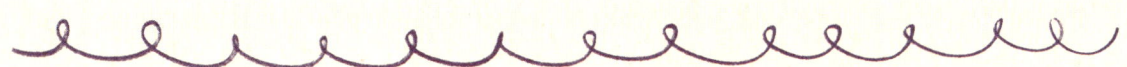

Dinner is served! Let's dig into a tasty pizza and some spaghetti by candlelight. Personalize the pizza by adding your favorite toppings, whether that's pepperoni or mushrooms, or both!

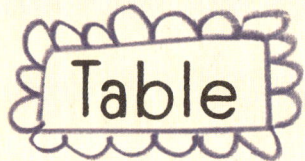

Table

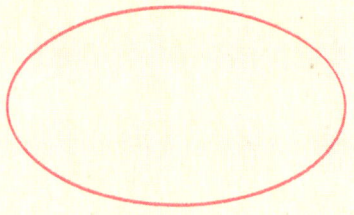

1. Draw a wide oval.

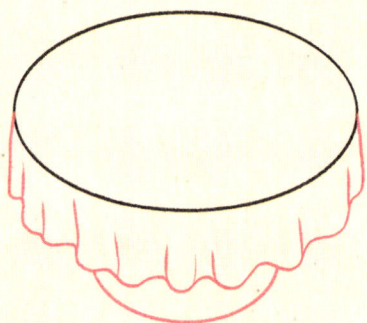

2. Draw two vertical lines at each end of the oval. Connect the two vertical lines with a wavy line and add some folds on some of its curves. Below, add a half circle for the base of the table.

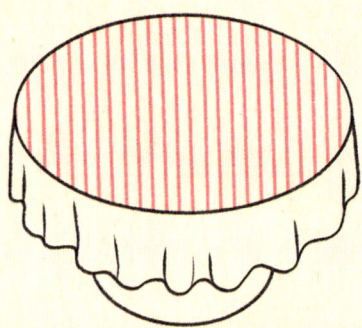

3. Add a series of vertical lines in the oval.

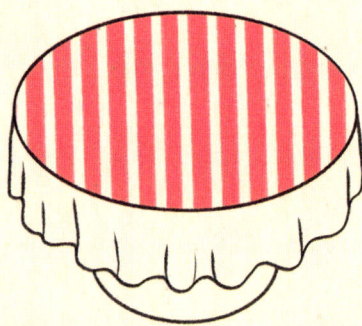

4. Color in every other space between the vertical lines.

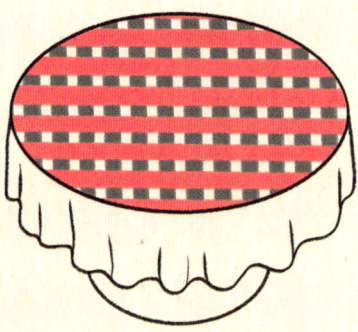

5. Create the same series of lines and coloring sequence horizontally in the oval. The overlapped vertical and horizontal lines should be darker.

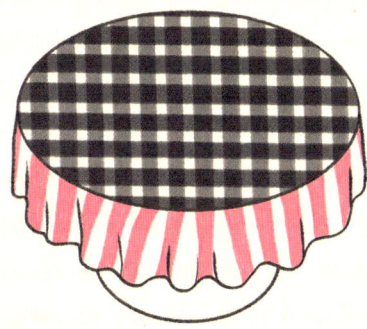

6. Draw thicker vertical and angled lines on the skirt of the tablecloth.

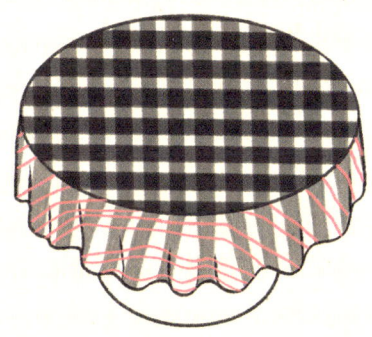

7. Draw a series of horizontal curved lines on the skirt of the tablecloth.

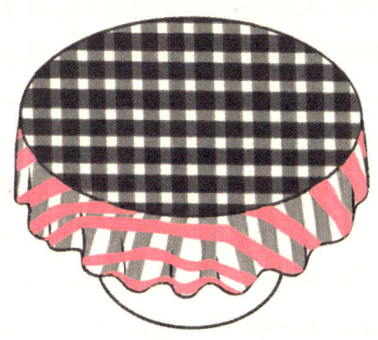

8. Color in every other space between the horizontal lines of the skirt to finish the checkered pattern tablecloth.

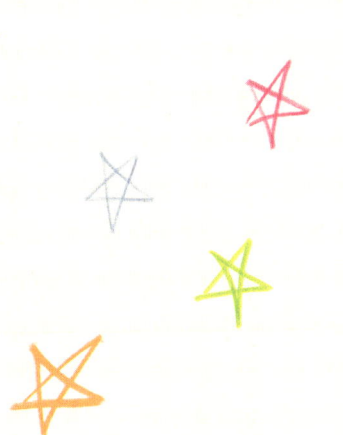

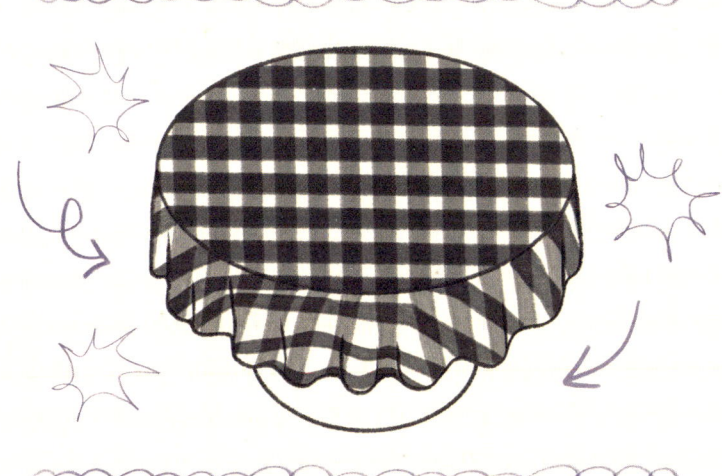

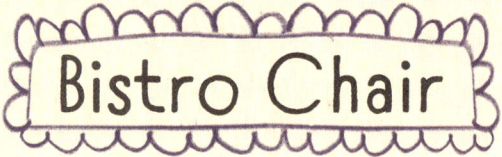

Bistro Chair

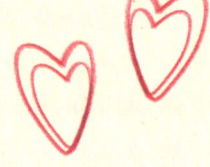

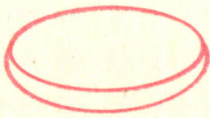

1. Draw an oval with a curved line connected at each end.

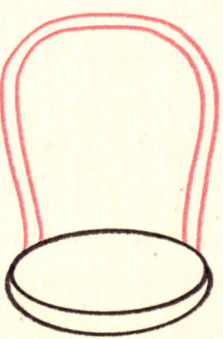

2. Add a double-lined, upside-down U shape above the seat.

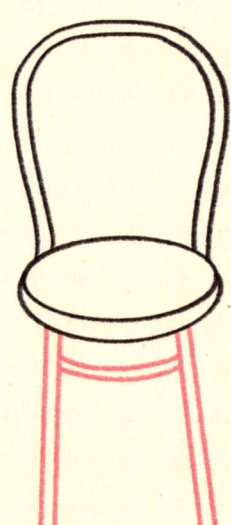

3. Add two vertical rectangles below the seat for the front legs. Draw a double-lined curve below the seat and between the front legs.

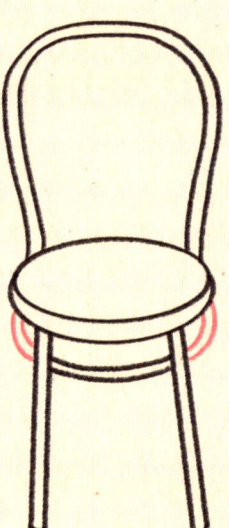

4. Add two double-lined curves on either side of the front legs and connected to the seat.

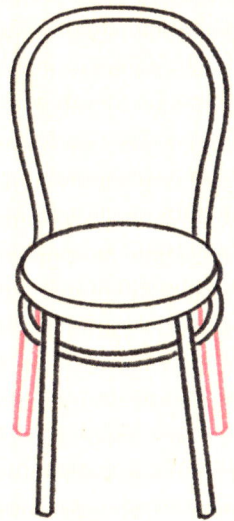

5. Draw the back legs—slightly shorter than the front legs—on each end of the seat.

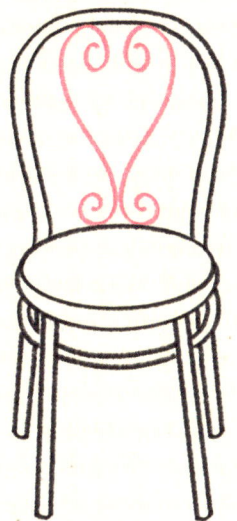

6. Add mirrored S lines with curlicue ends inside the U shape.

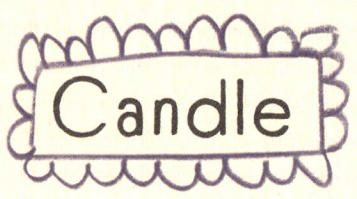 **Candle**

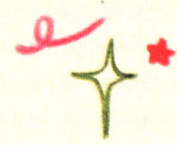

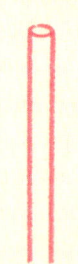

1. Draw two parallel lines with an oval at the top.

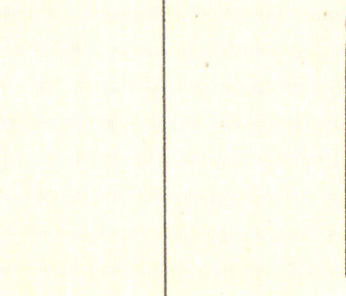

2. Draw a line at the top with a flame.

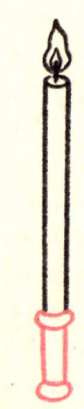

3. Draw two curved lines above and below shorter parallel lines.

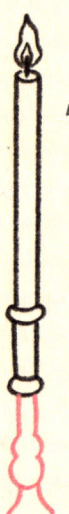

4. To the bottom of the candlestick, draw parallel lines followed by two circles with open ends. Add a curved shape below.

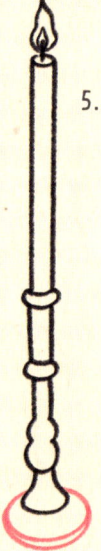

5. Finish with the base of the candle. Draw an oval with a curved line connecting each end of the oval.

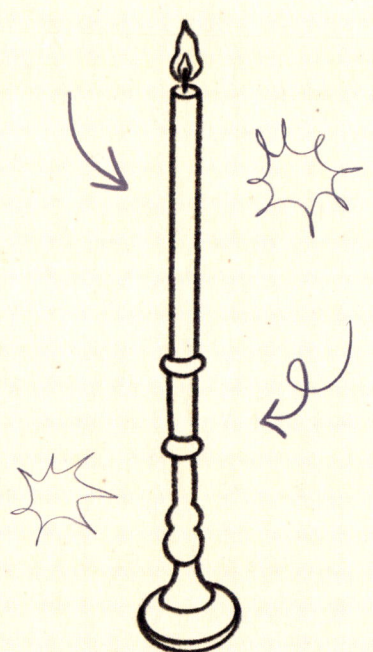

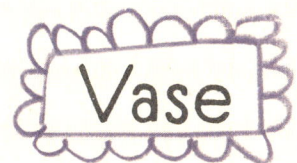

Vase

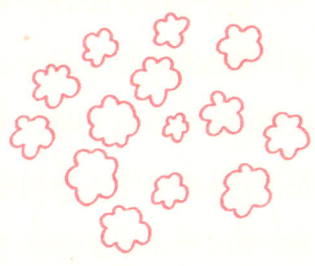

1. Draw a group of flower shapes in varying sizes.

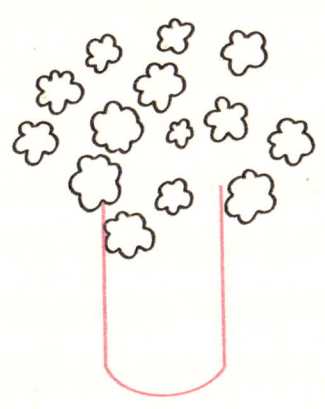

2. Draw two parallel lines connected by a curved line at the bottom.

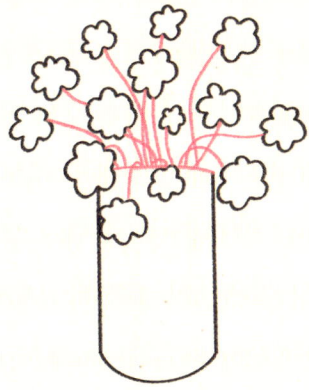

3. Close off the top of the vase with a straight line. Add the stems from the flowers to the top of the vase, even if the flowers are below the opening of the vase.

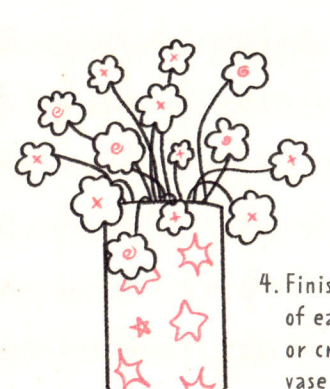

4. Finish with the centers of each flower using swirls or crosses. Decorate the vase with stars.

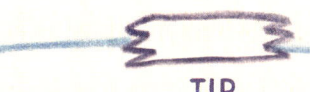

TIP

Choose your favorite flowers to fill your vase from Common Things in Your Room (page 14).

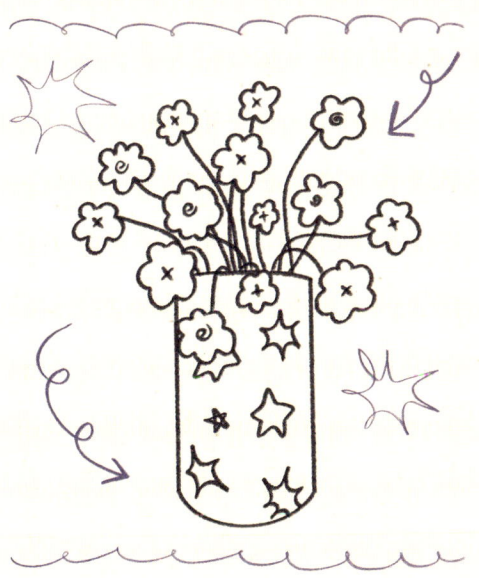

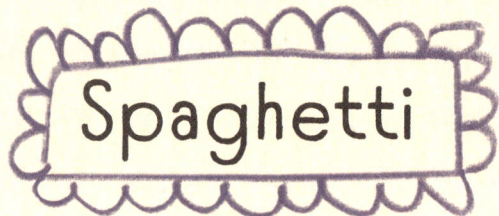

Spaghetti

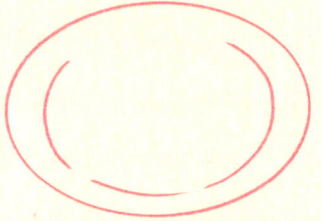

1. Draw a Plate (page 66).

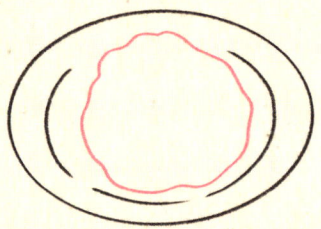

2. Within the curved lines, draw an imperfect circle using wavy lines.

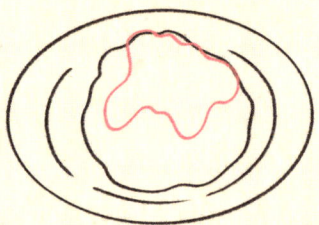

3. Draw an irregular shape for the sauce inside the imperfect circle.

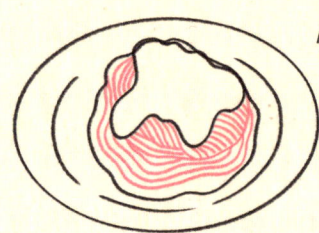

4. Draw a series of curved lines in the imperfect circle for the strands of spaghetti.

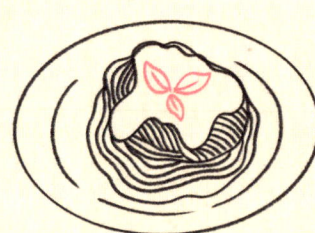

5. Top the sauce with basil leaves pointed in different directions—*bon appetit!*

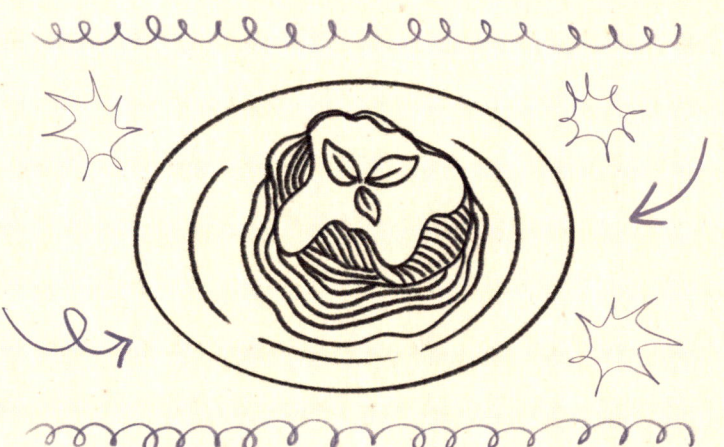

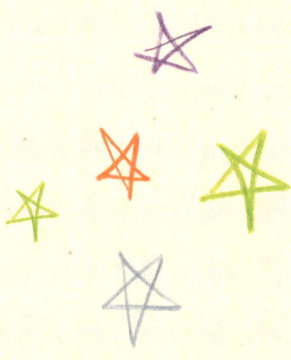

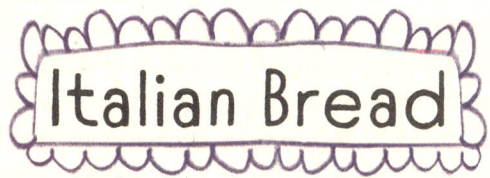

Italian Bread

1. Draw a straight line with bent ends.

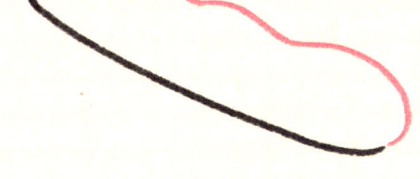

2. Connect a curved line with four bumps to each end of the straight line.

3. Draw four scores along the bread, like leaves with delicate lines through the shapes.

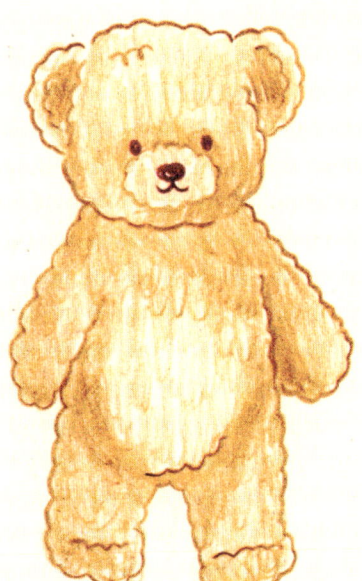

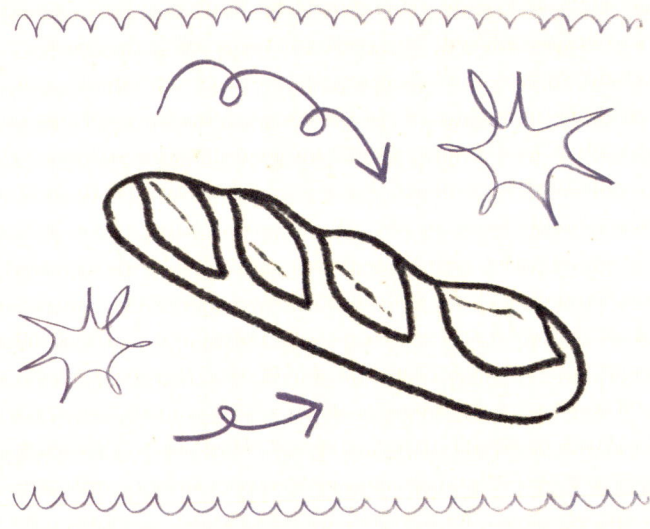

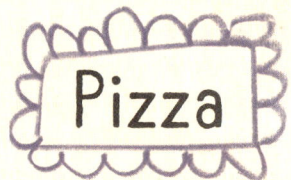

Pizza

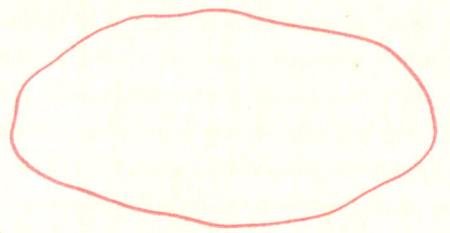

1. Draw an oval with slightly wavy lines.

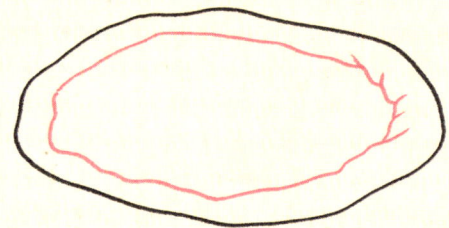

2. Add another oval inside with slightly wavy lines and short lines on the right edge for the thick crust.

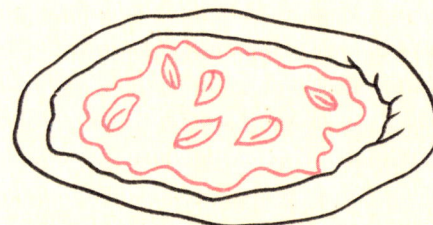

3. Add an irregular shape inside the ovals with extra wavy lines. Additionally, add basil leaves inside the irregular shape.

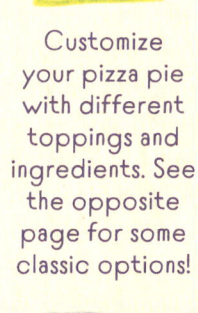

Customize your pizza pie with different toppings and ingredients. See the opposite page for some classic options!

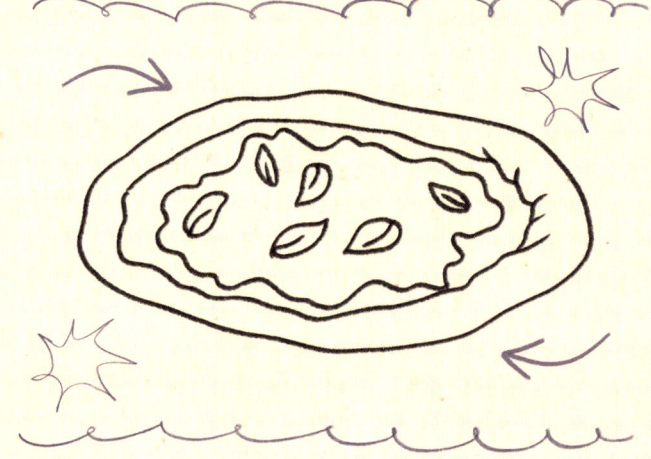

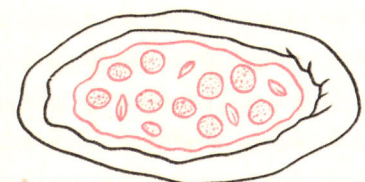

PEPPERONI

Draw circles on the sauce with little dots inside.

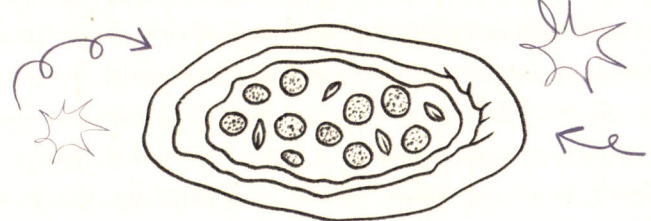

HAM & MUSHROOM

On top of the sauce, draw squares of various sizes for the ham and mushrooms shaped like hammers.

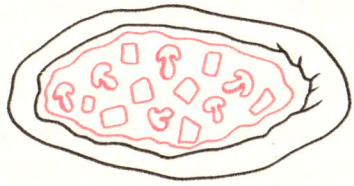

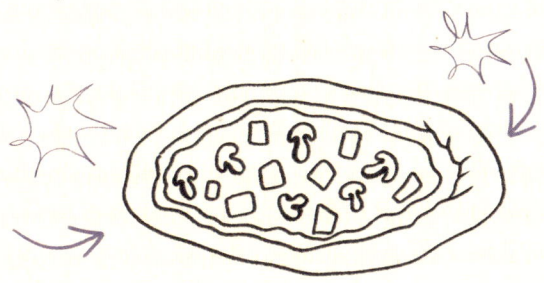

MARGHERITA

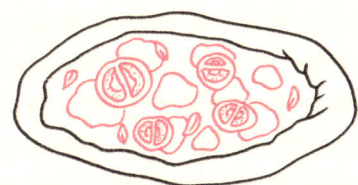

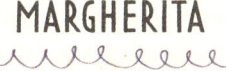

For the sliced tomatoes, draw circles with two mirrored half circles inside, add a curved line on the inside each half circle, and add dots inside the rest of each half circle. For the mozzarella, add wavy-lined circles behind and beside the sliced tomatoes.

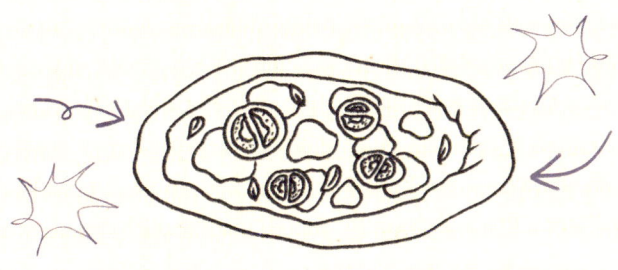

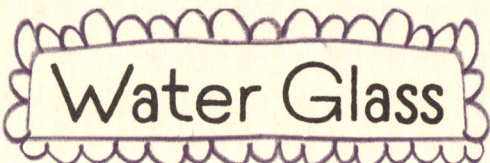

Water Glass

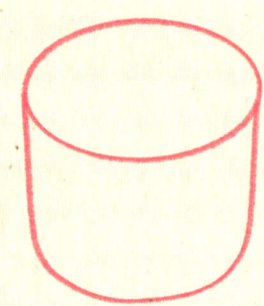

1. Draw an oval. Draw two parallel lines on each side connected by a curved line at the bottom.

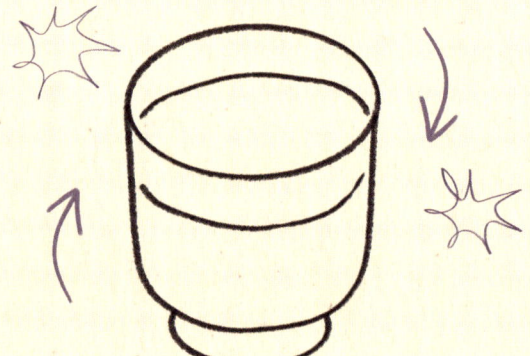

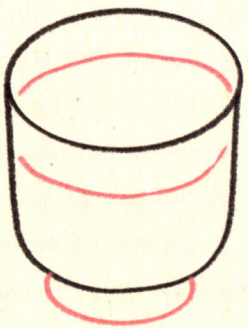

2. Draw another oval below the other with open sides for the water. Finish with the base using a curved line.

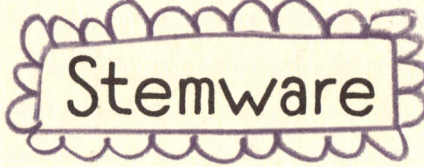

Stemware

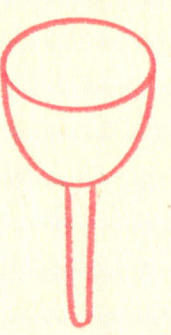

1. Draw an oval with a curved line connecting the edges of the oval. Add the stem of the glass below with a tall rectangle.

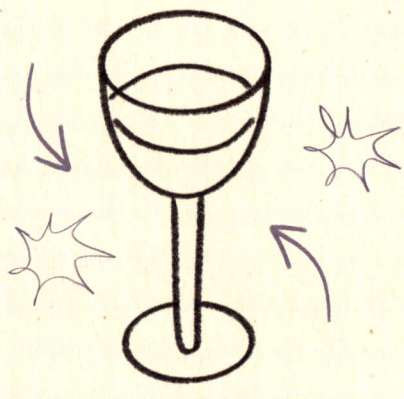

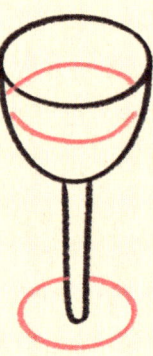

2. Draw an oval just below the opening of the glass for the beverage. Add the base of the glass with a wide oval, slightly smaller than the lip of the glass.

String Lights

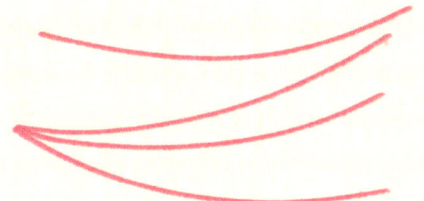

1. Draw four curved lines. The bottom three are connected on one side.

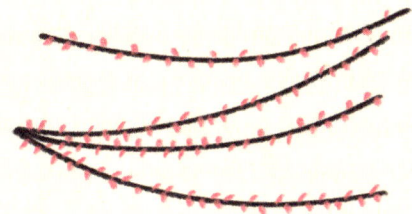

2. Draw short lines above and below each line.

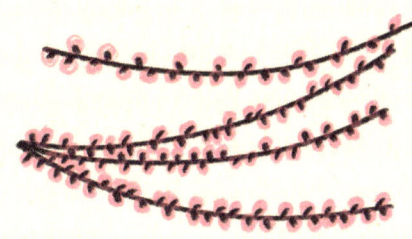

3. Finish by coloring the light around each short line. Choose your color, but yellow is the classic choice.

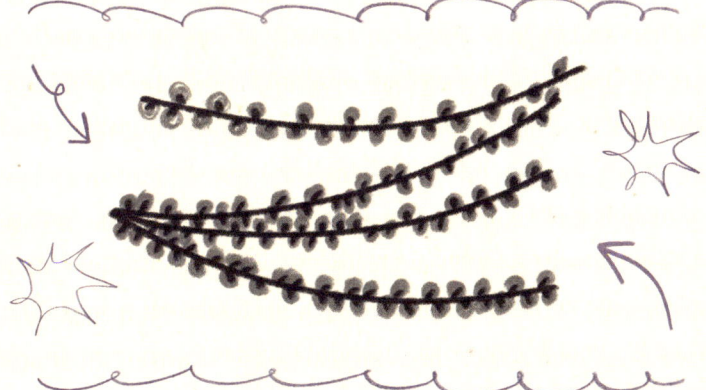

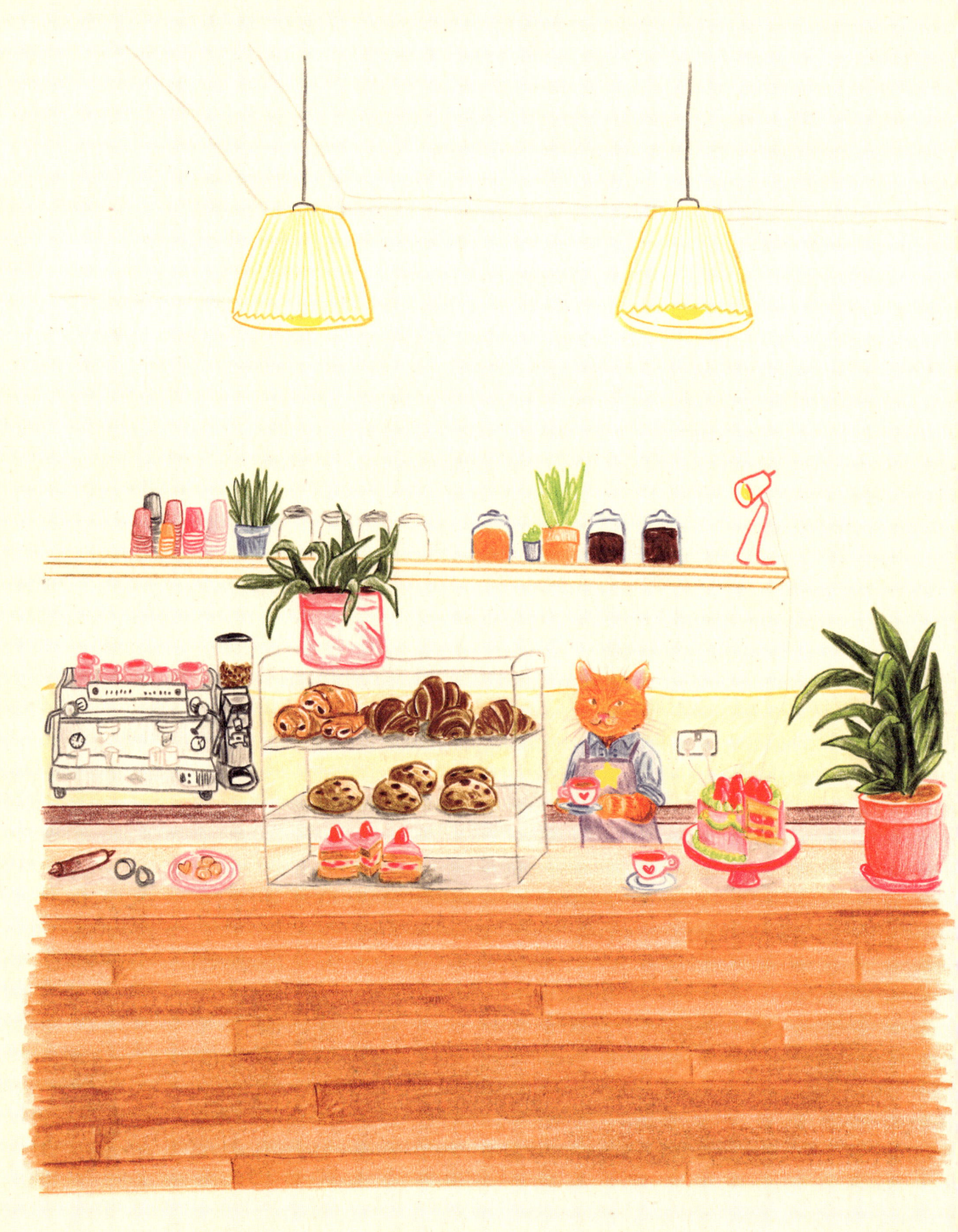

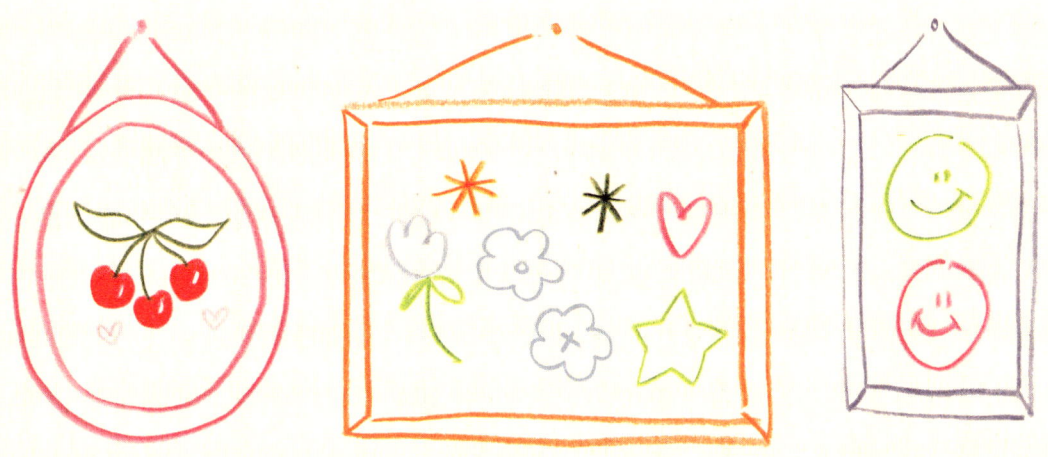

Cute Cat Café

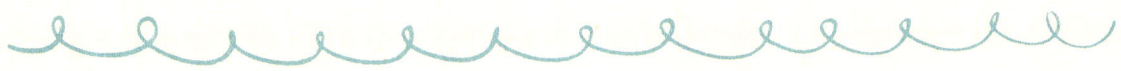

Fancy a mug of purrfectly brewed coffee?
You've come to the right place! Add some
greenery to your café by taking elements
from Snug as a Bug Bedroom (page 35). If
a slice of cake isn't your cup of tea, why
not add an appetizing waffle from Berry
Sweet Morning (page 63) to your order?

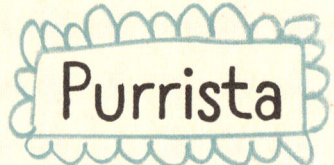

Purrista

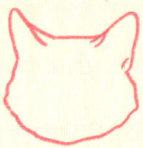

1. Start by drawing the head of the cat: a round face, triangular ears, and short lines around the ears for detail.

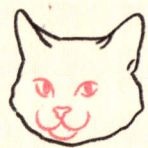

2. Draw two dots with curved lines above and below for the eyes. Draw two semicircles on either side of the T-shaped snout and a semicircle below for the mouth.

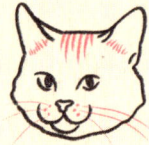

3. Finish the face by adding short lines in the ears and on top of the head for the fur. Add three dots in the cheeks and whiskers on each side!

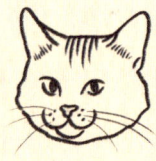

4. Below the face, dwraw an Espresso Cup & Saucer (page 99).

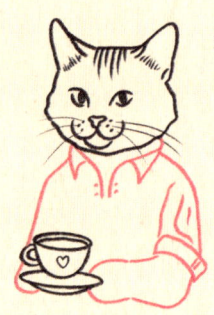

5. Draw a button-up with a triangular collar, curved edges for the shoulders, and a rectangle for the rolled-up sleeve. Add a rounded-edge rectangle near the cup for the barista's paw.

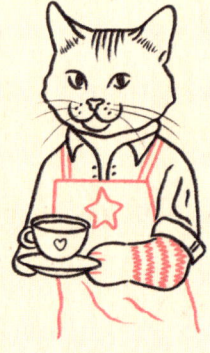

6. Draw zigzagged lines along the arm and lines on the paw. Finish with the Apron (opposite page) using a design of your choice!

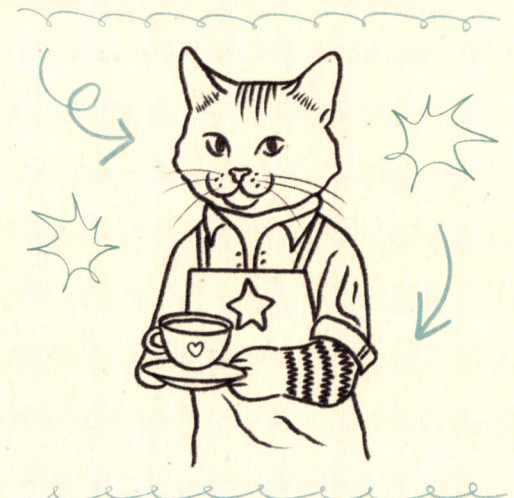

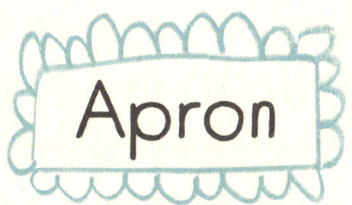

Apron

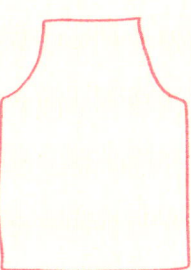

1. Draw a rectangle with the top corners cut out with curved lines.

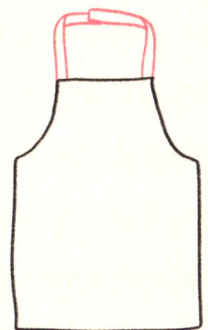

2. Draw a double-lined square above the rectangle. Draw lines through the corners for the folds and a line in the middle for the Velcro fastener.

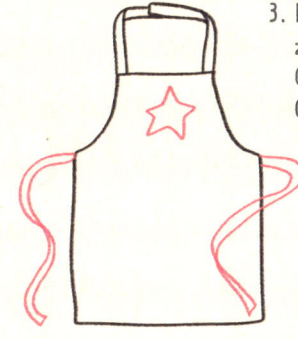

3. Draw two wavy double-lines starting beneath the arm openings and closed off at the ends. Design your apron with something from Common Things in Your Room (page 14). Choose a sun for Sunny Day Café or a smiley face for Brew Haha!

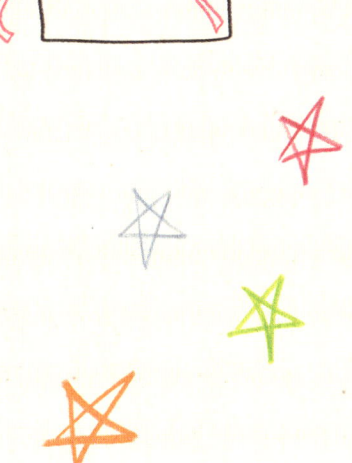

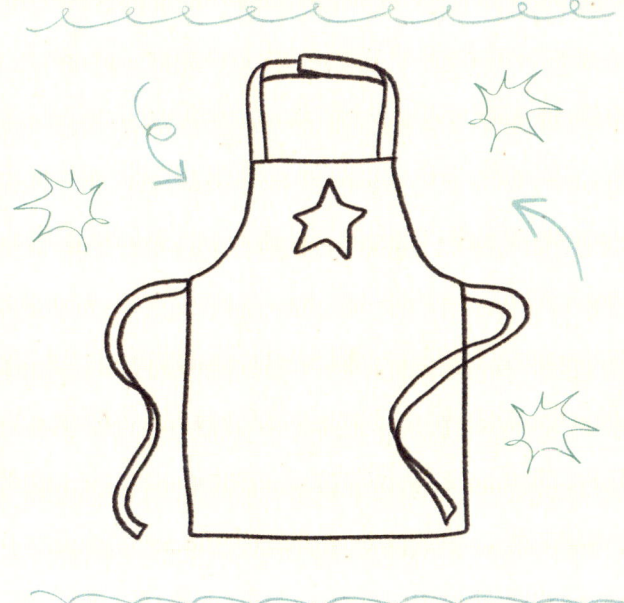

Espresso Machine

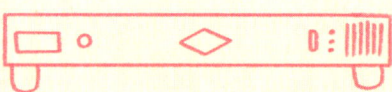

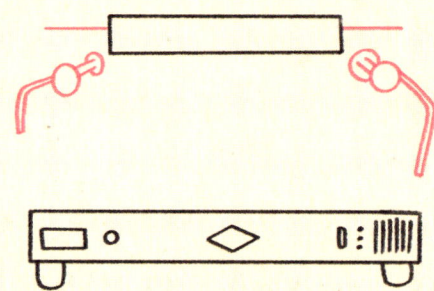

1. Draw two wide rectangles, the top one smaller than the bottom. Add two half circles to the base for the legs, in addition to rectangles, dots and circles, a diamond, and lines for details in the bottom rectangle.

2. Draw two horizontal lines on each side of the top rectangle. Below each line, add mirrored steam wands by drawing hooked rectangles and circles on a knob.

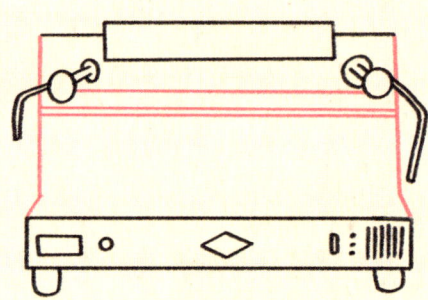

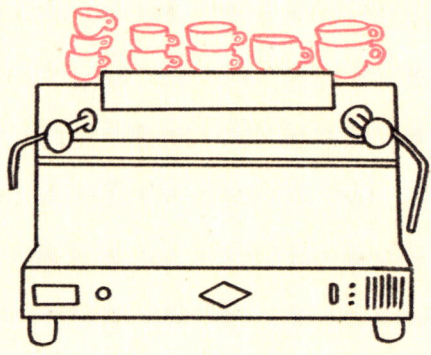

3. Draw the body of the machine with three horizontal lines below the steamers and two vertical, bent lines on either side of machine.

4. Add stacked Espresso Cups (page 99) on top of the machine.

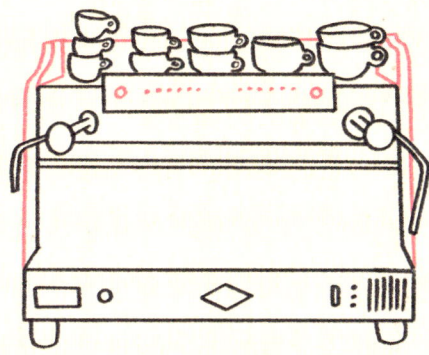

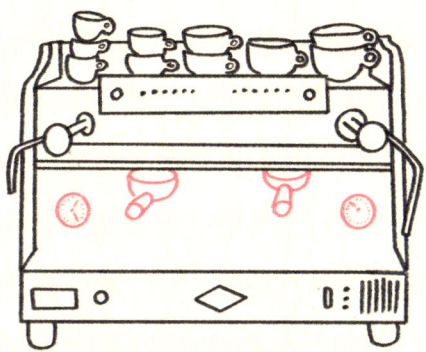

5. Add circles and dots to the top rectangle. Draw curved lines on each side of the machine and a straight, horizontal line behind the teacups.

6. Add two portafilters, similar to the Pan (page 70), above the drip tray, with two temperature and pressure dials, similar to the Wall Clock (page 61), on either side.

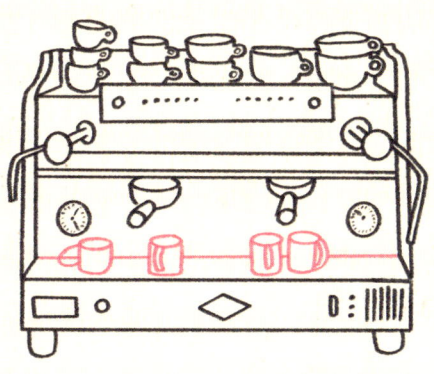

7. Draw a horizontal line below the dials to finish the drip tray. Finish with various Warm Mugs (page 29) on the drip tray.

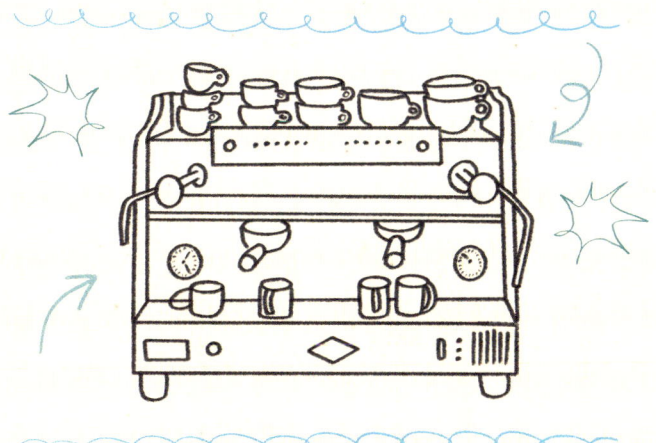

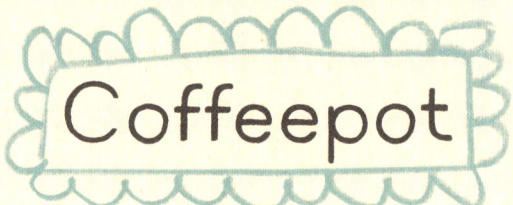

Coffeepot

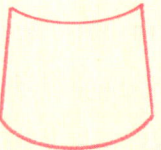

1. Draw a rectangle with a curved top and bottom.

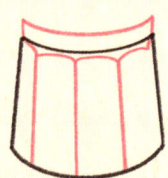

2. Add a shorter curved-edge rectangle above. Add vertical lines to the bottom rectangle that meet a scalloped line at each bend.

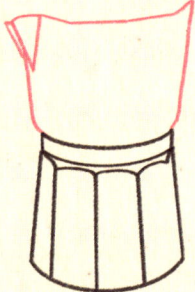

3. Draw two angled, vertical lines connected by a horizontal line with four bends. Add a triangular spout on the left edge.

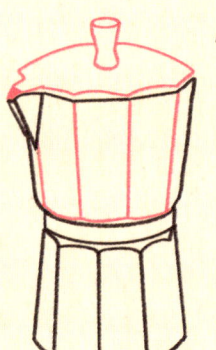

4. Draw the half circle for the lid, with a scalloped edge on the bottom and a rectangular shape at the edge to meet the triangle spout. Draw vertical lines below each bend.

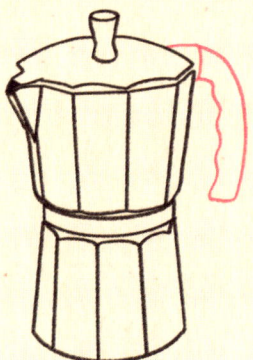

5. Finish with the handle. Add a square shape behind the lid and a curved rectangle with bumps along the pot-facing side for grip.

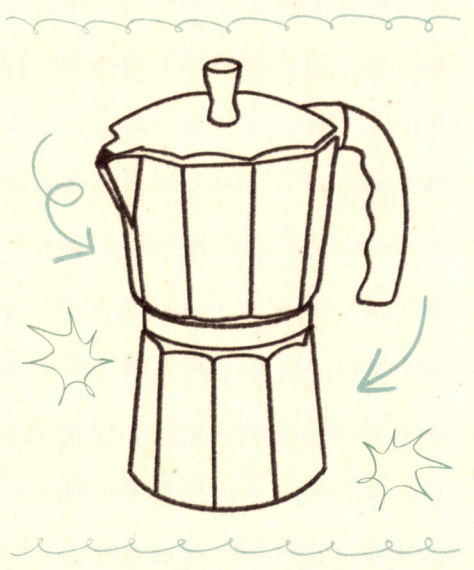

Espresso Cup & Saucer

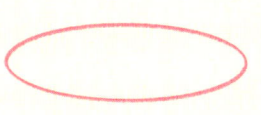

1. Draw a wide oval.

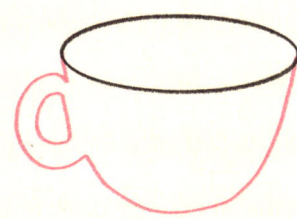

2. Connect a curved line below the oval from one end of the oval to the other. Add a C-shaped handle on one side.

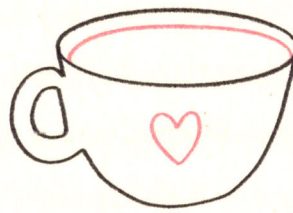

3. Draw a curved line in the opening of the cup for the espresso. Add a heart to your cup—I love coffee a latte!

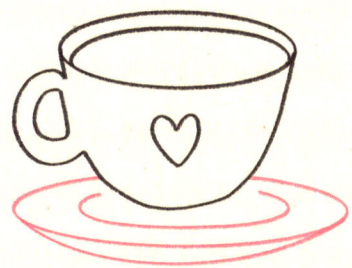

4. Finish with wide ovals, one inside the other, below the cup with a curved line beneath for the saucer.

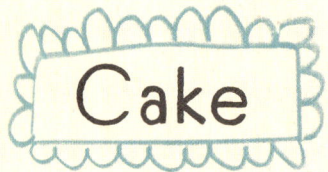

Cake

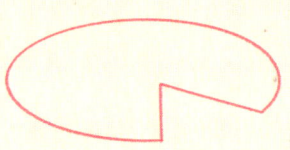

1. Draw a wide oval with a triangle cut out of the bottom right.

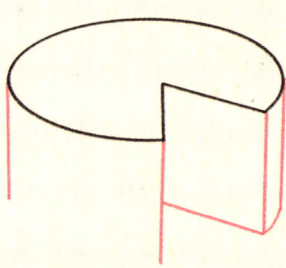

2. Draw vertical lines below the shape from each side of the oval and from the triangle corners. Add an angled line between the middle vertical lines.

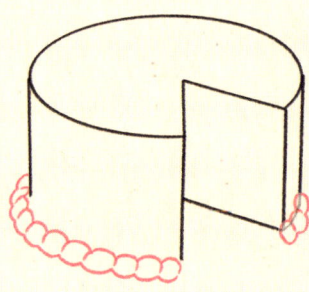

3. Add a series of circles at the bottom following the curved line but not in the triangle cutout.

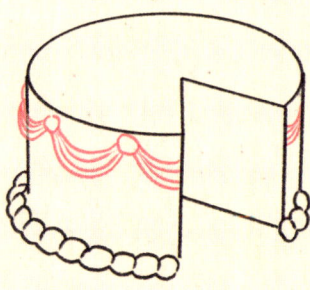

4. Add a few circles connected by stacked curved lines on the side of the cake but not in the triangle cutout.

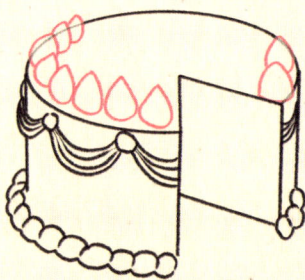

5. Draw triangles with curved bottoms around the top of the cake, but skip the back.

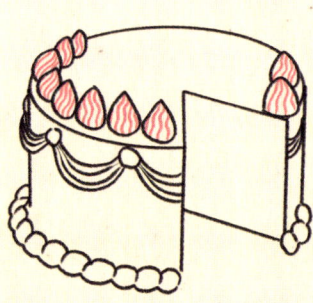

6. Add wavy lines to each triangle to add texture to the frosting.

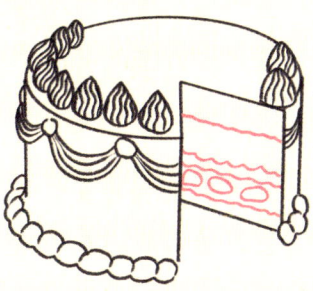

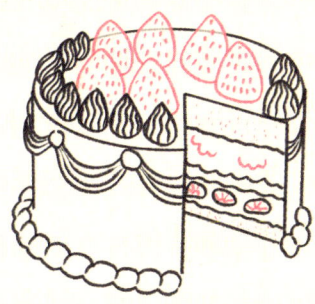

7. Draw angled, jagged, and wavy lines for the layers of the cake inside the triangle cutout. Near the bottom, add several ovals for embedded strawberries.

8. Add six strawberries to the top of the cake with little dots for seeds and pointed tops. They are slightly larger than the frosting dollops. Add details inside the cake with small dots, small curvy lines, and a sunrise design in the ovals.

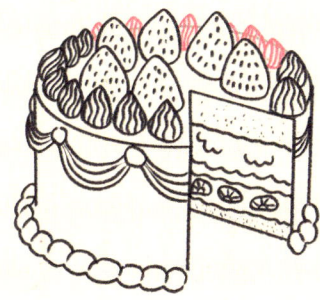

9. Finish with frosting dollops behind the strawberries to finish the circle around the cake.

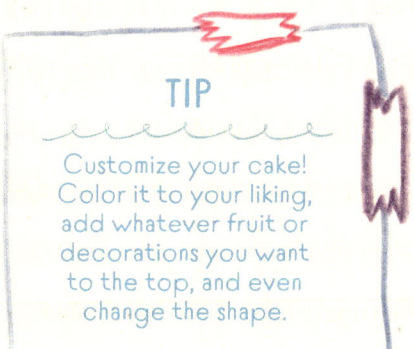

TIP

Customize your cake! Color it to your liking, add whatever fruit or decorations you want to the top, and even change the shape.

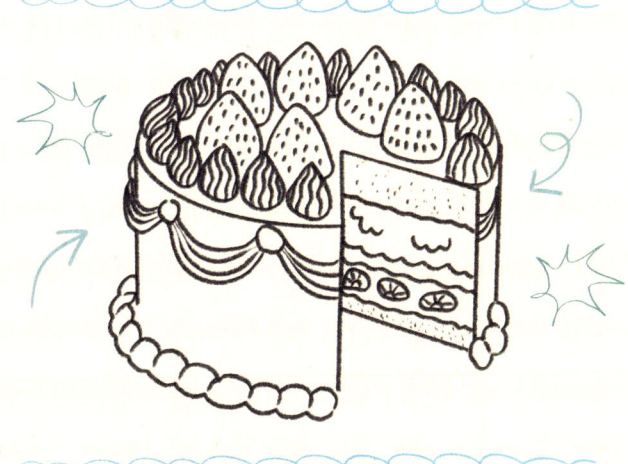

Cake Stand

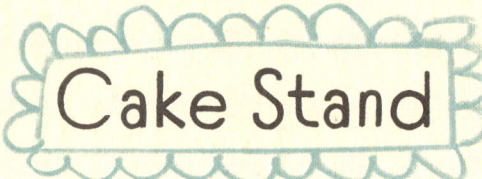 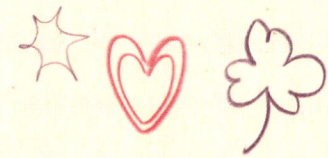

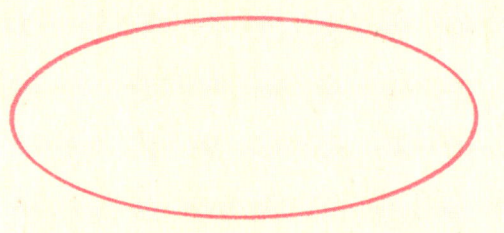

1. Draw a wide oval.

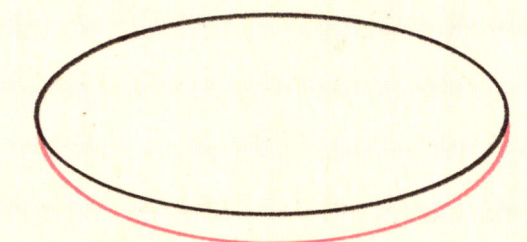

2. Draw a curved line beneath the oval.

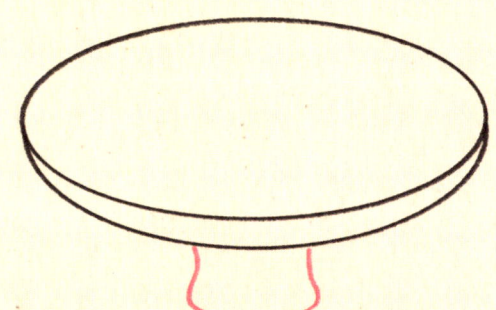

3. Finish with the stand. Draw an open-topped square with pinched sides.

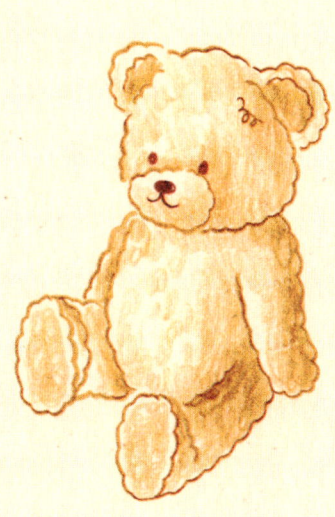

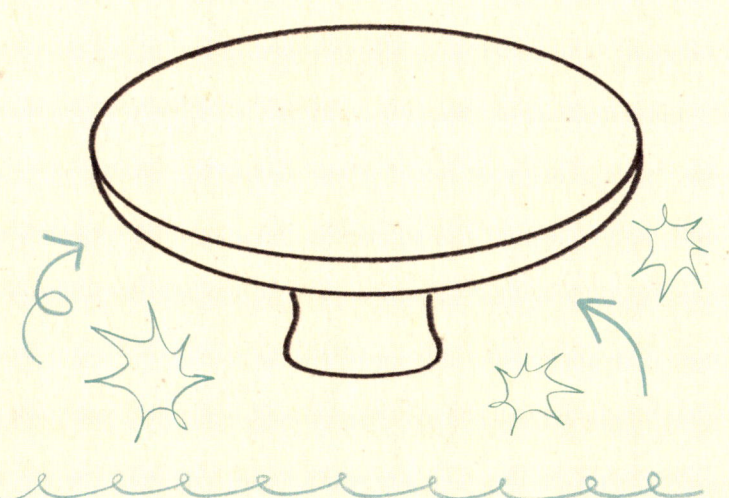

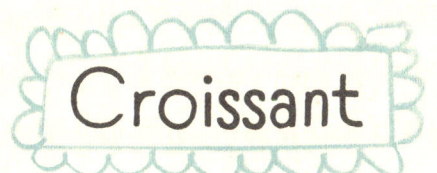

Croissant

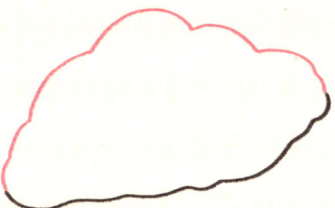

1. Draw an angled line with a series of ridges and curved edges.

2. Connect another line above with a series of curved lines like a cloud.

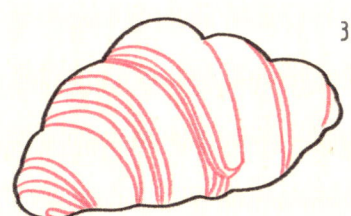

3. Finish with the croissant laminations using curved lines through the croissant shape, some close to each other and others not.

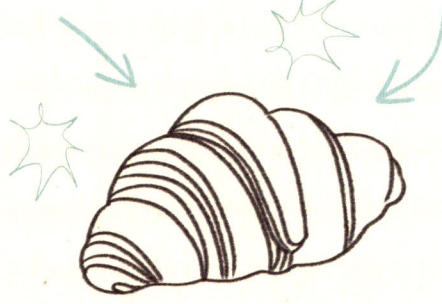

Pain au Chocolat

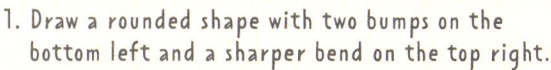

1. Draw a rounded shape with two bumps on the bottom left and a sharper bend on the top right.

2. Draw two ovals above the bumps and a series curved lines above and below the ovals for the pastry lamination. Add a line on the other end of the pastry for the lamination.

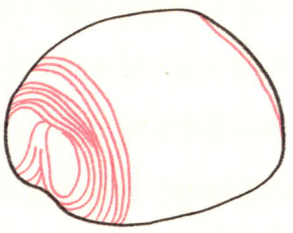

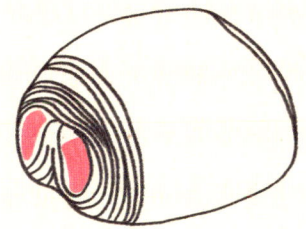

3. Add two large, filled-in ovals within the other ovals for the chocolate filling.

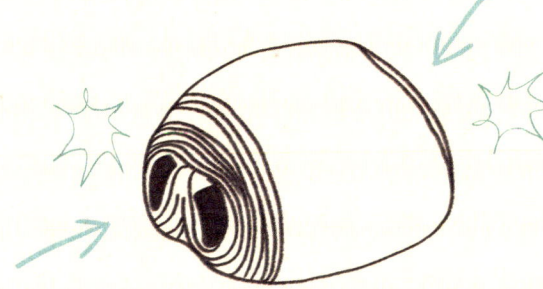

Chocolate Chip Cookie

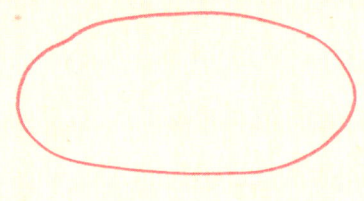

1. Draw an imperfect, wide oval.

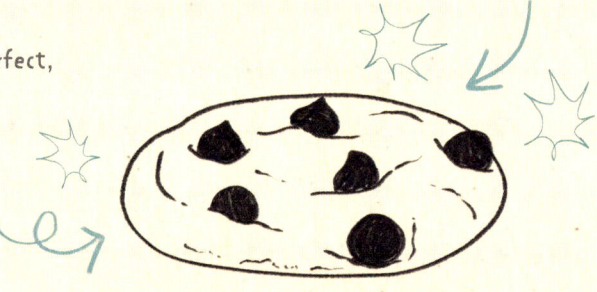

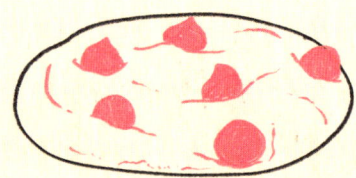

2. Add the chips as filled-in circles with pointed tops. Add small, curved lines beneath each chip and around the edges for the ridges of the cookie.

Linzer Cookie

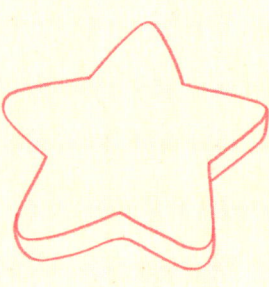

1. Draw a star shape with a line along the bottom of the shape and along the bottom right arm.

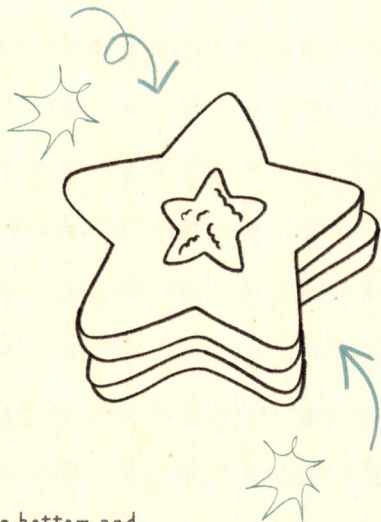

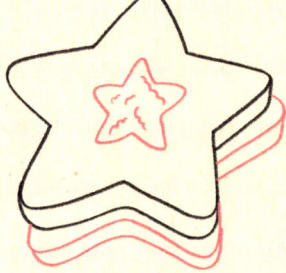

2. Draw two more lines along the bottom and the right side for the second biscuit. Add a smaller star shape on top of the cookie with little curved lines inside for the jam detail.

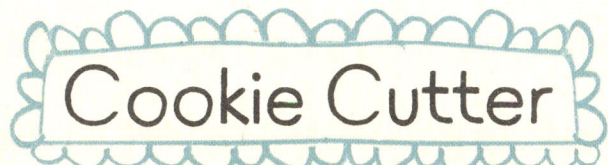

Cookie Cutter

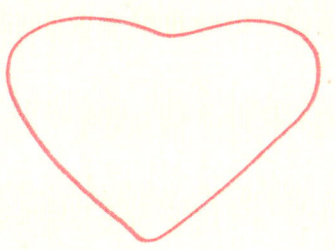

1. Draw a heart shape with no points.

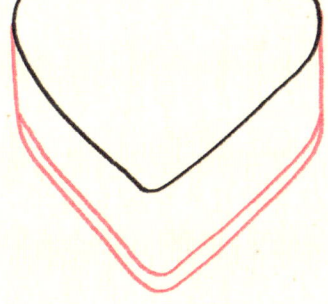

2. Draw short, vertical lines on each side of the heart. Then, draw a double line parallel to the bottom of the heart.

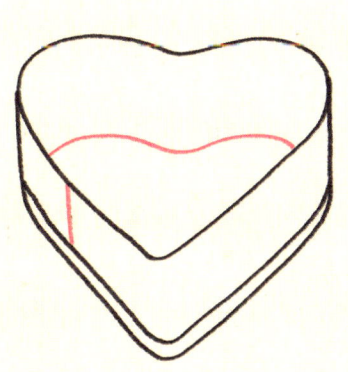

3. Add a line parallel to the top of the heart inside the shape and a vertical line along the side of the cookie cutter.

TIP

Make your cookie cutter any shape you want by starting with a different shape.

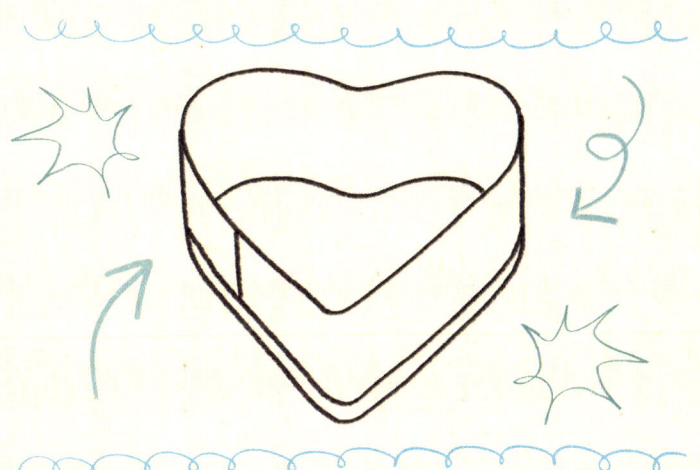

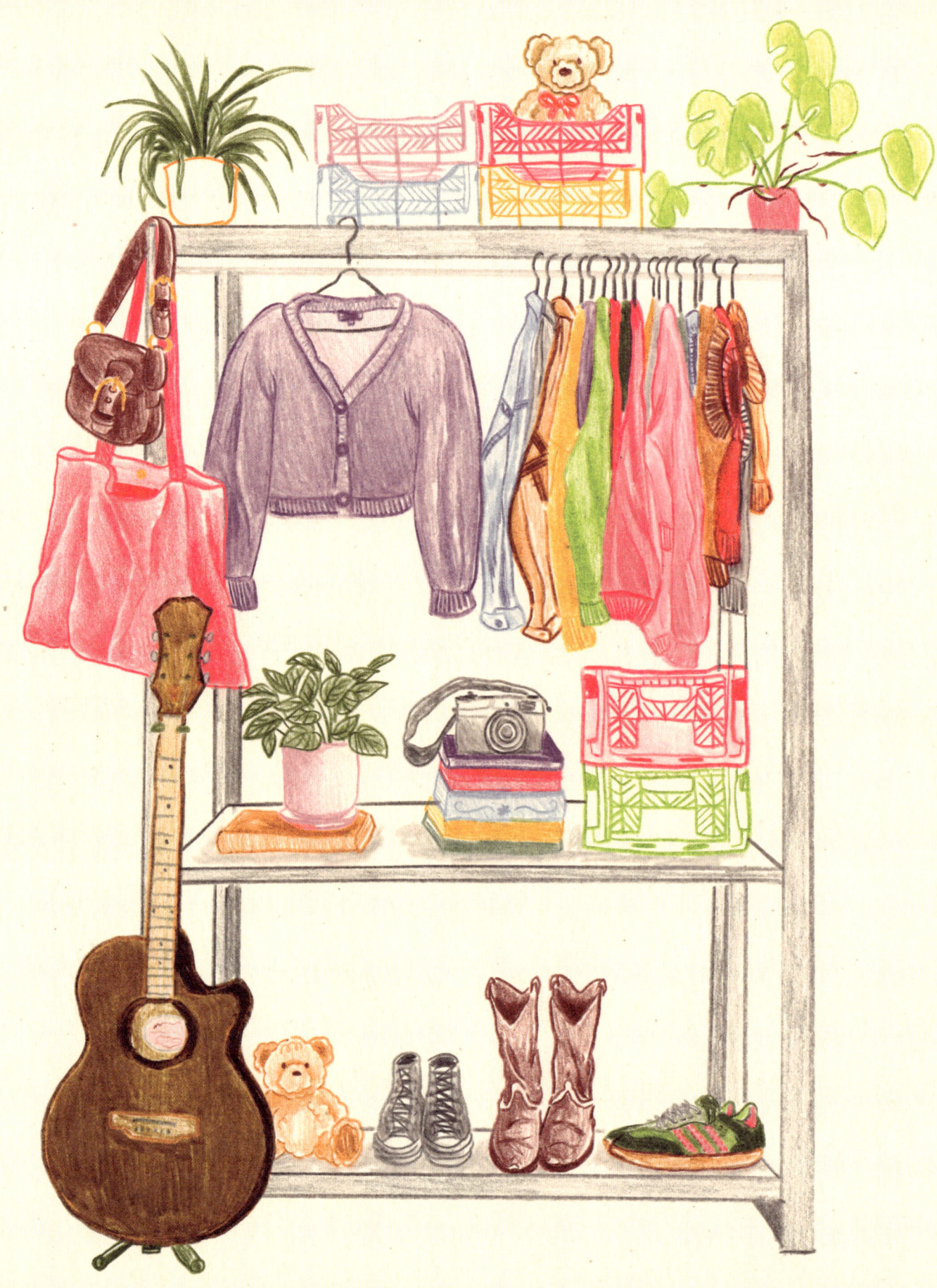

Charming Closet

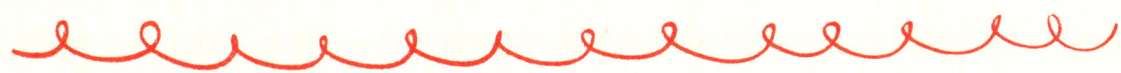

Time to choose your outfit for the day! Wrap up in a knitted cardigan or add some fun to your day by pairing a skirt with Western boots. Decorate your closet with little trinkets and a radio from Cozy Gathering Space (page 49)!

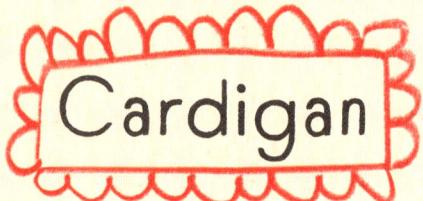

Cardigan

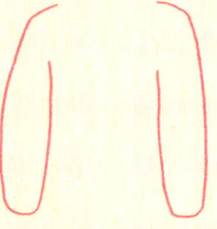

1. Start with the arms of the cardigan with rounded edges. Leave the top, inside parts open.

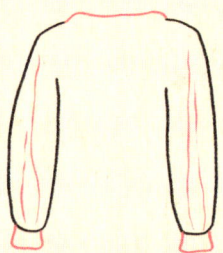

2. Add the neck of the sweater by connecting the arms with a curved line. Draw the ends of the sleeves with small rectangles and creases on the sleeves with straight lines.

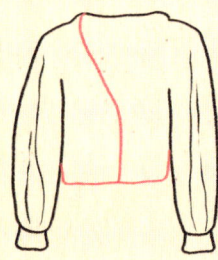

3. Draw the bottom of the sweater with a horizontal line halfway between the sleeves. Draw a bent line down the center of the sweater.

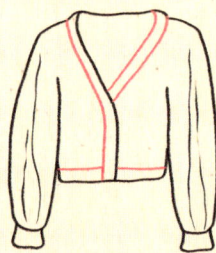

4. Add another angled line from the right side of the neck to the center of the sweater to create a V-neck. Draw parallel lines along the hems of the neckline and waistline.

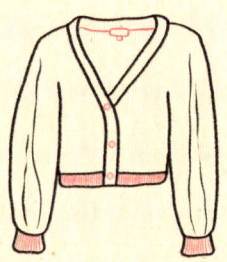

5. Draw a horizontal line inside the sweater and a tag in the center. Finish with buttons below the V-neck and vertical lines along the waistline hem and end of the sleeves.

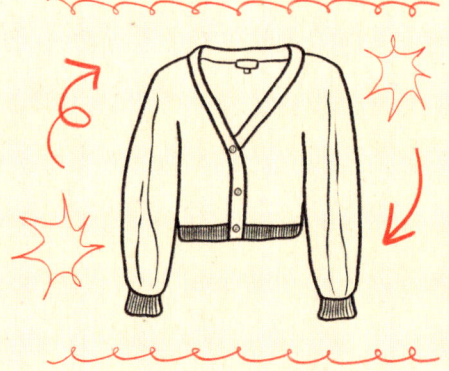

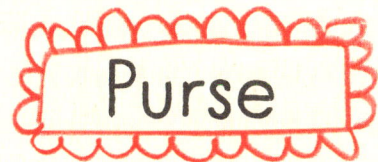

Purse

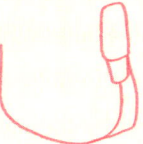

1. Draw the U-shaped bottom of the purse, a curved line along the right side, and a rectangle on top of a square on the right side.

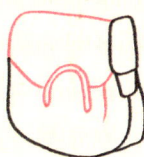

2. Draw a curved line to create the body of the purse. Draw two curved lines meeting toward an upside-down U shape for the bag flap and buckle.

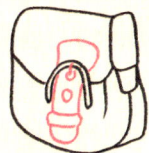

3. Add a buckle through the upside-down U shape with a belt loop at the bottom and two belt holes below the U shape.

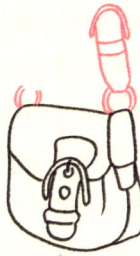

4. Add two double-lined circles with open tops on each end of the purse. On the right side, connect a belt strap to the circle with a buckle at the top.

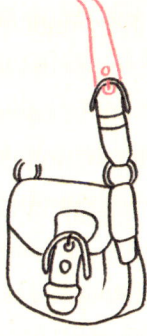

5. Add a circle above and below the buckle. Draw curved lines that almost meet at a point above the buckle.

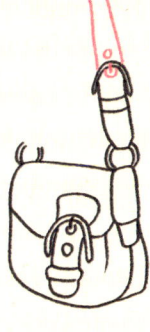

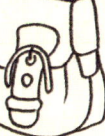

6. Finish the rest of the strap. Add two circles along the back strap.

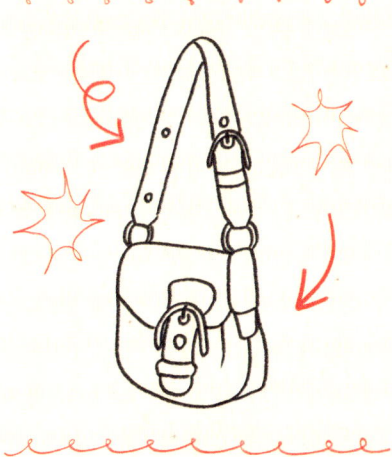

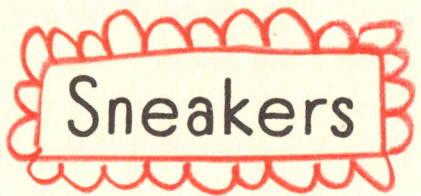

Sneakers

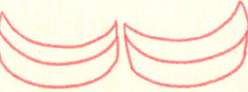

1. Draw two sets of curved and stacked rectangles beside each other.

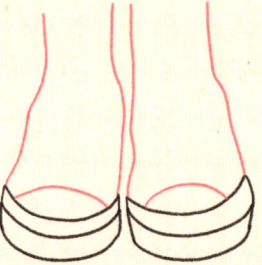

2. Add curved lines above the rectangles. Draw four lines from the ends of the rectangles, with bumps for the toes and ankles. Make sure the shoes are skinnier at the top.

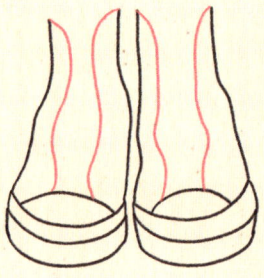

3. Inside each shoe, draw two wavy lines that connect the tops to the curved line at the bottom. The middle is as wide as the top.

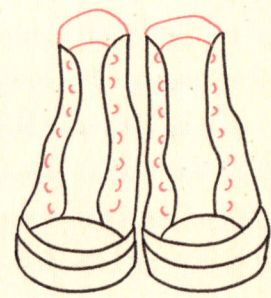

4. Add two curved lines at the top of each shoe. Draw C- and backward C-shaped lines surrounding the wavy lines inside the shoes.

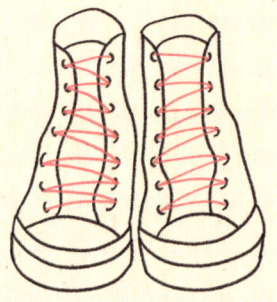

5. Finish with a jagged line following one C-shaped line to another backward C-shaped line, from the top to the bottom of the shoe.

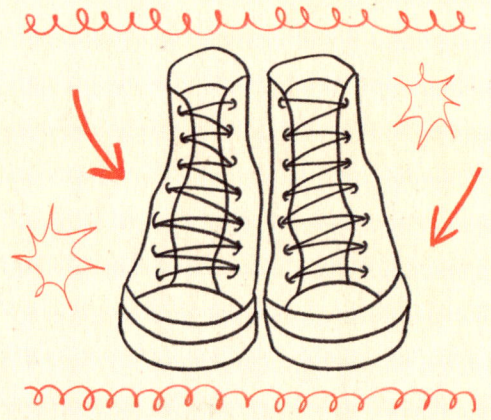

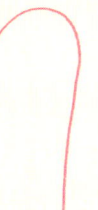

1. Draw a curved line like a question mark.

2. Connect a straight line to a curved line for the foot. Make sure there is a sharp V on the top of the boot.

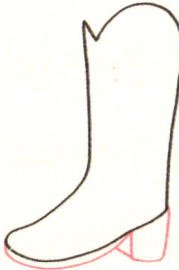

3. Draw a curved line below the bottom of the boot and a rectangle for the heel. Add a short line from the rectangle to the curved line for dimension.

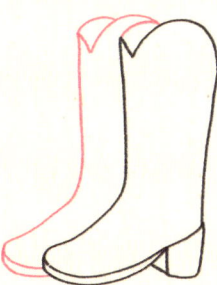

4. Duplicate the left half of the boot behind the finished boot.

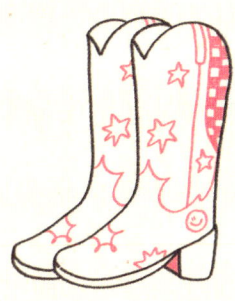

5. Decorate your boots! Add stars, bold patterns like a checkerboard, and fun, jagged lines. Color in the space beside the heel for shadowing.

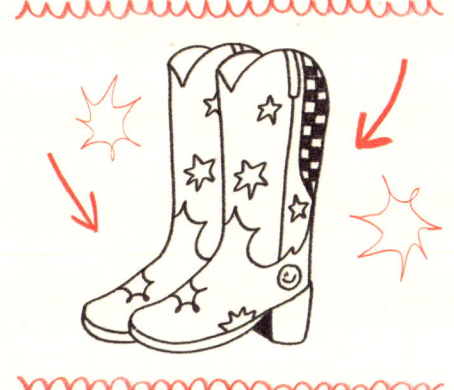

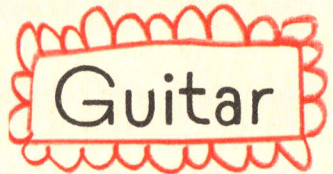

Guitar

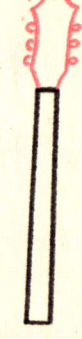

1. Draw a long, skinny rectangle for the neck.

2. Draw a shorter rectangle with cut-off corners for the head and three small circles on either side for tuning pegs.

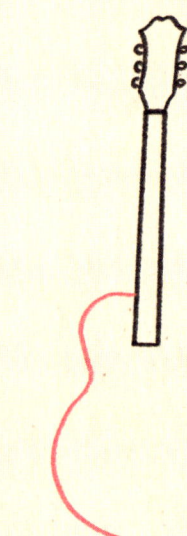

3. Draw a curvy line like a backward three on the left side of the neck.

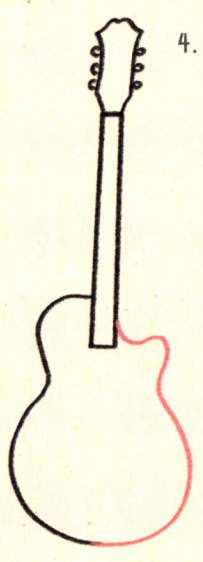

4. Draw a curvy line like a three on the right side of the neck with a more pointed top and connected to the other side. The right side should be slightly shorter than the left side.

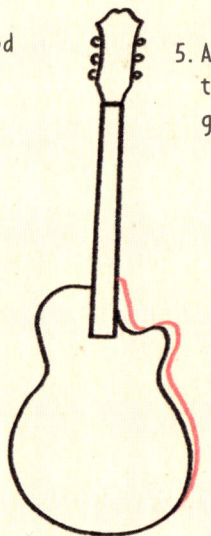

5. Add another line along the right side of the guitar body.

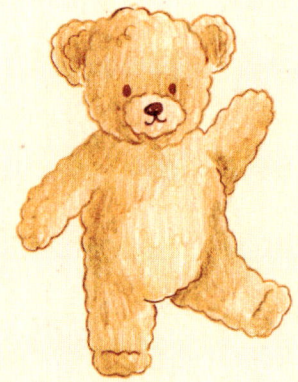

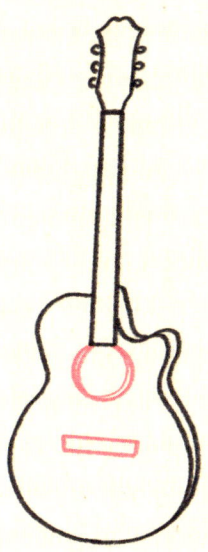

6. Draw a double-lined circle below the neck and a wide rectangle below the circle.

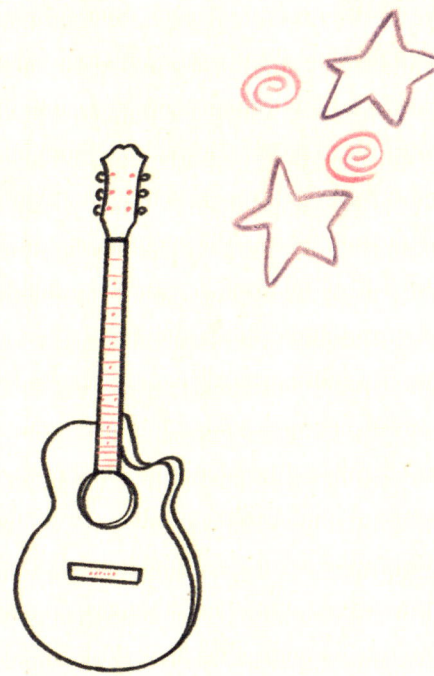

7. Add a series of dots within the wide rectangle, the neck, and the head. Add horizontal lines along the neck as well.

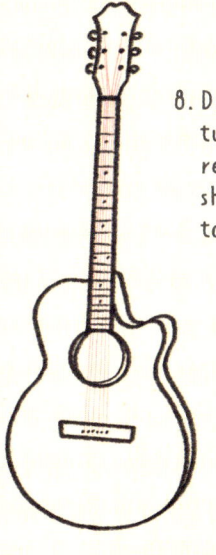

8. Draw lines connecting the top tuning dots to the bottom rectangle dots. The lines should end up being parallel to each other on the neck.

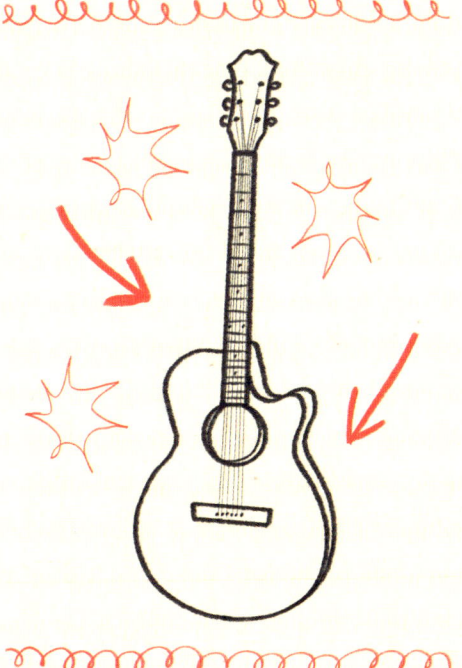

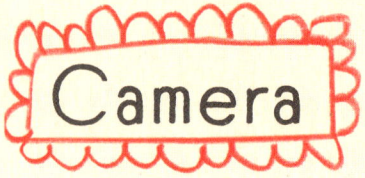 

Camera

1. Draw a rectangle with rounded corners.

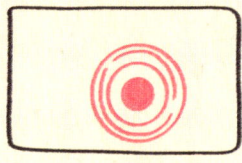

2. Draw a large dot on the right side of the rectangle. Draw two circles around the dot with two curved lines between the circles.

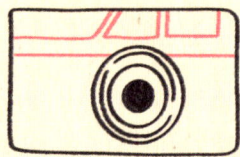

3. Add a horizontal line through the top of the lens and three rectangular shapes with slanted sides along the top of the camera.

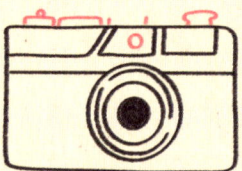

4. Draw a circle inside the middle shape, two rectangles on top of the camera, two lines on the top, and a mushroom-shaped button on the top right.

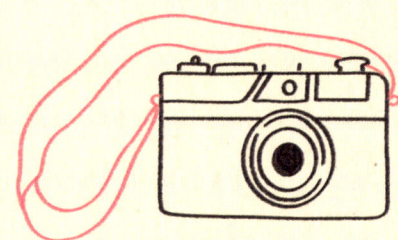

5. Finish the strap of the camera. Add two circles on each side of the camera, connected to long, curved lines. Add a line through the strap for the fold.

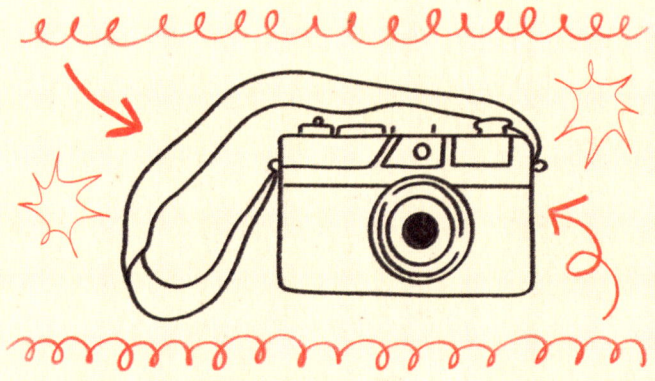

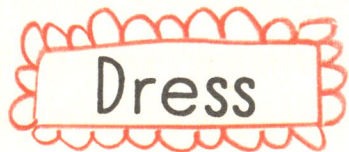

Dress

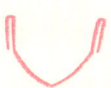

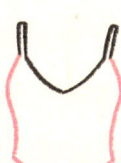

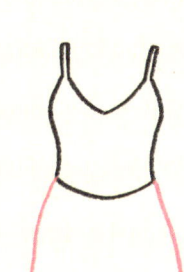

1. Draw a V connecting two thin, open-bottomed rectangles.

2. Draw mirrored lines shaped almost like an S and a curved line below connecting the two.

3. Draw two lines billowing out from the waist.

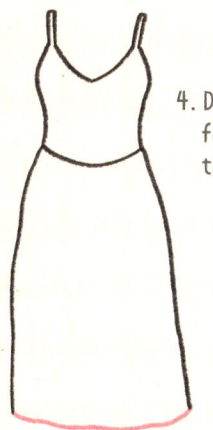

4. Draw a curved line for the bottom of the dress.

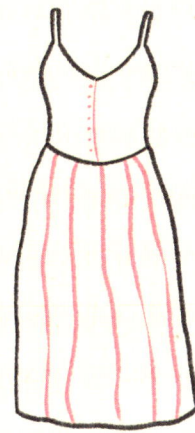

5. Finish with vertical, wavy lines on the bottom of the dress, a vertical line down the top of the dress, and dots to the left of this line for buttons.

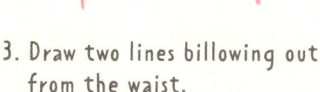

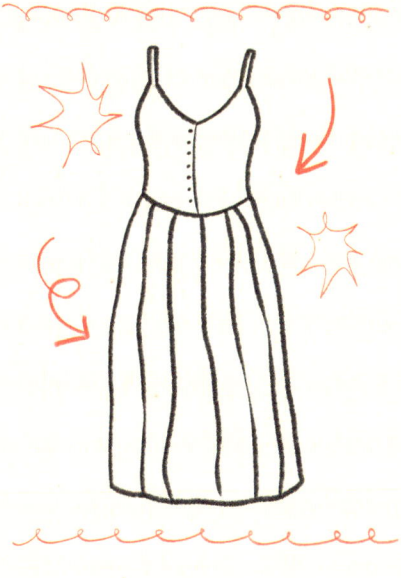

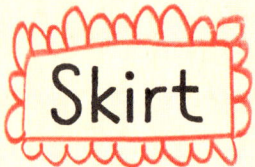

Skirt

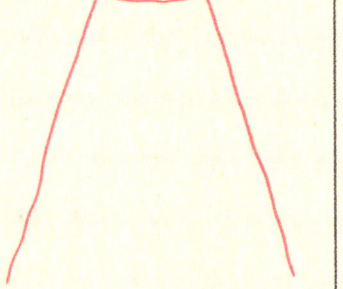

1. Draw two angled lines connected by a curved line for the waistline.

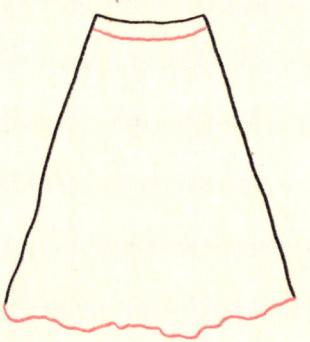

2. Draw another curved line beneath the waistline and a jagged line for the bottom.

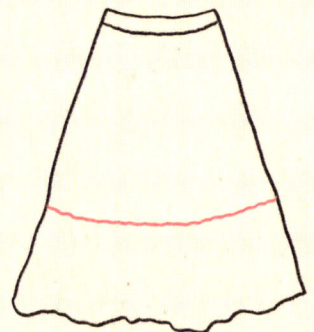

3. Draw a curved line through the bottom half of the skirt.

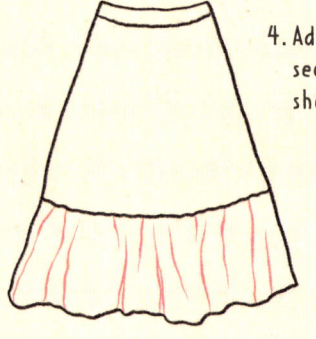

4. Add creases in the bottom section of the skirt using short and V-shaped lines.

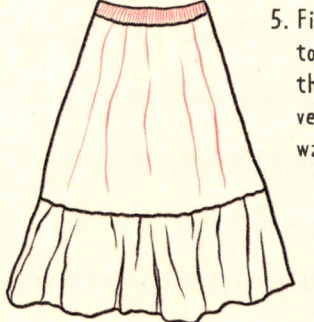

5. Finish with more creases to the top section of the skirt and a series of vertical lines along the waistline.

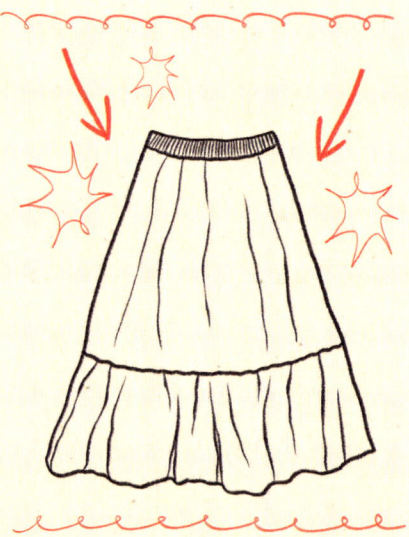

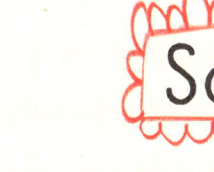

Scarf

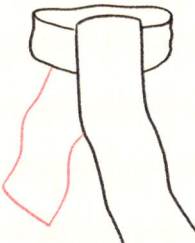

1. Draw a long rectangle with bends. Draw two shorter rectangles on either side of the long rectangle, as well as a curved line above to connect these shorter rectangles.

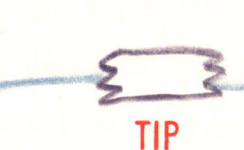

TIP

Color in alternate spaces between lines for a bolder striped scarf.

2. Add another long rectangle to the left of the other with similar bends.

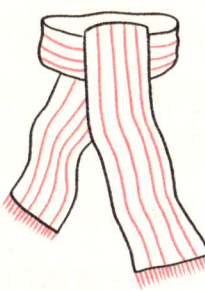

3. Add short lines on the ends of each long rectangle for the tassels with a series of vertical lines inside each. Draw horizontal lines inside the short rectangles.

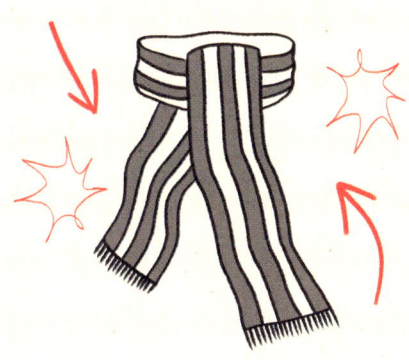

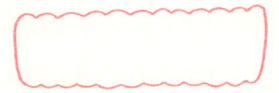

1. Draw a wide rectangle with scalloped edges on the top and bottom.

Hat

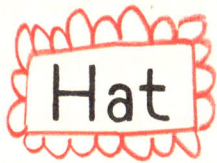

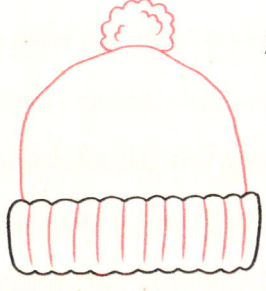

2. Draw an upside-down U starting from each side of the rectangle. Finish with a pom-pom on top using a half circle with a scalloped edge and two bumpy lines inside.

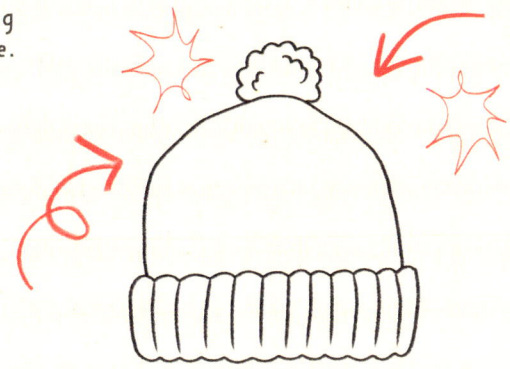

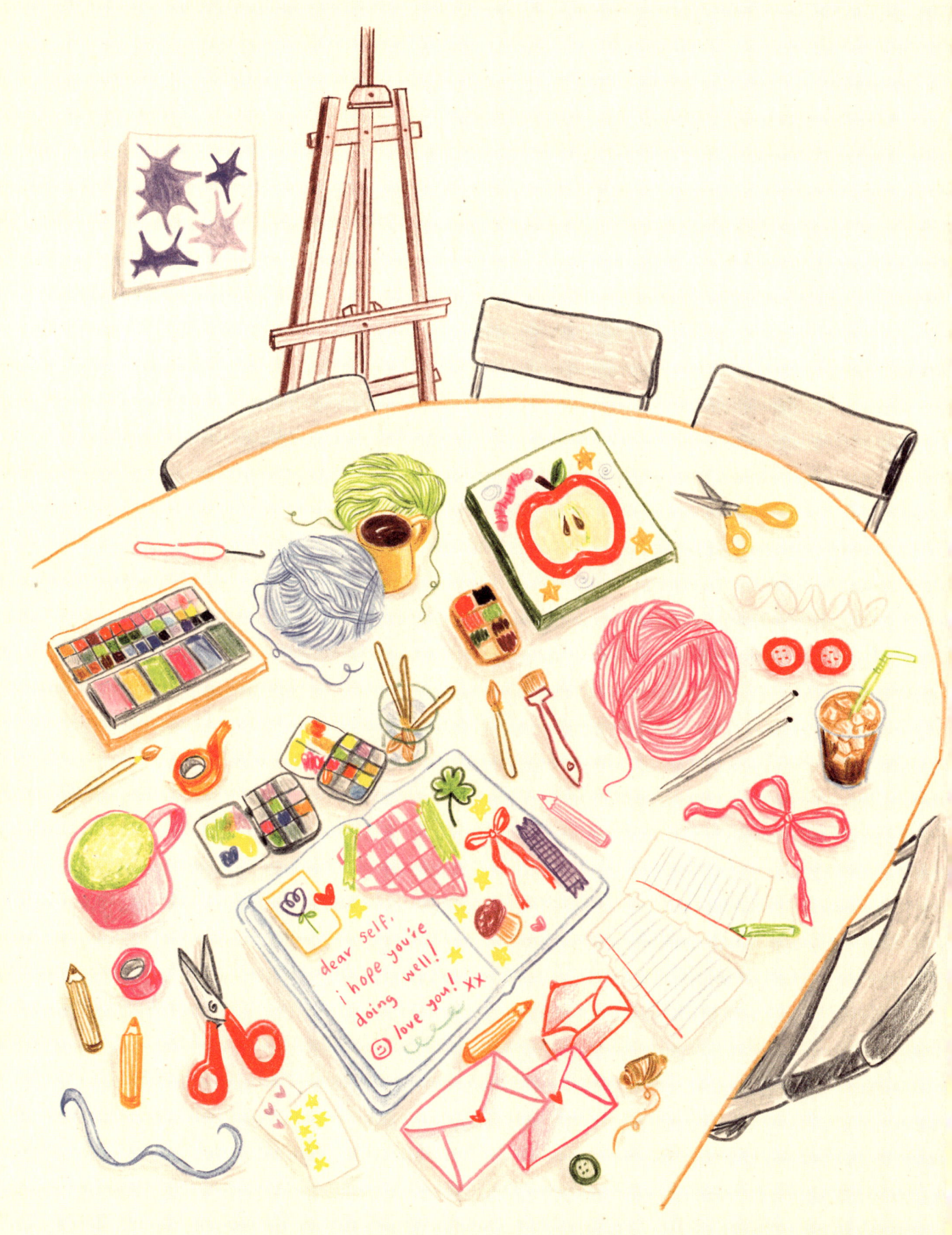

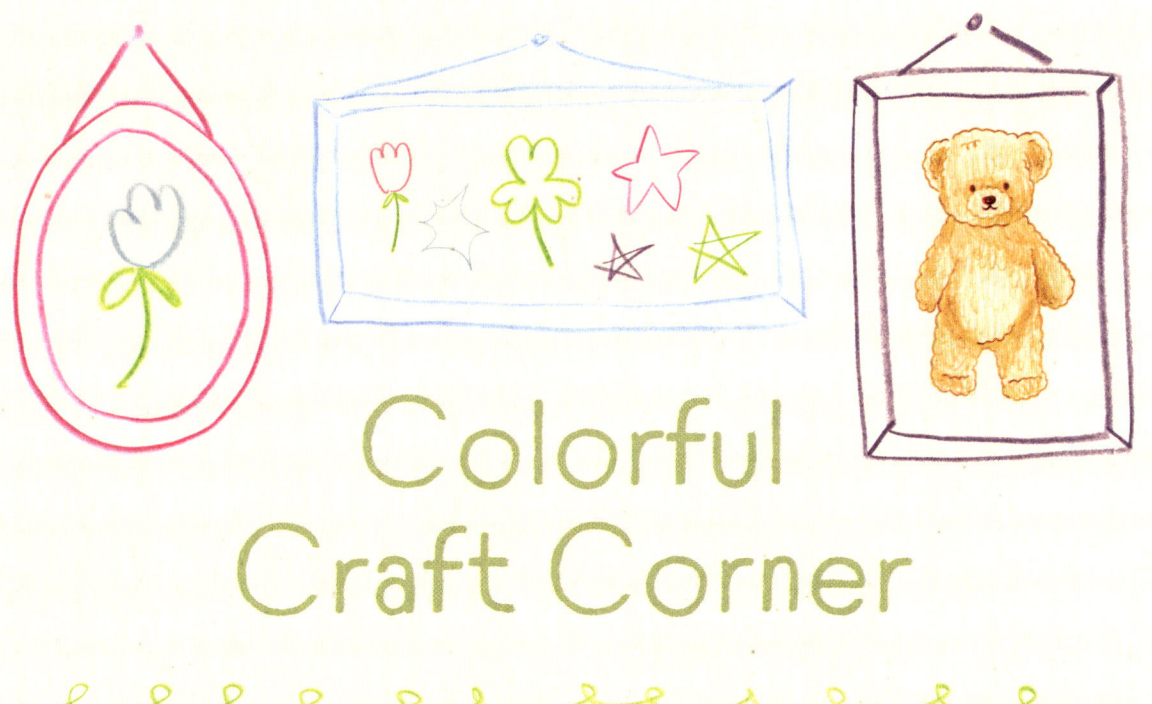

Colorful
Craft Corner

It's time to put all those stickers to use! Grab your sketchbook, canvases, and journals and get creative! Add elements from Serene Study Nook (page 21) to ensure you have all the stationery goodies you desire and from Common Things in Your Room (page 14) to personalize your canvases and stationery.

Easel

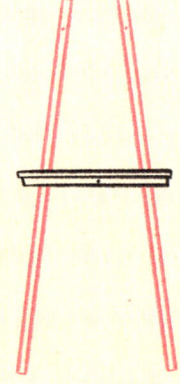

1. Draw a long, wide rectangle on top of another with a dot in the middle.

2. Draw two long, tall rectangles angled toward each other and split in the middle by the wide rectangles. Add two dots at the top of these tall rectangles.

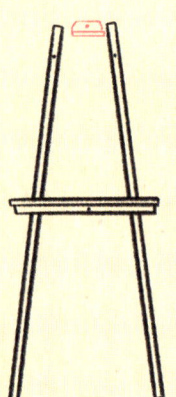

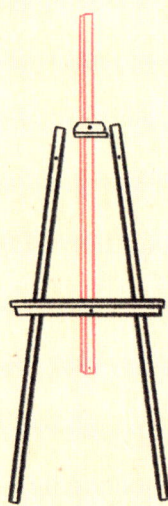

3. Between the two long, tall rectangles, draw a small rectangle with cut-out corners and a dot in the middle on top of a thinner rectangle.

4. Draw a long, tall rectangle through the small rectangle and the long, wide rectangles in the middle. Add a dot at the bottom of the rectangle and a parallel line to the right of the rectangle for dimension.

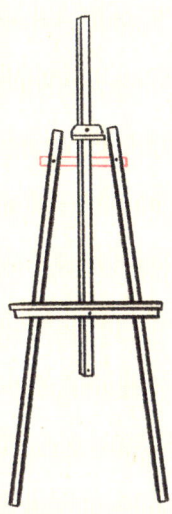

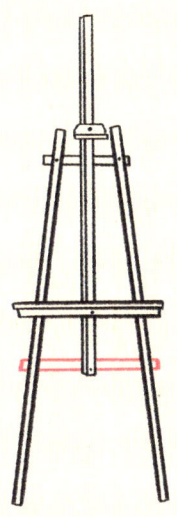

5. Draw a wide rectangle behind the three long, tall rectangles meeting at the dots of the two long, tall rectangles.

6. Draw a wide rectangle behind the three long, tall rectangles near the bottom of the middle rectangle.

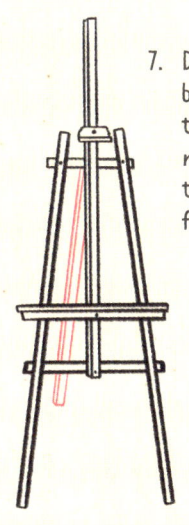

7. Draw an angled rectangle from behind the top wide rectangle to just below the bottom wide rectangle. Add a parallel line to the left of the rectangle for dimension.

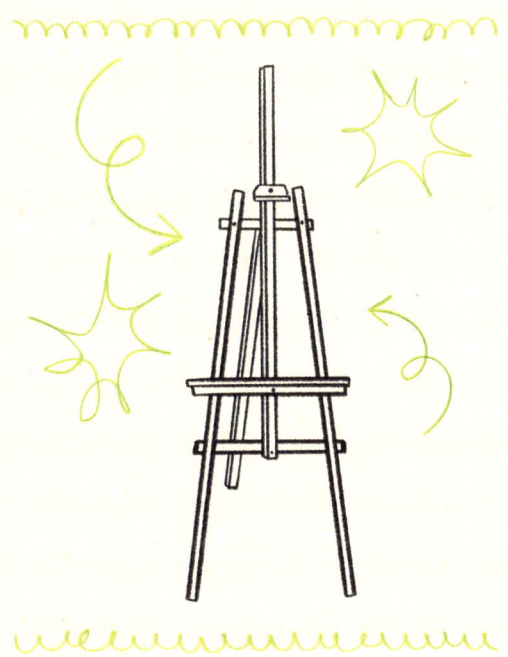

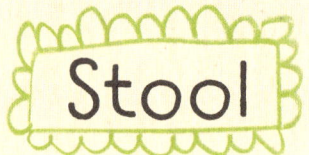

Stool

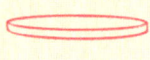

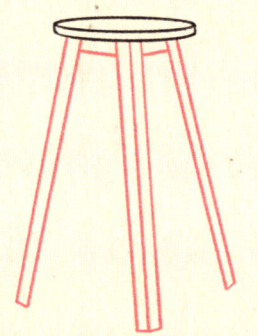

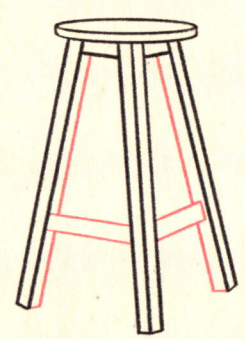

1. Draw an oval with a curved line beneath connected by two vertical lines at each end.

2. Draw three long chair legs extending from the seat. Add a line through the middle leg for dimension and two horizontal lines to connect the legs near the seat.

3. Draw a line with a bend at the end mirrored on the side legs. Add double-lined, horizontal lines to connect the legs.

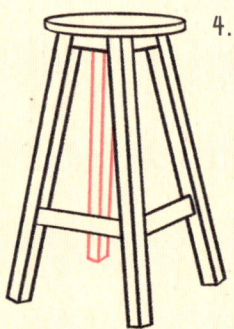

4. Add the back leg with a rectangle—which also has a thicker, middle line for dimension—behind the middle front leg.

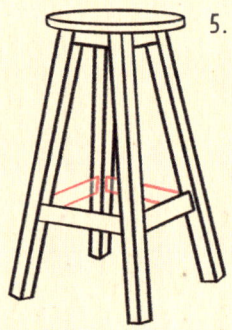

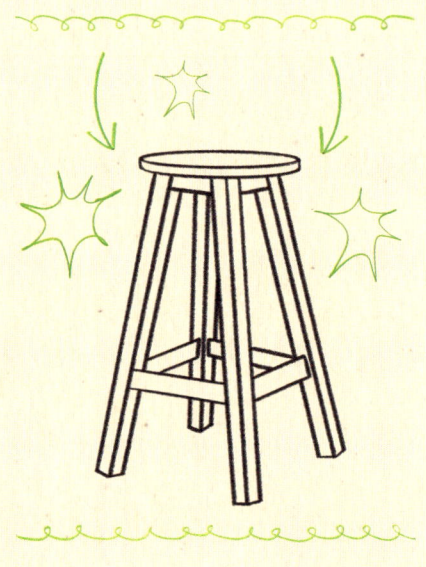

5. Finish with two more double-lined, horizontal lines connecting the side legs with the back leg.

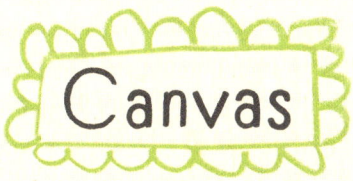
Canvas

1. Draw a square.

2. Draw a parallel line on one side and below the square. Connect the three corners with a short line.

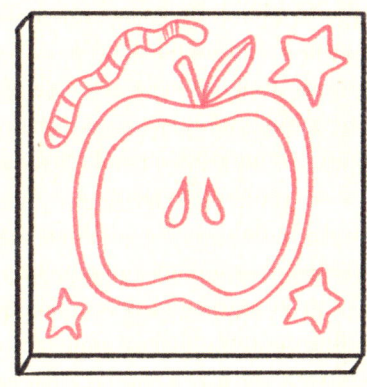

3. Design your canvas! Add stars, an apple, and a worm—or do your own thing. Take inspiration from Common Things in Your Room (page 14).

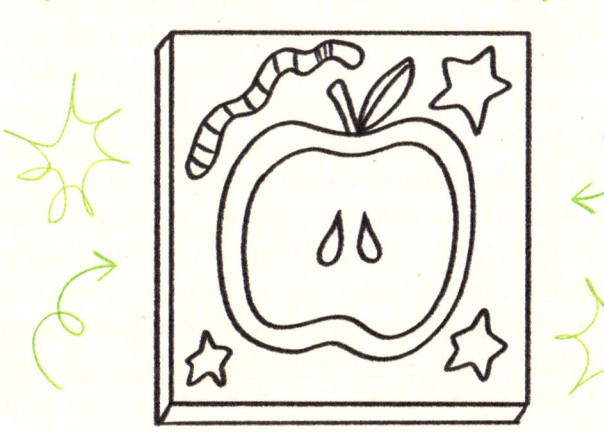

Paintbrushes

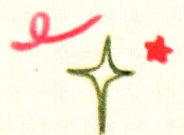

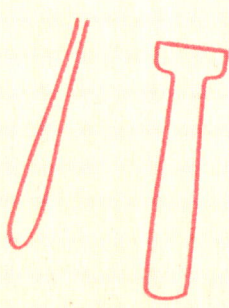

1. Draw the handles with a round-bottomed, open-topped rectangle next to a T shape.

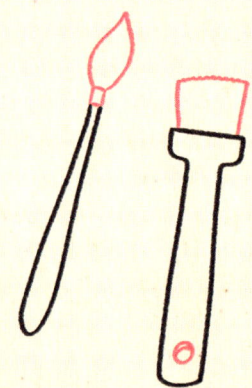

2. Add a leaf shape and small square to the left brush. Add a rectangle to the right brush with a zigzagged top and a circle to the handle.

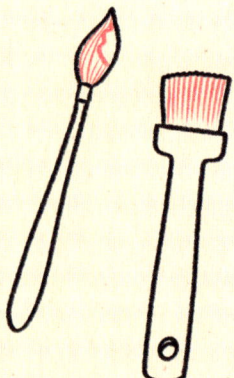

3. Add vertical lines to each of the brush heads. Add a little wavy shape on one to add a little paint.

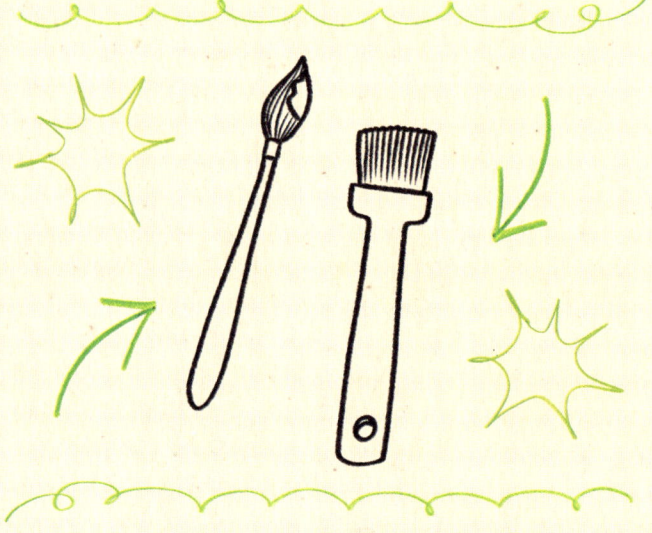

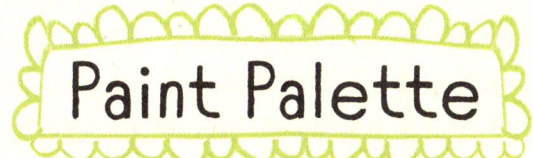

Paint Palette

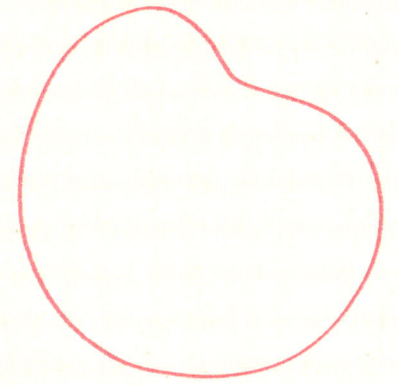

1. Draw a bean shape.

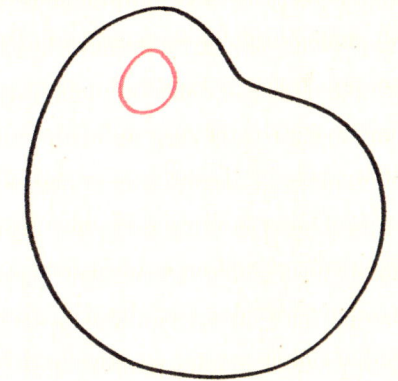

2. Add a small oval inside.

3. Finish with a group of irregular shapes and imperfect circles on the palette. Add some color to your canvas!

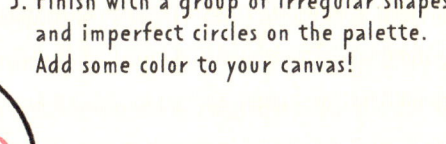

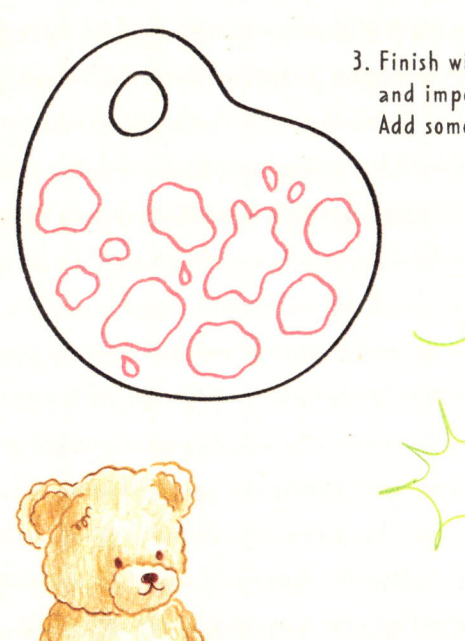

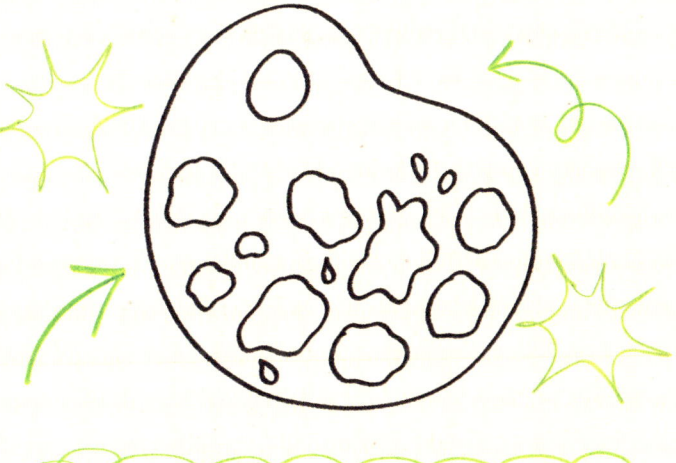

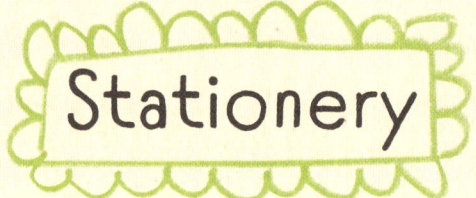

Stationery

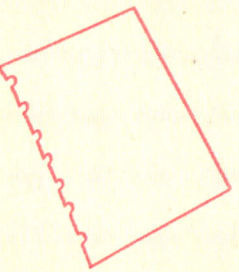

1. Draw an angled rectangle with half circles cut out of the left side.

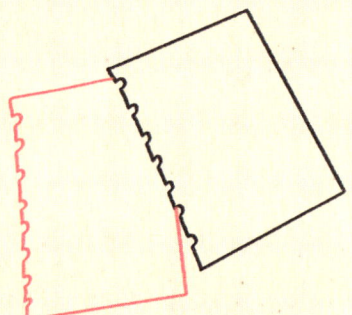

2. Duplicate the rectangle at a different angle beneath the first rectangle.

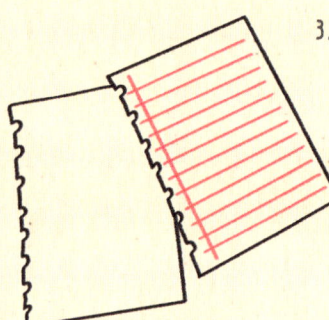

3. Add a vertical line down the left side of the right page and a series of horizontal lines across the page. The vertical line should be bolder than the horizontal lines.

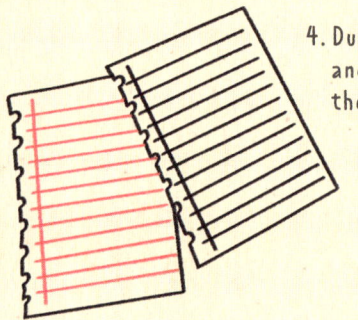

4. Duplicate the vertical and horizontal lines on the left page.

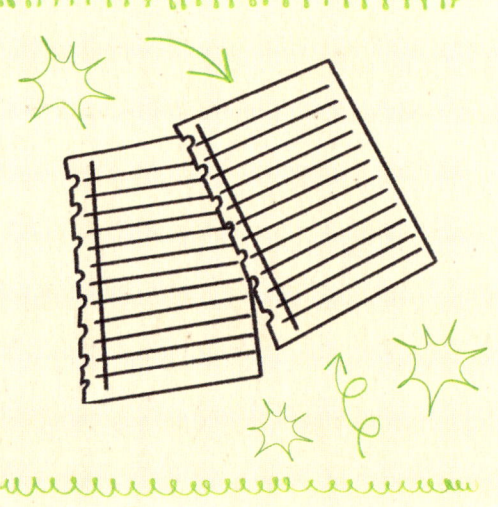

Envelopes

1. Draw an angled rectangle.

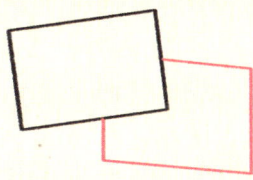

2. Add another rectangle beneath the first rectangle.

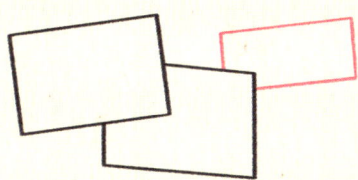

3. Add a thinner rectangle beneath the top right of the second rectangle.

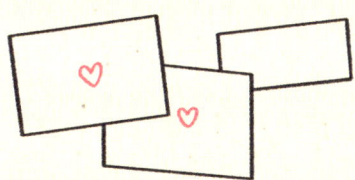

4. Add two hearts to the center of the first two envelopes.

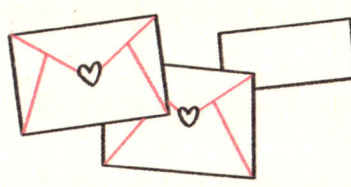

5. Draw lines connecting the top corners to the heart in the center of each envelope. Add two more lines connecting the bottom corners to the other lines.

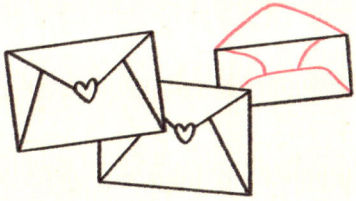

6. For the final rectangle, add a triangle on top of the shape as well as two curved and mirrored lines connected to a curved line from each bottom corner. You've got mail!

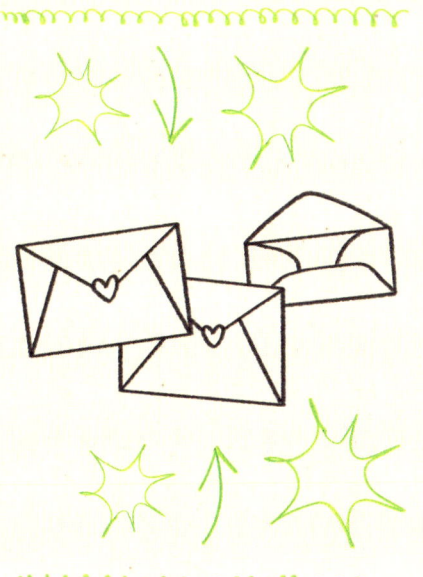

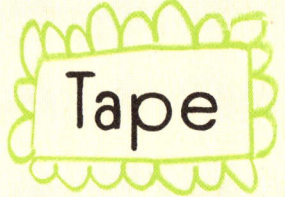

Tape

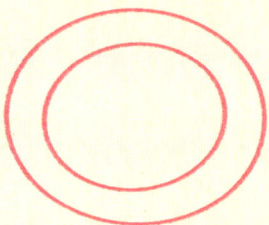

1. Draw two circles, one inside the other.

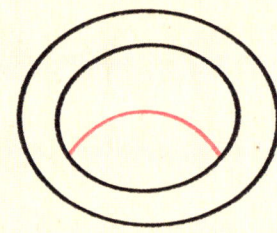

2. Draw a curved line inside the interior circle.

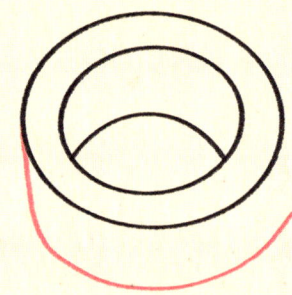

3. Draw a curved line below the circles connected by a vertical line on the left end.

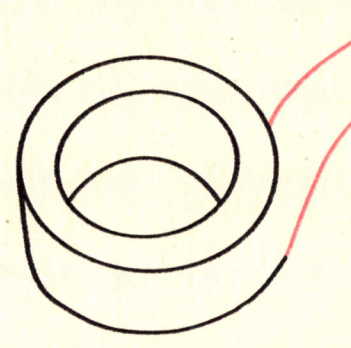

4. Draw a curved rectangle on the right side with a jagged end.

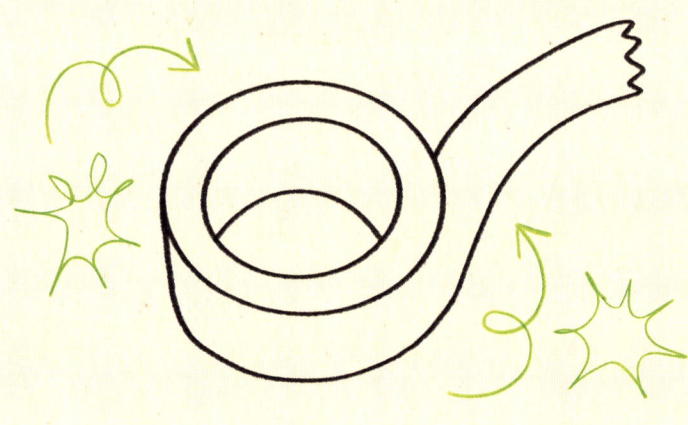

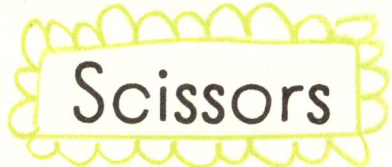

Scissors

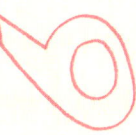

1. Draw a lowercase B shape at an angle.

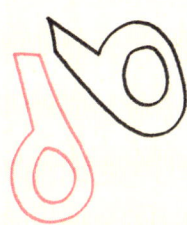

2. Mirror the lowercase B shape.

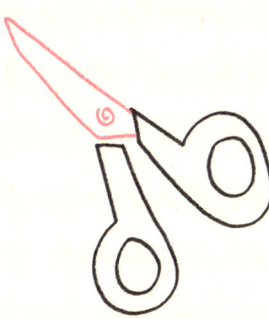

3. Draw a line parallel to the first B shape with a sharp tip. Add a slanted line to meet the tip of the mirrored B shape and a swirl at the bottom of the blade.

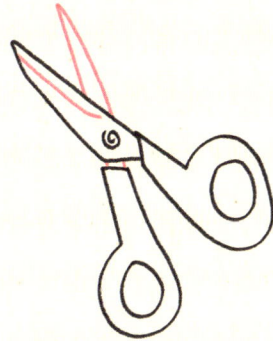

4. Add a triangular blade parallel to the mirrored B shape and a straight line in the middle of the left blade.

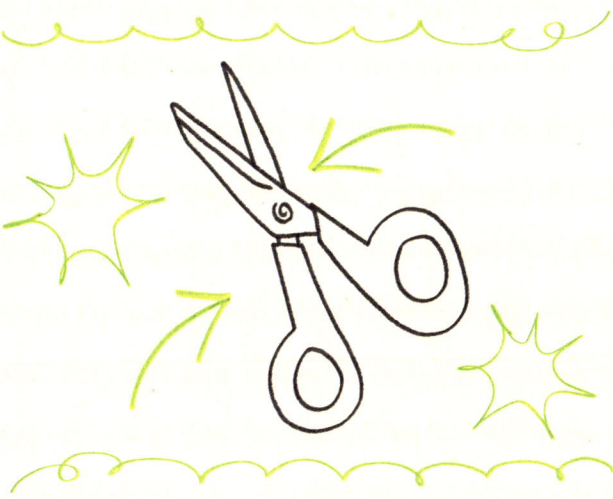

Knitting Needles

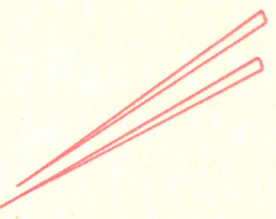

1. Draw two thin, long triangles.

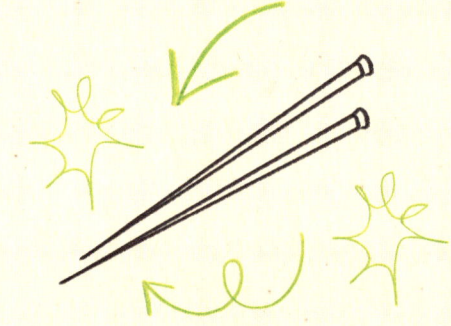

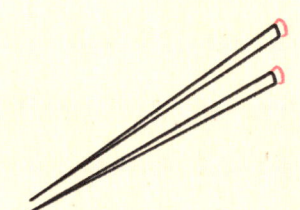

2. Add an oval to the non-pointed end.

Yarn

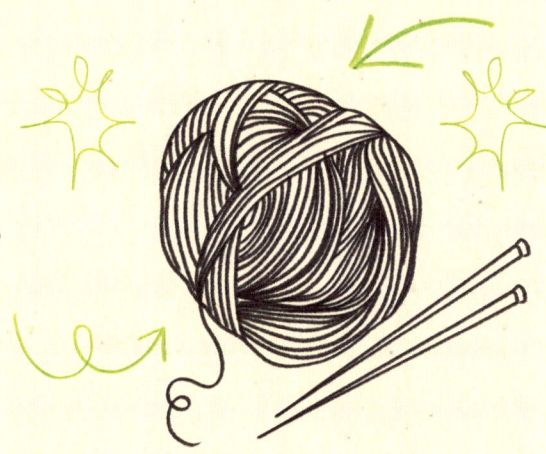

1. Draw an imperfect circle beside Knitting Needles (above).

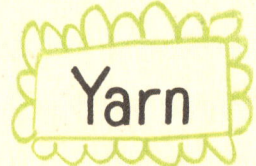

2. Add a series of curved lines oriented in different directions. Add one curlicue line outside of the circle for a loose string.

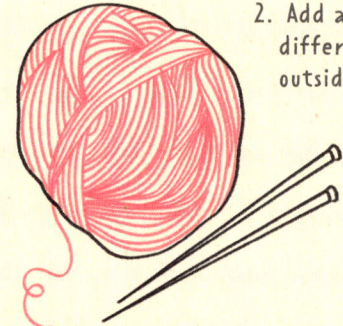

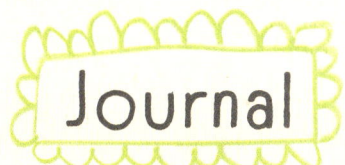

Journal

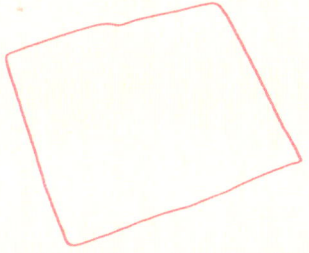

1. Draw an angled rectangle with a bump in the middle of top edge.

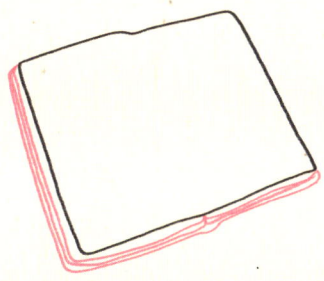

2. Add three lines along the left side and bottom connected at the top left and bottom right corner. Add a divot at the bottom middle for the spine.

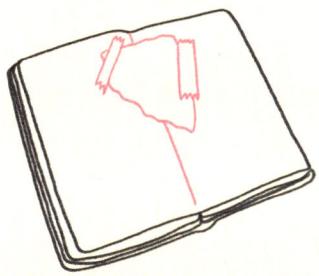

3. Draw an irregular triangle in the center of the book and two rectangles with zigzagged ends on each side for tape. Draw a line down the center of the journal—from the spine and parallel to the sides—behind the taped-on paper.

TIP

Add a motivating quote from Quote Inspiration (page 12) or get ideas from Common Things in Your Room (page 14), like a bow or smiley faces, to decorate your journal.

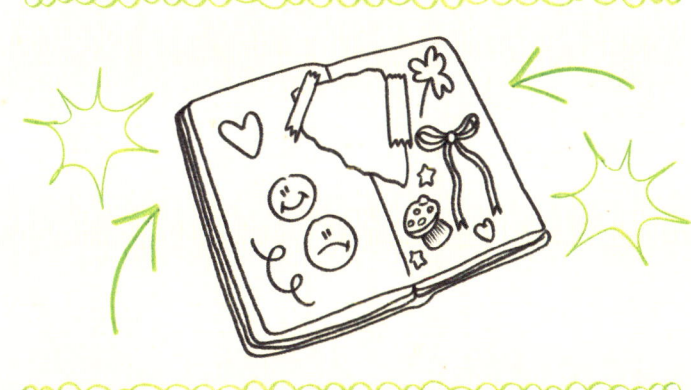

Sketchbook Craft

Tiny Button Book Guide

Equipment

→ Paper or cardstock
→ Pencil
→ Scissors
→ Glue stick or glue dots
→ Buttons

I'm excited to share a fun and easy craft project to make a mini sketchbook using buttons and paper. The technique used to fold the paper is called an "accordion fold" or a "fan fold." This folding technique is a great way to create a compact and portable book for personal journaling or creating. It could also make a great gift for your loved ones!

How to Create a Fan Fold

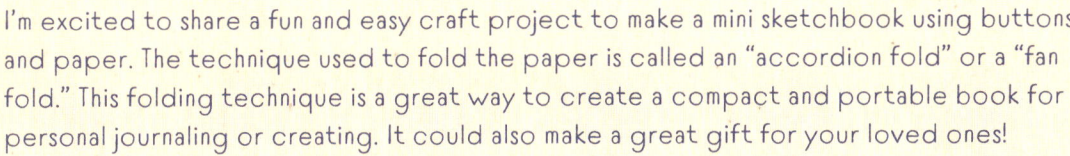

1. Fold over the edge of the paper 1 to 2 inches (3 to 5 cm) and make a crease.
2. Flip over the paper. Do the same fold in the opposite direction.
3. Continue to fold the remaining paper, making sure to turn it over each time and to keep the same length.
4. Once finished, you have made what looks like a concertina or accordion.

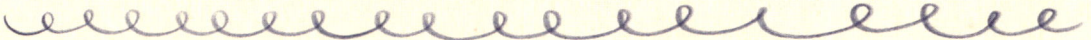

Tips for Making Your Button Sketchbook

• The longer your piece of paper, the more pages your sketchbook will have. However, this does also mean it will be harder to cut through with scissors.
• You can use any size buttons! I personally use 2 by 2-inch (5 by 5 cm) buttons. Please note that if you use smaller buttons, it may be a little trickier!
• Use a bone folder, ruler, or even the back of a spoon to create sharper creases.
• Please ensure that you cut inside the two pencil lines on your paper. This allows the uncut edges to form the folds and attach each page together!
• Once you have cut your circle book out, your edges may be slightly jagged. Use your scissors to carefully tidy them up before gluing your button covers on.
• Mix up your designs by using colored paper to create your mini button sketchbook!
• For ease and speed, I recommend using glue dots to stick your buttons and paper together.

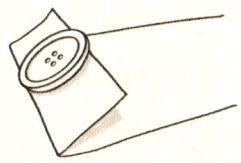

1. Place your button on the short edge of the paper. Make sure your button slightly hangs over the top and bottom and then fold once. This ensures your pages will be the same size as your button!

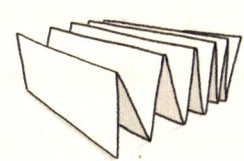

2. Fold the remaining paper using the fan fold method.

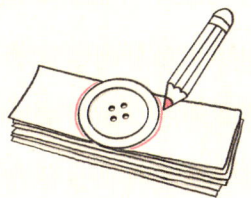

3. Place the button on top of the folded paper, double-check the top and bottom of the button overhang slightly, and draw on each side using a pencil.

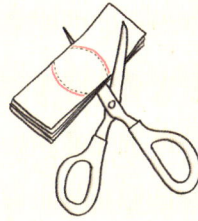

4. Cut slightly inside your pencil lines. Do not cut it all the way around.

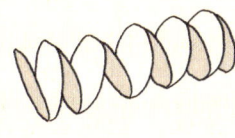

5. It should look like this once cut!

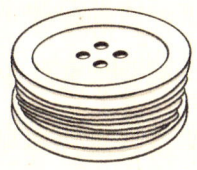

6. Apply glue to the back of your button, whether you're using glue dots or a glue stick.

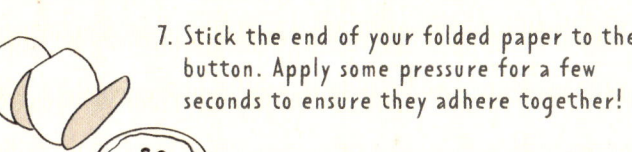

7. Stick the end of your folded paper to the button. Apply some pressure for a few seconds to ensure they adhere together!

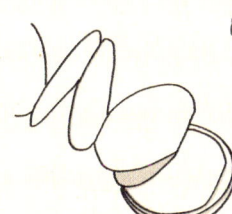

8. If using a glue stick, please allow up to ten minutes for your tiny book to dry before decorating. If using glue dots, there is no drying time required!

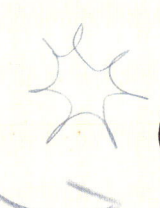

9. Get creative! Use your favorite art supplies and decorate the pages of your new Tiny Button Book!

Coloring Pages

It's not over yet! Here are some more interior scenes and mindful doodles in my style that you can color in *your* style and decorate to your preference. Here's an example of how I color my work: I love colorful art and sweet things! Use these pages as inspiration for your own scenes and doodles.

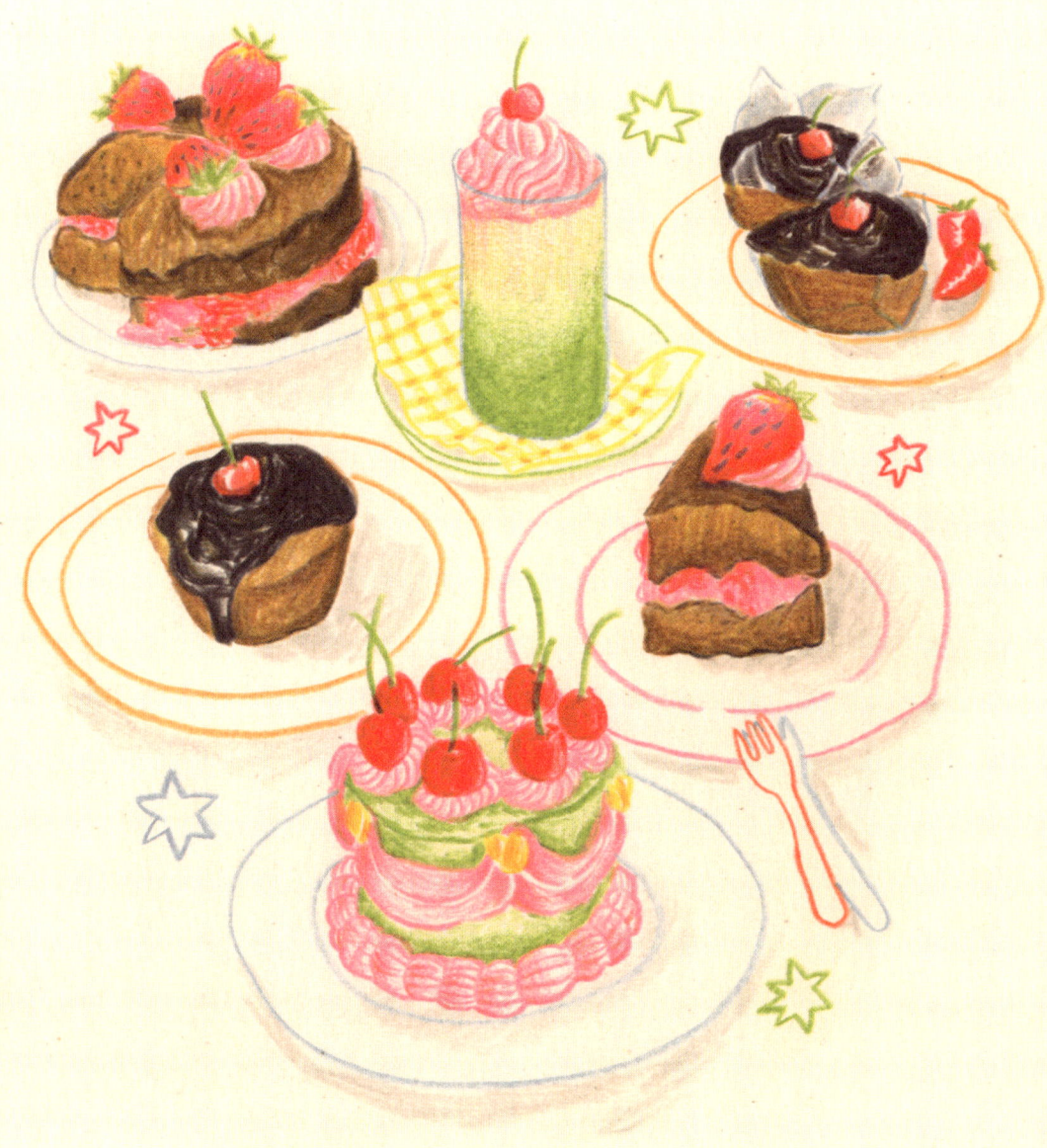

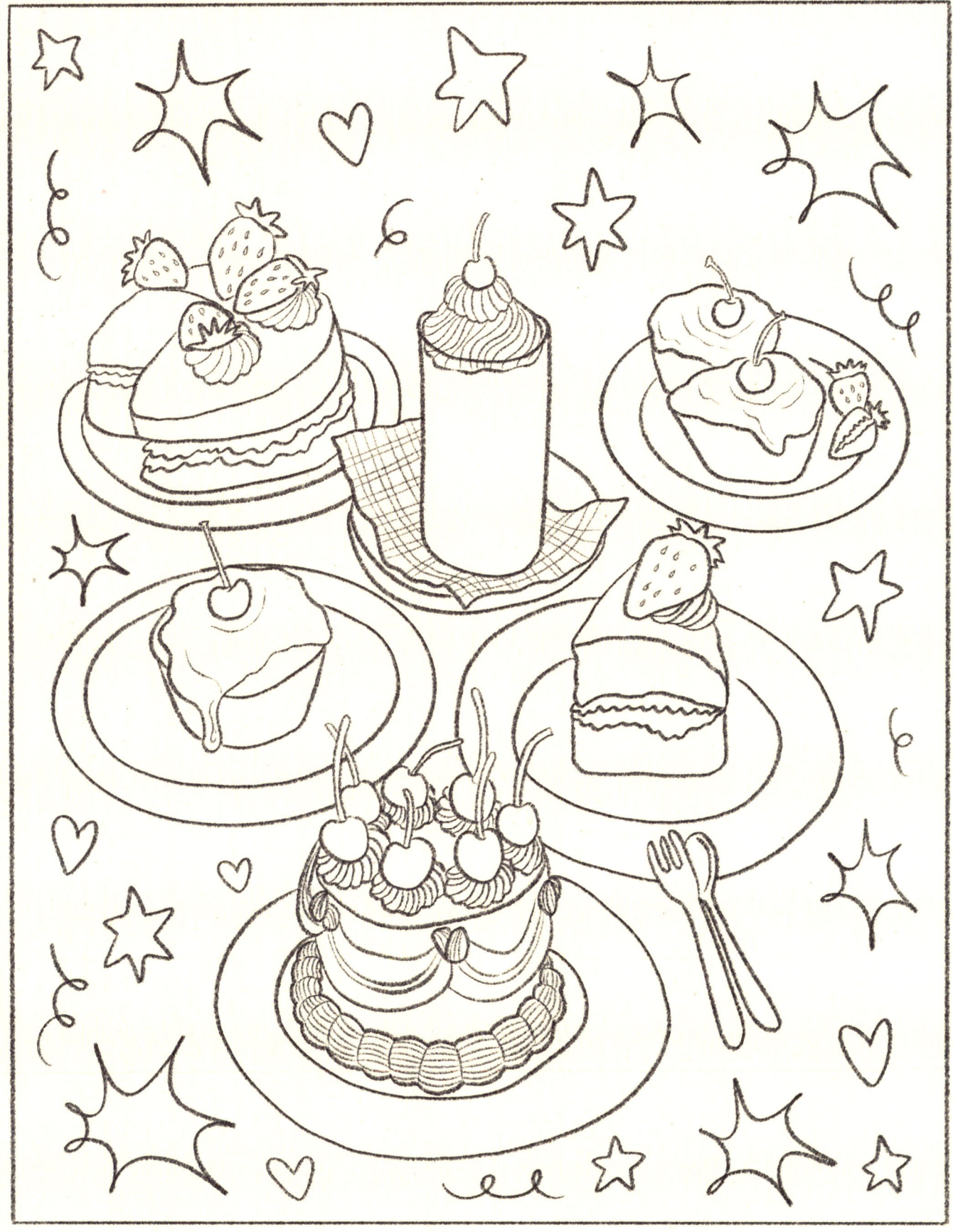

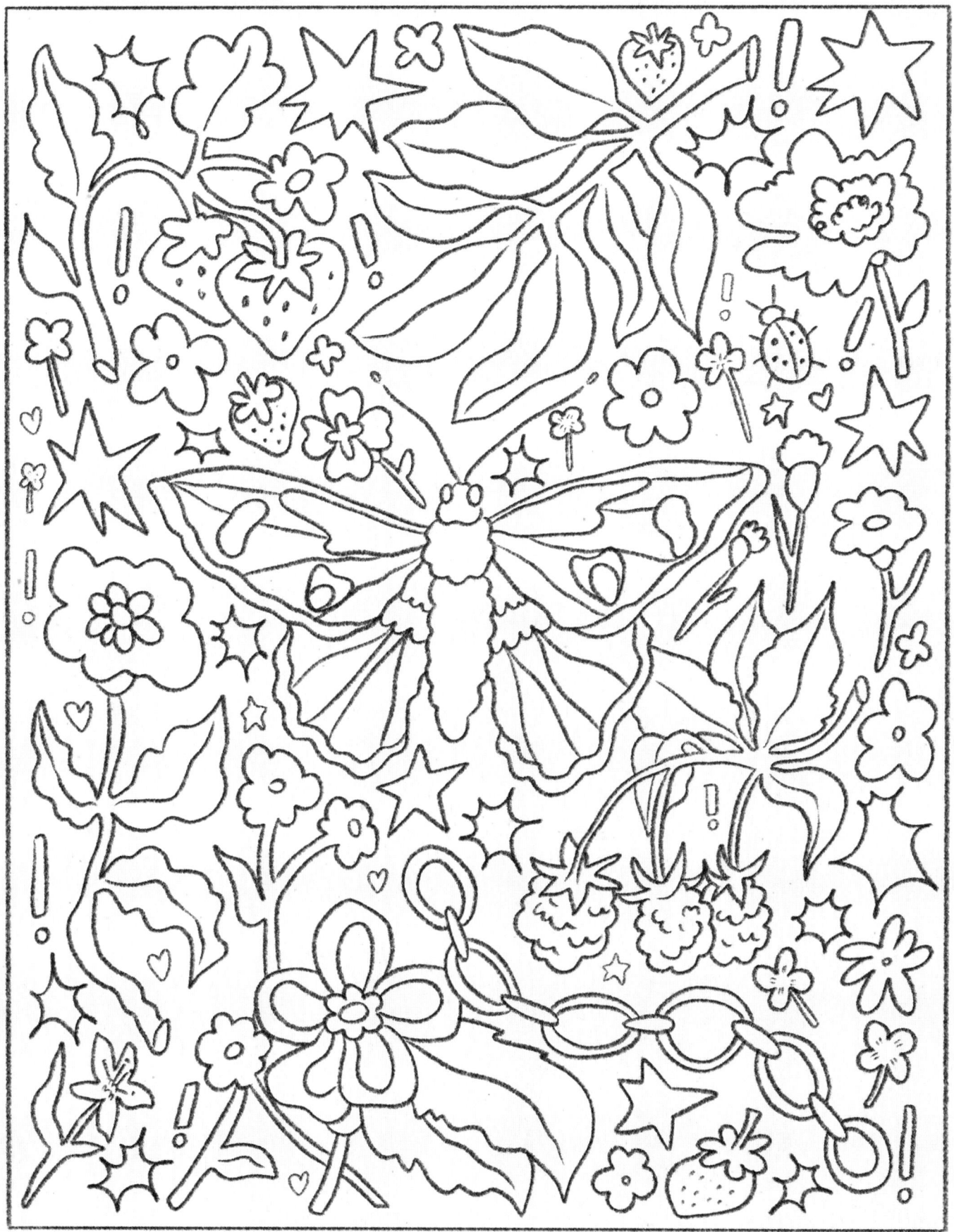

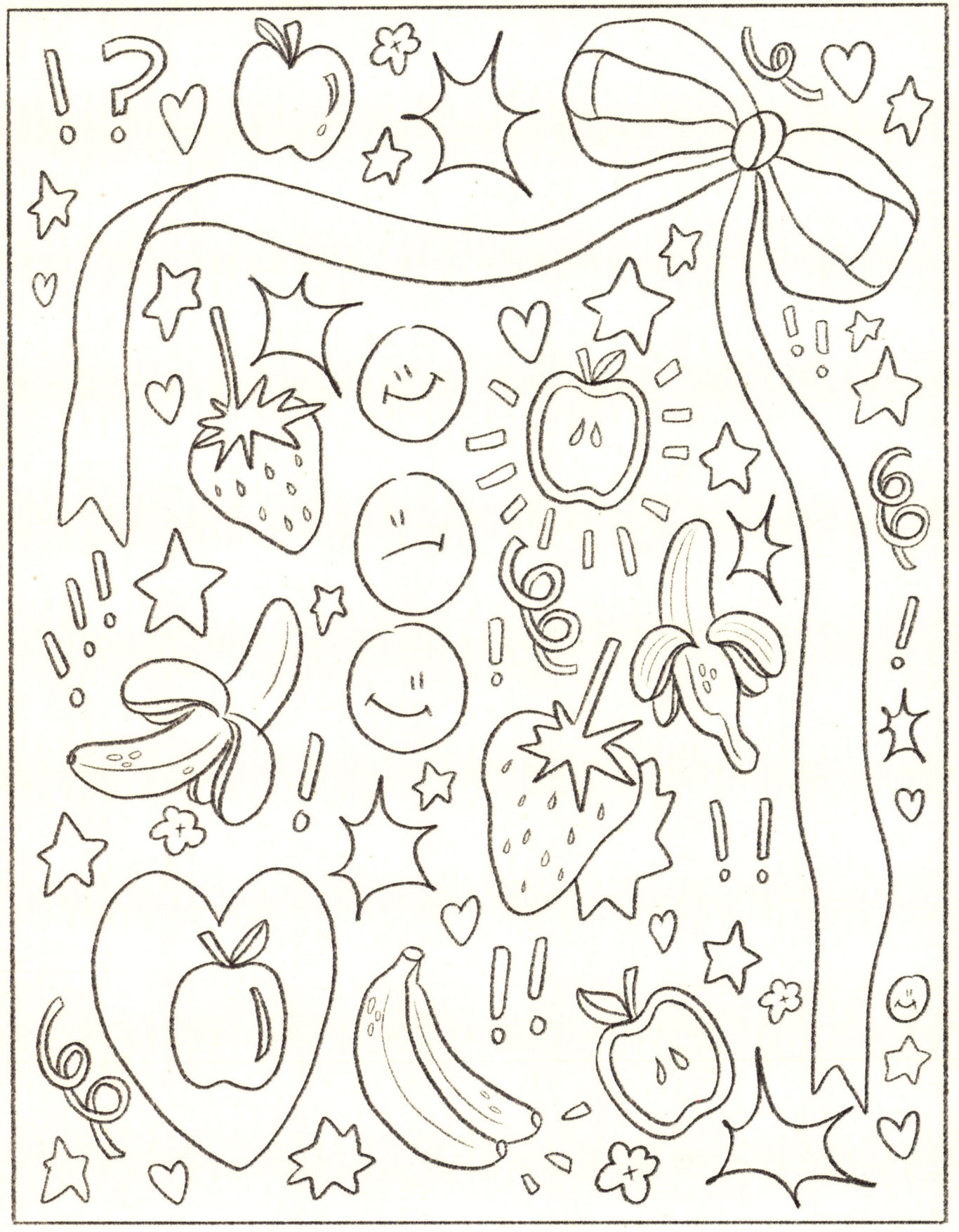

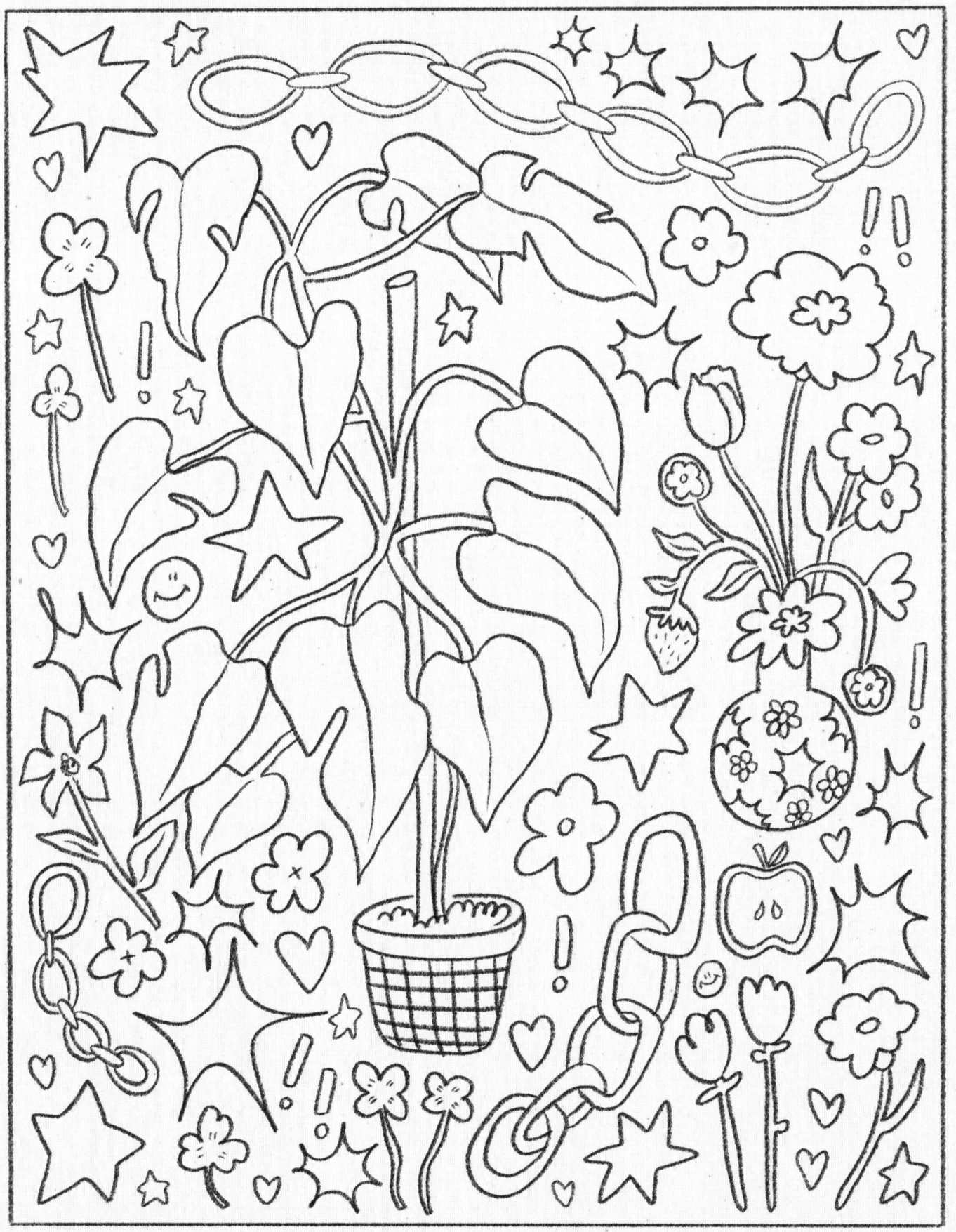

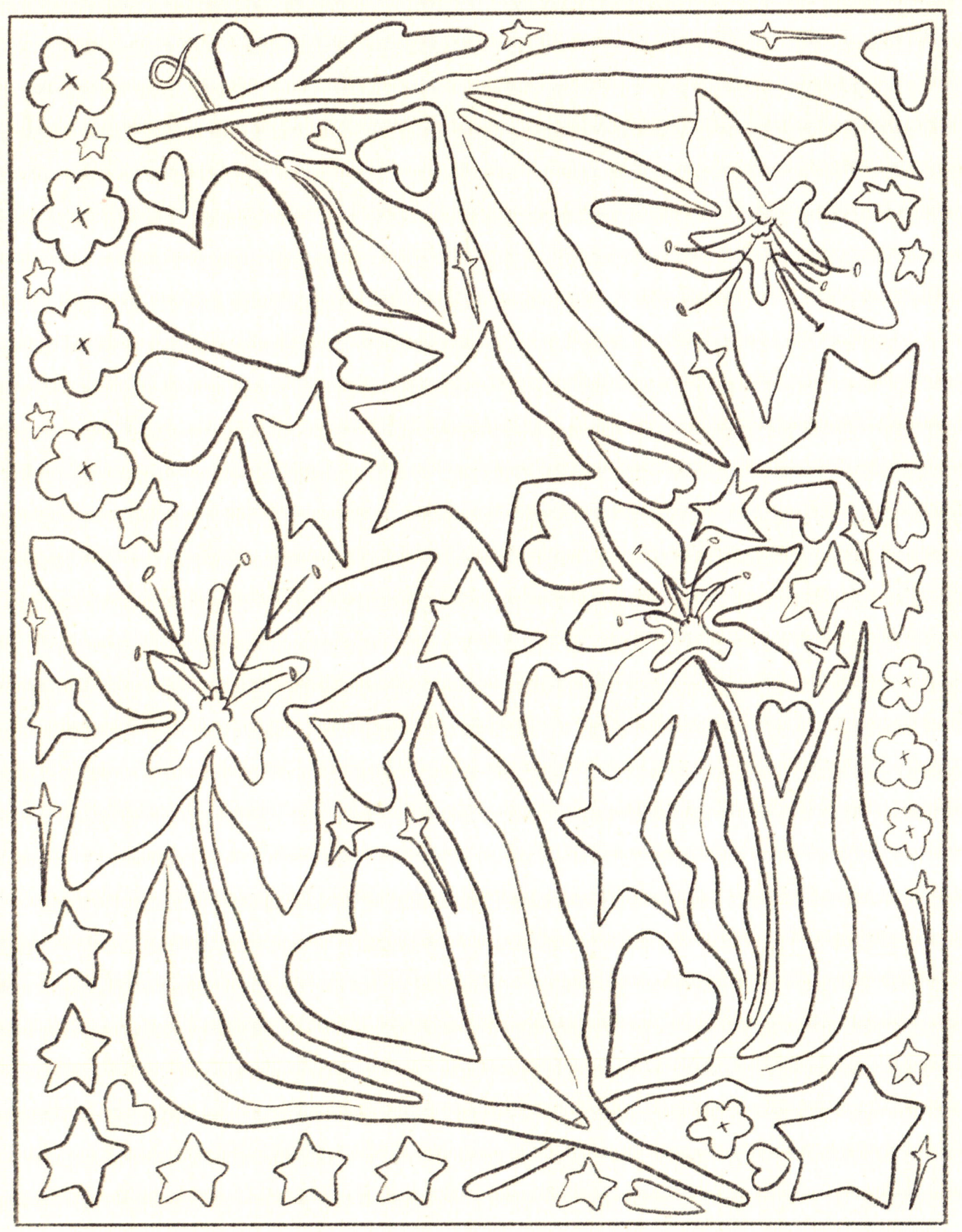

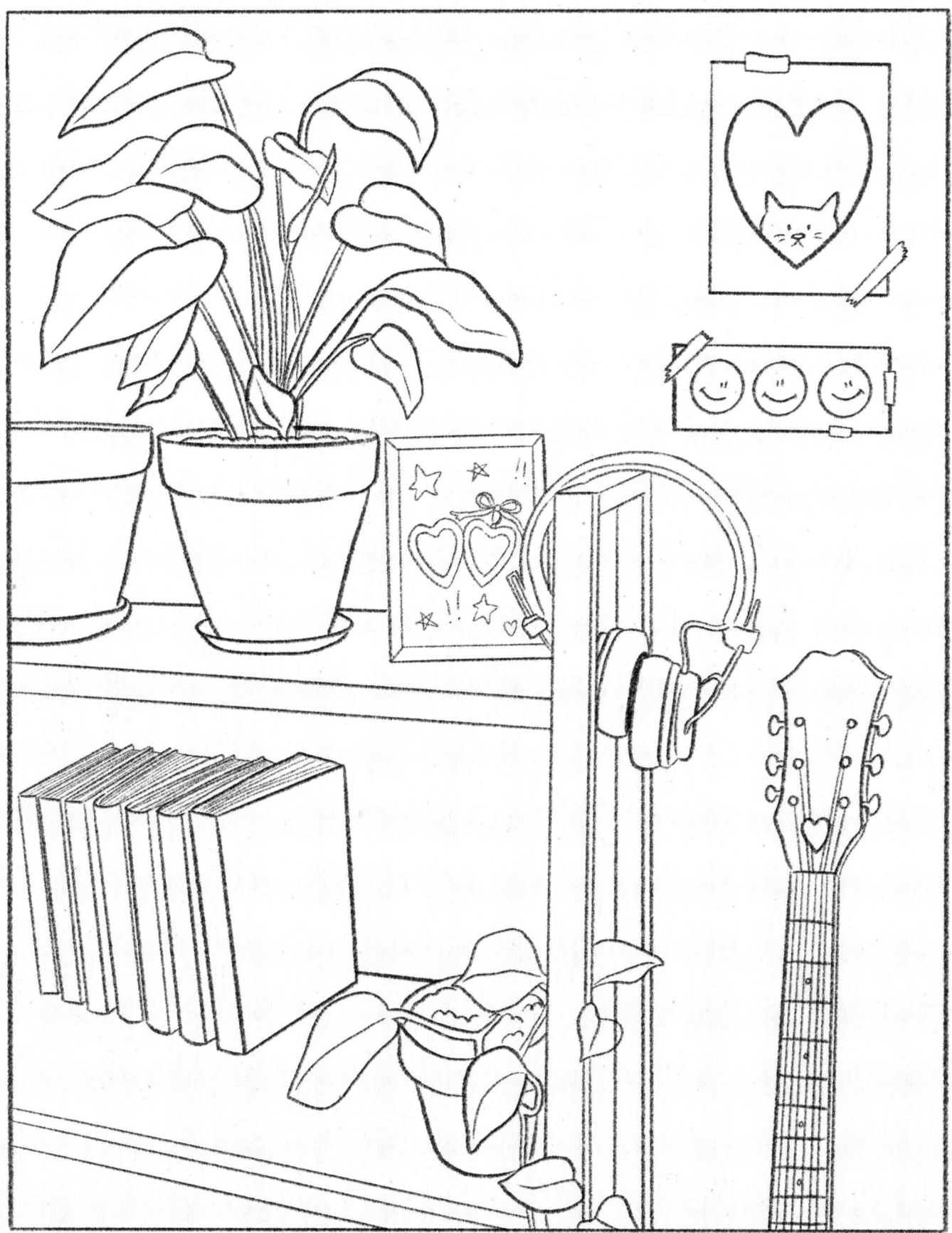

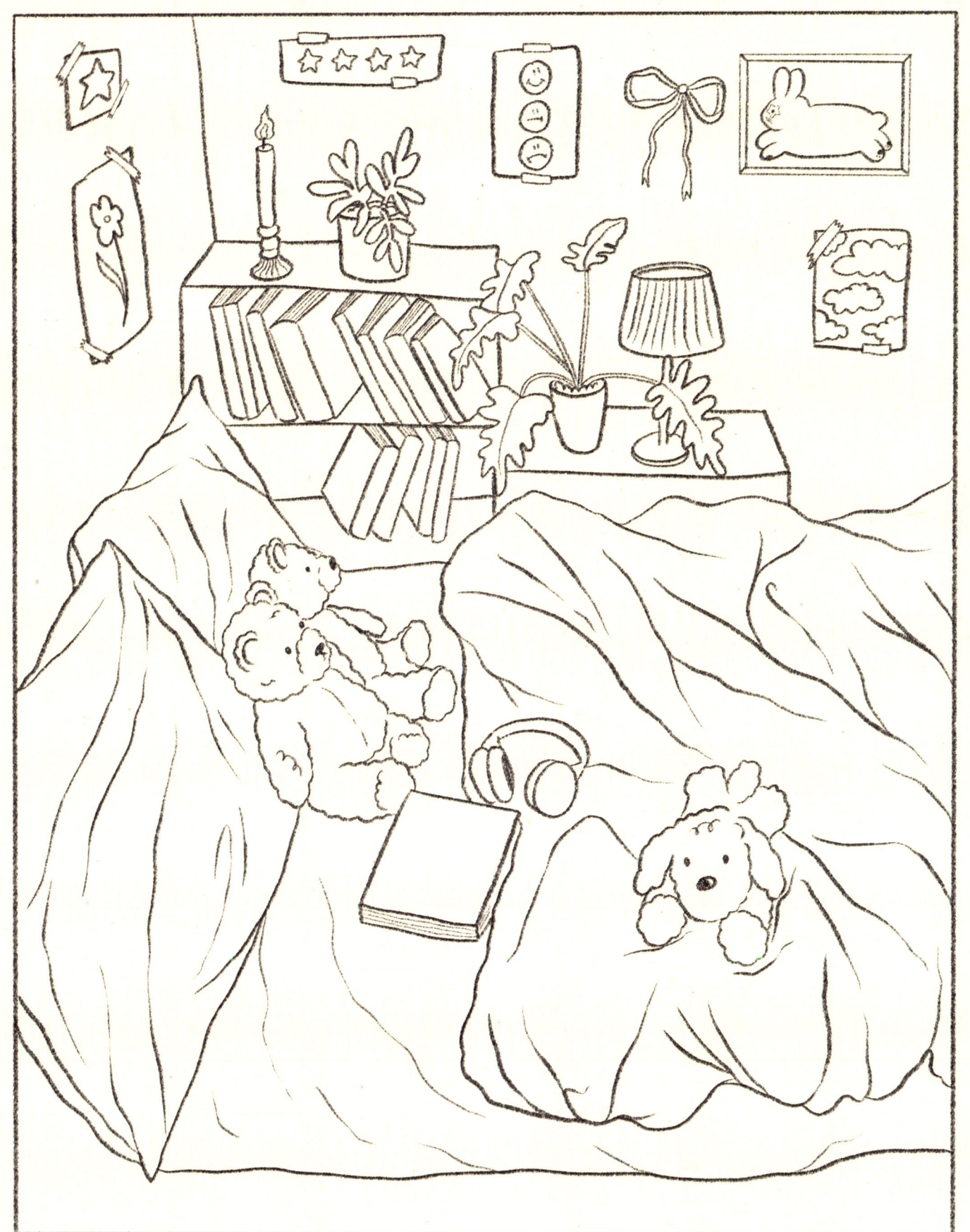

Acknowledgments

I would like to express my sincere thanks to the Quarto team, especially Sarah O'Connor, my wonderful editor. Her guidance and support were invaluable throughout the process of creating this book. She worked so hard to help make this book what it is and offered me constant encouraging feedback to my millions of questions! For that I am truly so grateful and appreciative of her passion and dedication throughout this project, and the book wouldn't be the same without her!

With heartfelt gratitude to my parents, Melanie and Anthony, whose unwavering love and support have been my constant anchor. Thank you for all the home-cooked meals and day trips to ensure I took some time for myself.

Thanks to my partner, David, for always believing in me, even when I doubted myself. And to my cat, Otis, for providing lots of love and constant company. I mean, he literally has his own chair in my art studio...

And finally, to the creative world around me, thank you for constantly inspiring me.

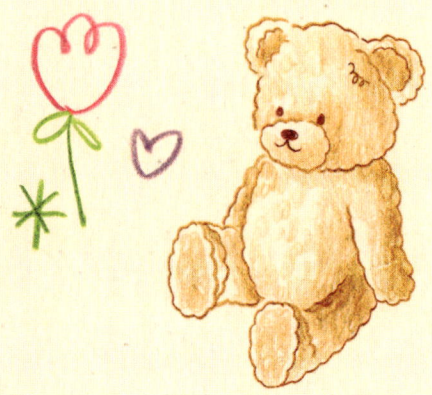

About the Author

Erin Siney is an illustrator and crafter based in the North East of England. Erin has always found joy in the simple act of doodling with colored pencils, a hobby that has followed her throughout her life. During her second year of studies of her Illustration and Design BA(Hons) degree, Erin decided to turn her passion into a reality by creating a freelance art business to share her art and uplifting doodles with the world. She hopes to add a touch of whimsy to someone's day. After the completion of her Fine Art MA degree, Erin has continued to grow her online business and create more products to sell in her online store, ranging from coloring books, art prints, stickers, to even a collection of handsewn pencil cases and purses!

First published in 2025 by Rock Point, an imprint of The Quarto Group,
142 West 36th Street, 4th Floor, New York, NY 10018, USA
(212) 779-4972 Quarto.com

EEA Representation, WTS Tax d.o.o.,
Žanova ulica 3, 4000 Kranj, Slovenia.
www.wts-tax.si

Rock Point titles are also available at discount for retail, wholesale, promotional and bulk purchase.
For details, contact the Special Sales Manager by email at specialsales@quarto.com or by mail at
The Quarto Group, Attn: Special Sales Manager, 100 Cummings Center Suite, 265D, Beverly, MA 01915, USA.

10 9 8 7 6 5 4 3 2 1

ISBN: 978-1-57715-547-8

Digital edition published in 2025
ISBN: 978-0-7603-9852-4

Library of Congress Cataloging-in-Publication Data

Names: Siney, Erin author illustrator
Title: Sweet spaces : learn to doodle the coziest corners / Erin Siney,
    creator of eggsdoodz.
Description: New York, NY : Rock Point, 2025. | Summary: "Learn how to draw
    cozy interiors and trendy motifs through step-by-step tutorials in Sweet
    Spaces"-- Provided by publisher.
Identifiers: LCCN 2025007375 (print) | LCCN 2025007376 (ebook) | ISBN
    9781577155478 paperback | ISBN 9780760398524 ebook
Subjects: LCSH: Interior architecture in art | House furnishings in art |
    Drawing--Technique
Classification: LCC NC825.15 S56 2025 (print) | LCC NC825.15 (ebook) |
    DDC 743/.84--dc23/eng/20250430
LC record available at https://lccn.loc.gov/2025007375
LC ebook record available at https://lccn.loc.gov/2025007376

Publisher: Rage Kindelsperger
Creative Director: Laura Drew
Editorial Director: Erin Canning
Managing Editor: Cara Donaldson
Editor: Sarah O'Connor
Art Direction and Cover Design: Beth Middleworth
Interior Design: Kim Winscher

Printed in Huizhou, Guangdong, China TT072025